AMERICAN IDEAS
OF EQUALITY

AMERICAN IDEAS OF EQUALITY

A Social History, 1750–2020

Carl L. Bankston III

CAMBRIA
PRESS

Amherst, New York

Requests for permission should be directed to permissions@cambriapress.com, or mailed to:
Cambria Press, 100 Corporate Parkway, Suite 128, Amherst, New York 14226, USA.

Library of Congress Cataloging-in-Publication Data

Names: Bankston, Carl L. (Carl Leon), 1952- author.

Title: American ideas of equality : a social history, 1750-2020 / Carl L. Bankston III.

Description: Amherst, New York : Cambria Press, [2021] |
Includes bibliographical references and index. |
Summary: "Using a variety of data sources, this book describes how the views we hold
regarding this fundamental national value developed as products of our cultural history from
the origins of the American republic to 2020. It traces how cultural transmission, political
and economic structures, and communication technology have shaped this core American
value. The book begins with the early days of the American republic and follows ideological
changes through the era of the self-made man, the rise of corporate society, the New Deal,
the post-World War II era, and the era of Civil Rights. It ends with a detailed discussion of
how this history has resulted in some of the most divisive political and social controversies
of the twenty-first century. Most studies of equality have taken this as having a single, clear
meaning. Most often, this has been either how much equality of opportunity exists now
or has existed in the past, or how much equality of condition exists now or has existed in
the past. They rarely consider that people can be equal or unequal in different ways, and
that what we mean when we talk about equality or engage in debates about it has been
shaped by historical experience. This book is a work of historical sociology that examines
the forces that have shaped and re-shaped this fundamental cultural value. The book leads
readers through an exploration of how different stages of American history have led to
thinking about equality in terms of independence from hierarchy, the opportunity for self-
creation, access to services and resources, widespread upward mobility, and equality across
social categories. It takes a unique multi-disciplinary approach, combining intellectual and
cultural history with political, economic, and sociological analysis. No other book offers
this kind of analysis of the both the historical origins and contemporary consequences of a
cultural concept at the core of American national life. American Ideas of Equality will interest
academic researchers, students, and general readers interested in American studies; cultural,
economic, and political history; political science; and sociology"-- Provided by publisher.

Identifiers: LCCN 2020045623 (print) | LCCN 2020045624 (ebook) |
ISBN 9781621965558 (library binding) | ISBN 9781621966944 (paperback)
ISBN 9781621965930 (epub) | ISBN 9781621965923 (pdf)

Subjects: LCSH: Equality--United States. | Social stratification--
United States. | United States--Race relations. | United States--
Social conditions. | United States--Economic conditions.

Classification: LCC HN90.S6 B357 2021 (print) | LCC HN90.S6 (ebook) |
DDC 305.50973--dc23

LC record available at https://lccn.loc.gov/2020045623

LC ebook record available at https://lccn.loc.gov/2020045624

For Cynthia

TABLE OF CONTENTS

LIST OF FIGURES

Acknowledgements

I thank Tulane University for generously supporting me during a semester sabbatical that enabled me to complete this book. Thanks are also due to Stephen J. Caldas for reading and commenting on an earlier version, to the reviewers for their helpful criticisms and recommendations, and to Cambria Press for their help and guidance in the publication process.

AMERICAN IDEAS
OF EQUALITY

The Problem of Equality

A Complicated Notion

In my university classes on social stratification, I frequently ask students whether they see "equality" as a desirable goal for a society. They always say that they do, characterizing movement toward greater equality in American society as progressive and as the way of social justice. So, I ask them, do you think that we should all receive the same incomes or live in uniform houses? Very few students agree to that, but they often do say that smaller gaps in material well-being than we have today would be desirable, without being able to specify just how much those gaps should be reduced. Pressed, they will generally explain that the kind of equality they favor is a competitive inequality. Everyone should have the same opportunity to obtain unequal rewards. But wouldn't competition for jobs or offices make the desired positions more unequal, I ask, since increasing demand raises market value? And wouldn't the unequal results tend to make future competition unequal since more and less successful competitors, or their children, would not be starting from the same places?

Sometimes the students will tell me that what they mean by equality is really political equality or equality under the law. But if political equality means that every individual has exactly the same voice in governance as every other individual, then the attainment of this state is unlikely in most real-world situations if it were ever even possible. Even in a small community that practices direct democracy, some people will be more engaged, more vociferous, or more persuasive than others, meaning that some will have greater influence. Coalitions and selective cooperation among some groups of people will result in differences in power to direct decision-making.

Even within such small communities, wealth, as well as persuasive ability, weighs heavily on decision-making. Those with greater resources have more influence. In a large and complex society, access to means of communication or ownership of those means greatly magnifies the influence, so that formal political equality is not only consistent with inequality of power but can also contribute to it.

Equality under the law faces problems of both economic and political inequality. As Anatole France wrote, "*La majestueuse égalité des lois, qui interdit au riche comme au pauvre de coucher sous les ponts, de mendier dans les rues et de voler du pain*" [the law, in its majestic equality, forbids the rich as well as the poor to sleep under bridges, to beg in the streets, and to steal bread].[1]

A few students will tell me that for them equality means a true equality of condition, with all individuals in the same situation. However, if this means that all have the same shares in goods and resources, then some power must control distribution—hence, attempts to achieve and maintain economic egalitarianism often imply concentration of political control. In Weberian terms, control over distribution shifts inequality from class to party.

Other students will say that they use the term "equality" to mean the equal representation of members of racial, ethnic, or gender categories in desired positions or equality of outcomes among those categories. This is a reasonable response, given the inequities of our history. Again, though, this is a type of unequal equality because it would make variations in power or life chances occurrences within these categories, instead of among them. The pursuit of what I call "categorical equalization" in this book also entails the intensified use of political control.

It is not my intent to argue for or against any of these versions of equality in this book. Nor do I propose to make a case for any particular brand of market or socialist economy. Instead, the purpose of this study is to explore the ways in which the fundamental American commitment to something called equality have evolved and shifted over the course of the nation's history. Although we often use this term without reflection as if we know exactly what it means, it refers to a protean concept that has taken different forms and received varying emphases in different periods. The modern notion of equality among human beings is ambiguous and involves self-contradictions and paradoxes. Social, economic, and political realities have frequently been inconsistent with expressed ideals of equality, and reconciling ideals with realities has entailed selective awareness.

In the following pages, I argue that the essential but troublesome American concept of equality has been a product of interrelated historical forces. One of these is cultural transmission. No society creates its stock of ideas entirely anew, and the past remains always with us, although the values and images we receive from the past require modification to fit changing circumstances. Another force is the economic and political setting of a given period. Equality of opportunity, for example, depends on the availability of opportunities. Political equality depends on the structure of government. Yet a third force is communication. Ideas clearly exist in communication, so the media shape ideas.

SUMMARY OF THE ARGUMENT

The American nation began with debates over the nature of social and economic equality and over the implications of equality for the establishment of government. The break with European domination involved an ideological break with hierarchies of inherited status, with aristocracy. Early American views of equality, then, were founded on the independence of individuals from hierarchy. But this very independence, some worried, might bring about a new inequality, in the form of a "natural aristocracy." This was an early form of the contradiction between equality of condition and equality of opportunity. Over the course of the nineteenth and twentieth centuries, an ideology of individual, self-reliant upward mobility combined with the compartmentalization of excluded groups to enable Americans to reconcile the contradictory parts of the national ideal of equality.

The ideology of the "self-made man," communicated through the ubiquitous medium of newspapers, came under pressure from a changing economic environment and evolved over the decades, but continued to be a critical part of our system of beliefs. In the late nineteenth century an expanding industrial economy, with heavy immigration to fill the bottom ranks, encouraged Americans to see their society as providing perpetual opportunity for upward mobility. However, African Americans, who provided much of the unskilled labor, particularly in agriculture, continued to be compartmentalized. A distinction between gender-based public and domestic spheres also continued to compartmentalize women.

In the late twentieth century, two developments, along with the rise of mass visual media, began to bring the contradictions in our commitment to equality to the surface. First, the rise of the affluent society after World War II created the expectation that upward mobility should not simply be an opportunity for all individuals, but a reality for all members of society. Second, the recognition that previously compartmentalized groups had been excluded stimulated demands for promoting and subsidizing the upward mobility of the least advantaged.

In the twenty-first century, expanding demands for categorical equality came increasingly into conflict with inherited and more individualistic notions. The technology-finance economy caused economic opportunities to contract even as expectations that universal upward mobility should be the norm continued. New electronic media gave rise to a boutique communication economy catering to specialized identities, perceptions, and resentments. Technological change both fostered economic concentration and stimulated the flourishing of identity groups competing over narrowing resources in an era of fragmentation and polarization.

Readers may note, especially in the later chapters of the book that treat more recent historical developments, that few solutions to problems of inequality are offered. This is intentional. The goal of this book is to provide a descriptive and interpretive history of concepts of equality for the sake of understanding social problems, not prescribing remedies for them. Nevertheless, I do include some very brief thoughts at the end about the importance of compromise in a diverse society with differing and frequently conflicting views on the meaning of one of its foundational principles.

Readers should also keep in mind that this book is an effort to identify how ideas of inequality have evolved over the course of American history. As observed in the opening paragraphs, inequality is a complicated notion. The focus of this book is not with analyzing every kind of inequality or equality, but rather exploring which kinds have received public attention over the course of our history and why.

ORGANIZATION OF THE BOOK

Chapter 1 examines equality as a foundational ideal of the early American republic. Although there were wide regional variations in stratification at the time of the American Revolution, the rural nature of early North America and the availability of land for settlement and speculation encouraged the desire for independence from England and the idea that equality was a matter of individual independence from Old World hierarchy. The agrarian basis of this equality of independence made advocates of urban, commercial interests suspect in the eyes of Jeffersonian egalitarians. The reaction against hierarchy also raised an early version of debate over the implications of individual achievement. Might the old aristocracy of birth be replaced by a "natural aristocracy" of ability, effort, and luck that would reestablish hierarchy? The ideal of an equality of independence was also deeply inconsistent with the institution of slavery, an inconsistency generally managed by compartmentalizing an entire racial category.

Chapter 2 describes how the independent yeoman of the early years of the American republic became the "self-made man" in the years before the Civil War. The expanding boundaries of the nation increased opportunities for farm ownership and for success in manufacturing enterprises. The chapter looks at equality and mobility in the expanding nation through the eyes of two foreign observers, Alexis de Tocqueville and Frances Trollope. It explores the centrality of the image of the self-made man in the politics of an era characterized by widening male suffrage and by popular communication by newspapers, which became a primary way of expressing and popularizing equality as the opportunity for individual self-creation. The chapter concludes with sections on two major contradictions of the belief in the self-made individual: slaves and women.

Chapter 3 follows the transformation of the concept of the self-made man during the late nineteenth and early twentieth centuries, a time that saw the growth of major corporations, rapid urbanization, the growth of formal organizations such as public schools, and massive immigration. It explores the movement known as "progressivism" as a response to political, economic, and social centralization and bureaucratization. In the increasingly bureaucratic setting of the time, equality began to take on the implication of the equality of citizens before a central, organizing state. The popularity of success literature reflected the view that self-made men were those who could draw upon their own talents and energies to rise in a corporate bureaucratic environment. This environment also placed an increased emphasis on formal education as a way of fitting individuals into a corporate environment and as a way of enabling competition for success. The great wave of immigration that accompanied the expanding economy both fostered the ideal of America as the land of opportunity and produced a system of ethnic stratification. While racial segregation maintained African Americans in many ways at the bottom of the stratification system, it also provided, in terms of ideals at least, a parallel path to self-made success, as reflected in the popular autobiography of Booker T. Washington.[2] Although women were still generally compartmentalized in a separate domestic sphere, the concept of the abstract citizen, equal in formal organizations began to challenge gender segregation.

In chapter 4, I look at the further development of the bureaucratic society during the time of the New Deal. I argue that one of the chief characteristics of the bureaucratic society was the unequal equality of individuals in hierarchical organizations, which laid the foundation for what would later become known as "meritocracy." The enhanced role of government in this bureaucratic society also encouraged the development of a concept of social citizenship, which included enhanced federal responsibilities for the welfare of citizens. The equality of citizens lay in their claims on the benefits and resources provided by the government. Economic distribution, as measured by shares of income, became more equal during this period, setting expectations for greater equality of condition that would be promoted by governmental intervention and regulation, with the equality of citizens seen in terms of consumption. The emergence of mass media, in the form of radio, helped to absorb individuals into the social citizenship of the bureaucratic society. Political attempts to spread benefits and guarantees of participation and material security across broad swathes of a national population stimulated thinking of equality in categorical terms, largely defined by social classes. Formal education also responded to the corporate setting, as it took on more of a role of the political shaping of social citizens. Despite the beginning of thinking about equality in terms of social categories, political pressures continued the bracketing out of Black citizens. The chapter ends with looking at the emergence of contested ideas of equality during the New Deal period.

Chapter 5 describes these contested ideas as largely slipping into the background during the boom post–World War II years, mainly the late 1940s and 1950s. Following the war, the country enjoyed rapidly increasing levels of production and consumption, along with a relative equalization of incomes known as the Great Compression. A wider distribution of income was accompanied by structural upward mobility —an increase in desirable, well-paid, prestigious occupations requiring high levels of education. American society began to look like a race that everyone had the opportunity to win, and, following a pattern established by the New Deal, the government played an active role in subsidizing these opportunities through support for mortgages, education, and other sources of upward mobility. In higher education in particular, one of the consequences was the appearance of a new "natural aristocracy," in the form of what was now called a "meritocracy." At the time, though, the questions that an elite of achievement might pose about social and economic equality, raised in the early republic, were obscured by the increasing structural mobility, making it look like there was "room at the top" for everyone. An undercurrent of criticism of what appeared to be a homogenizing, conformist culture did appear, though. Along with this critical undercurrent, the very expectation that success and material well-being should be universally available provoked objections from other social critics, who pointed out that some were still excluded. Faith in the capacity of policy led these critics to argue for more active political intervention to bring all into the realm of abundance and opportunity. Television contributed high consumer expectations and to national centralization. The period saw the ideal of categorical equality—equality applied to groups as opposed to individuals—begin to challenge traditional individual-level concepts. Legal challenges to racial discrimination in schooling were initially based on meritocratic ideals of individual opportunity, but these would also lead to efforts at categorical equalization.

Chapter 6 follows by tracing efforts at group equalization during the 1960s and early 1970s. The era of the civil rights movement placed a new focus on group equalization, drawing attention to previously suppressed contradictions in traditional American concepts of equality. This was the consequence of four main developments. First, the material abundance of the postwar years had encouraged thinking of the nation's primary challenge as one of extending high standards of living throughout the society. Second, mass communication promoted consumer expectations across all parts of the society. Third, mass communication also provided a national theater for members of groups excluded from benefits and opportunities. Fourth, the expansion of governmental social intervention encouraged thinking about improving standards of living in general and equalizing life chances across categories of people as problems that could be solved by means of public policy. The chapter gives particular attention to how the model for thinking about equality developed by the civil rights movement expanded to categories beyond race. It considers how policies of categorical equalization in employment and education both incorporated earlier individual-level concepts of equality and conflicted with those concepts.

The final chapter brings the history up to the present time. In a discussion of the economic setting, the chapter points out that by the late 1970s the trend of general income equalization and structural upward mobility was over, even as Americans continued to expect that life chances and opportunities should improve. The development of an economy dominated by advanced technology and finance was one of the most important characteristics of this setting. Centralized mass communication gave way to the new social media that were part of the technology-finance economy. The new social media were both centralizing and decentralizing. In terms of ownership, knowledge-intensive and capital-intensive industries promoted an oligopoly. At the same time, though, the new social media produced a boutique economy of communication, encouraging the splitting of the society into interest and identity groups. This fragmentation contributed to the growth of a form of populism in American politics. At the same time, the narrowing of opportunities heightened the contradictions involved in trying to subsidize upward mobility for group equalization. This narrowing of opportunities during a time that government policies attempted to increase opportunities for excluded groups combined with competing forms of identity politics to reinforce partisan political polarization, as shown in voting patterns. Competing ideas about the nature of equality and the role of government in equalization encouraged disenchantment with the American political system, as well as polarization. The chapter concludes by considering how historically developed, conflicting ideas about equality had come to reflect a polarized and fragmented society.

NOTES

1. France, *Le Lys rouge*, 118.
2. Washington, *Up from Slavery*.

CHAPTER 1

EQUALITY AS INDEPENDENCE

WHITE YEOMEN, NATURAL ARISTOCRATS, AND SLAVES

THE IDEAL OF EQUALITY

Historian Gordon Wood, in his 1969 classic *The Creation of the American Republic*, observed that the ideal of equality was a formative part of early American culture. For Wood, the early American attraction to goals of equality grew out of the unsettling experience of the American Revolution, the severing of ties to the English hierarchy, and the rise of new individuals to political and social power during the bitter struggle for separation from Britain. In his 1992 book, *The Radicalism of the American Revolution*, Wood expanded this observation to argue that the conflict with the mother country inspired a deep transformation of American thought about social relationships during the years 1760 to 1825.

The years of turmoil during the American Revolution did shape an American rhetoric and ideology of equality. However, the ideal of a political body of equal individuals took such a strong hold because it emerged from a long historical experience before the establishment of the new nation, and the ideal developed in the ways that it did because the historical experience both promoted dedication to some form of equality and presented that dedication with grave challenges and contradictions. The intellectual currents of the eighteenth century, including the egalitarian theories of Jean-Jacques Rousseau and Thomas Paine, undoubtedly influenced the thinking of leading individuals in the American war of independence and the early republic. But the history and social setting of the period left them open to these kinds of ideas and created the need to reconcile thoughts about equality and inequality among citizens. As I will argue throughout this book, moreover, American thinking about social relationships has been complex and often complicated by the realities of our historical existence. In addition, the early period of the history of the United States produced the beginning of a tradition of political culture that has continued but changed over the years. The knot of ideas about equality in American minds today wraps around strands that come to us from the early years of our nation, but these have become interlaced, often without conscious public recognition, with later views.

The first national understanding of equality emerged from the pursuit of economic and social independence by individuals during the colonial period. This understanding was less a matter of Americans having the same standards of living or even being able to look forward to the same opportunities than it was a matter of being able to hold and farm land and thereby to live apart from a hierarchy of dependence. Land, more than anything else, provided the real basis of the early American economy; and much of the nation's history of expansion across the continent can be understood as the quest for more land by individuals seeking to support themselves and, in their quest, acquiring the view that each of them, whether scratching bare sustenance from a small plot or harvesting export crops from a vast plantation, could be self-supporting and self-contained. Even the appearance of a middling sort in the eastern cities owed much to the constant possibility of moving out of the cities.

By the time of national independence, the central political issue for most Americans was not the redistribution of wealth. It was whether the acknowledged and accepted inequalities of condition would subordinate some to others. Looking back to England, the citizens of the new nation saw that the hierarchy of dependence in Europe rested on inherited status. Thus, the great debate over stratification at the time of the adoption of the Constitution, the argument over natural aristocracy, was in large part fueled by concerns about whether the "well-born" would be able to re-create and a European-style hierarchy of dependence in the United States. From this very early time, Americans readily accepted differences in wealth, as long as those differences resulted from each person pursuing an independent course. Wealth from the accident of birth carried the taint of Old World hierarchy and raised the possibility of replacing what we now call acquired status with ascribed. Definitions of natural aristocracy were often complicated and contradictory, sometimes portraying the elite as a coherent social class to be balanced against other classes in maintaining equality and sometimes as a collection of individuals of talent. These differing definitions affected how people saw members of the elite and what kinds of responses they advocated to keep inequality of condition from threatening the political equality of independent yeomen or middling town dwellers.

As the original ideal of equality as independence arose, one of the most serious contradictions to this ideal became evident. The early American economy was based on slavery, in addition to land. If the availability of land shaped national ideas about equality, slavery directly contradicted them.

THE UNITED STATES OF REAL ESTATE

The American commitment to an ideal of equality grew in a society not only of extensive inequalities but also of great regional variations in stratification. Many of these variations can be linked to the class background of the settlers in different locations. The earliest wave of immigrants to the lands that became the United States were Puritans who came from the east of England in the years 1629 to 1640 and settled in Massachusetts.[1] Most of these early arrivals were from the middle ranks of English society, and the majority worked in skilled craft and trade occupations. Although people from the lowest classes in English society made up only a very small proportion of the settlers in Massachusetts, a little under one-fourth arrived as servants, so that some stratification definitely existed. The elite of the Puritan-based society of New England that came out of the Massachusetts settlement, though, consisted of the interconnected and intermarried leading families of ministers and magistrates. Heavily drawn from the eastern counties of England, the men of these families had attended the same schools before migration, with nearly half attending three colleges of Cambridge. [2]

Despite the clear existence of a New England elite, stratification was relatively modest in this section of the colonies. The mainly middle-ranking population of Massachusetts multiplied rapidly in the years following 1640 and settled much of the northeastern region of the future United States. High levels of literacy characterized the great mass of this population as well as the small upper elite. Wealthy ruling families had arisen in Massachusetts by 1760, but their power was insecure and they could be challenged by larger publics. Similarly, a proprietary gentry had come into existence in the mid-Atlantic states in the face of diversity of ethnicity and religion,

The governing elite of Virginia came closest to the aristocratic ruling class of England, although the two were distinguished by, among other characteristics, the commercial origins of the former.[3] By the time of the American Revolution, Virginia was largely ruled by wealthy planters whose position and power came from their crops and commercial speculations. More importantly, the Virginia planters exercised their powers primarily over their slaves, rather than over White freemen, regardless of how poor those White freemen might be.

In relative terms, then, early America was a fairly equal society. Comparing America's colonial elites with the English ruling class, Korn-bluth and Murrin observe that "North America was much more rural and had no set of men as wealthy as the families that governed England.

England had no class of laborers as exploited as the slaves of America. The most affluent 1 percent in England probably controlled over 40 percent of the wealth, and the richest 5 percent owned over 70 percent of the kingdom's land and personal property. In the colonies the yeomanry —roughly 60 percent of White householders—controlled 70 percent of the land. The wealthiest 5 percent in colonial society claimed only 30 percent. The most distinctive feature of the colonies was the relative economic autonomy of the middling orders. Thus, colonial society had a lower basement and a lower ceiling than England, and it also had far more people crowded into the middle."[4]

The emphasis on the rural character of colonial America and on land is important. The United States at its inception was an overwhelmingly rural society: 95% of Americans lived in rural areas in 1790, with an average population density of only 4.5 people per square mile, compared to 17.8 people per square mile in 1890 and 70.3 people per square mile in 1990.[5] In looking at these numbers, we should recall the United States at the end of the eighteenth century was limited to the relatively densely populated east and did not include the vast reaches that would be added with the Louisiana Purchase or the later Gadsden Purchase. In this spread-out, farming society, the early American version of what would later be called "equal opportunity" was based precisely on the ready availability of land. And it was the quest for land, more than anything else that created economic mobility, as well as geographic mobility.

In a work on expansionism as American foreign policy, historian and former State Department official Robert Kagan has observed that for the American colonists of the eighteenth century,

> The desire for land was not primarily a desire for profit. Some land speculators made fortunes off the lands they bought and sold. But for the vast majority of settlers, the benefits of expansion were of a more spiritual and political nature. Landownership equaled liberty, both in Lockean theory and in practice. Settlement on the ever-expanding frontier offered unprecedented freedom and independence, and a sense of honor, to hundreds of thousands

of families who would otherwise have lived a more dependent or oppressed existence in Europe or crowded in the cities on the Atlantic Coast. The endless supply of land meant that no one, except the slave, was condemned to spend a lifetime in the employ of someone else. Men earned wages only until they had enough money to buy land and move away. This was the original "American dream," one that Abraham Lincoln was still extolling a century later: the opportunity of every white male to abandon a wage earner's life for the independent life of the landowner.[6]

By examining tax lists from the late 1700s, Jackson T. Main determined that substantial upward mobility characterized early America. Even in older farm districts, many landless individuals acquired property between the 1760's and the 1780's. In new frontier areas, rates of land acquisition were high. In the cities, skilled workers could obtain credit and open shops, and relatively high wages enabled even poor workers to move up by learning trades. Most importantly, geographic and horizontal mobility raised chances for vertical mobility.[7]. The ever-present opportunity to move on to settle on available land held out the possibility of moving out and being on one's own, out of the power of a patron or employer. It also helped keep the labor market in the East Coast cities fluid and contributed to the independence of the relatively small numbers of urban workers by boosting demand for labor and making it relatively easy for workers to move from one employer to another. This early version of the land of opportunity was based on the opportunity to acquire land. Understanding this fact is crucial for understanding the westward push first to the center and then to the far west of the continent.

One might plausibly argue, in fact, that this driving hunger for land not only settled what would become the United States with European descendants but even created the United States as an independent nation. By the middle of the eighteenth century, settlers from the English American colonies were finding their plots of land by pushing relentlessly into the Ohio Valley, claimed by the French as well as the British. Control of the land so eagerly sought became the key to fortune. Stock companies, such as the Ohio Company, sought to bring together shareholders and obtain title to vast reaches of land. However, settlement brought the Americans, and by extension England, into conflict with the French, so the English government attempted to limit the settlement that was the source of independence, mobility, and fortune. The Seven Years War, known in America as the French and Indian War, began when Ohio Company stockholder and Governor of Virginia Robert Dinwiddie sent the youthful Colonel George Washington to establish a fort on the Ohio River in order to secure colonial property interests. The clashes between Washington's forces and the French escalated into a war between France and England. Although it resulted in victory for the English, the need to pay for this long and expensive struggle led England to attempt to extend new forms of taxation to the American colonies, provoking a colonial protest that expanded into a war for independence.

To describe the American Revolution as a struggle for independence is to emphasize "independence," not just separation from the original European homeland. Samuel Johnson, one of the most eloquent opponents of the Americans, described himself to James Boswell as "a friend to subordination." For Johnson, an ordered society required a hierarchy of dependents and patrons, and to opt out of such a hierarchy was to court anarchy. Indeed, one of the fundamental sources of disagreement and misunderstanding between the British and their troublesome American subjects concerned relationships of subordination. British communications repeatedly emphasized the theme of the subordinate position of the colonies toward the mother country and it was this, more than the mere payment of taxes, that sparked violent responses from recalcitrant colonists. The same quest for land that had led the Americans to start the French and Indian War later also produced a spirit of independence from ranked authority that made it difficult to command them to pay for the war.

It is important to note that equality as independence derived from land and from the resulting relatively high degree of control over labor power in towns was different from economic equality. In fact, landownership was one of the major sources of economic inequality. This was not just because some Americans owned vast tracts whereas others held small plots. In a mainly agricultural society with continuing immigration driving up the demand for land, landowners could count on steadily rising values. Speculation in land therefore became one of the earliest routes to wealth before and after the American Revolution. The brilliant, slippery French diplomat Charles Maurice de Talleyrand, during a period of disfavor in the turbulent years after the French Revolution in his own country, took advantage of his refuge in the United States to accumulate a tidy sum speculating in American land.

The idea of equality as the independence of landed freemen took on a quasi-mythical form in the thinking of Thomas Jefferson. Recognizing the importance of land speculation in creating inequality, Jefferson observed that "the greatest Estates we have in this Colony were made ... by taking up & purchasing at very low rates the rich back Lands which were thought nothing of in those days, but are now the most valuable lands we possess."[8] Jefferson saw little contradiction between great estates and equality because he understood equality as the absence of hierarchical dependence. Jefferson's model of society was one of independent farmers, each working his own land. He believed that Saxon England prior to the Norman Conquest had been based on allodial law, in which land belonged to the person who worked it, and he argued that American society should be a return to this old Saxon system. [9] "In the model he envisioned, the political structure would be built up from the community based on the local 'hundred' or county with its own court and administration"[10]

Jefferson's social vision makes it clear just how he managed to square social egalitarianism with a belief in the existence of superior individuals. All men (and Jefferson's ideas did apply chiefly to "men" in the narrower sense of male humans) were indeed not only created equal but also would live in equal circumstances insofar as none were dependent on others for support or patronage because each controlled his own agrarian base.

Some might indeed hold larger tracts, as Jefferson did, but this would not give larger land holders power over smaller holders.

With a basic social and economic equality assured by agrarian independence, the only real ranked inequality would be within a narrow range of political authority. Even Jefferson's counties would need administrators and judges. One way in which these leaders could be chosen would be through a popular vote. The likely candidates could also be trained and preselected over their lifetimes, though, through some program like Jefferson's 1797 educational scheme for basic education for all (White men) and a competitive pyramid of schooling for political leaders. Such a program would give the independent yeomen the basic learning not only to control their own livelihoods more effectively but also to recognize and support the special abilities of leaders. Given Jefferson's concept of a strictly limited government, his "natural aristocracy" would, in theory, pose few problems for the egalitarianism of a social structure existing largely outside the sphere of political power.

Jeffersonian agrarians, such as John Taylor of Caroline, emphasized landed property as the means by which each household (of Whites, at least) could maintain self-sufficiency. In his massive treatise on the agrarian ideal, Taylor attacked commercial activities as means of drawing off the abundance created by farmers and mechanics and concentrating this abundance in the hands of a powerful elite of investors.[11] To modern eyes the Virginia planters look like a feudal aristocracy, and the Hamiltonian merchants and bankers look like rising challengers to aristocratic ways. But from the agrarian point of view, it was Alexander Hamilton and his allies who wanted to impose a rank-ordered society along British lines by institutionalizing the commercial means of confiscating the products of the true, primarily agricultural, labor.

While the idea of a natural aristocracy posed few problems for Thomas Jefferson's concept of equality as land-based independence, it was more troubling for many other Americans, especially for those who did not share their placid faith in an America of self-sustaining yeomen. The possibility that some could rise above the conditions of others always contained the danger that hierarchy could be imposed. This possibility, summed up in the phrase "natural aristocracy," stimulated the most important debate about power and stratification in early American history.

The Debate over Natural Aristocracy

The availability of land as well as the independence and economic mobility resulting from this availability shaped American attitudes toward social relations. Through public debate and the building of governmental institutions, these attitudes began to take more coherent form in the early years of the republic. The controversy over the adoption of the Constitution, in particular, brought out the different perspectives on power, rank, and social order. Many of those perspectives come down to us in the writings of members of a political and intellectual elite, such as James Madison, Alexander Hamilton, John Adams, and Thomas Jefferson. However, we do have some more broadly based evidence from sources such as newspapers and broadsides, although the elites tend to be overrepresented in these. However, it is important to remember that even such profound intellectuals like Adams and Jefferson did not live outside of their society and that their observations were sophisticated distillations of the ideas of their times.

American beliefs and concerns over equality as independence coalesced at the turn of the eighteenth and nineteenth centuries in the phrase "natural aristocracy." Today, we remember this phrase either as a point of contention in the struggle between the Federalists and the Anti-Federalists over the adoption of the Constitution or a question of political philosophy in the late correspondence of John Adams and Thomas Jefferson. As figure 1 indicates, this term was closely associated with the historical period from the American Revolution through the early nineteenth century. Some caution should be used in interpreting this table because it shows the numbers of uses of "natural aristocracy" in all newspapers, broadsides, Congressional journals, and other printed ephemera. As the total number of printed documents grew and newspapers in particular increased in numbers during the nineteenth century, the occasions for the appearance of any set of words increased. Thus, the association of the term "natural aristocracy" with the nation's first decades and more especially with the turn of the century may be even stronger than this figure suggests.

Figure 1. Mentions of "Natural Aristocrats" or "Natural Aristocracy" in the Archive of Americana.

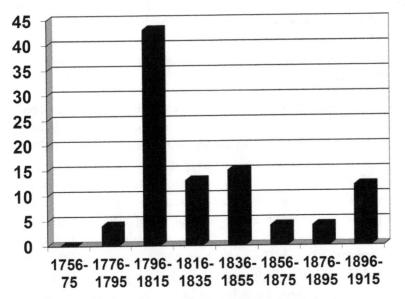

Source. *Archive of Americana*, Readax, https://infoweb-newsbank-com. Includes broadsides and ephemera, early American imprints, newspapers, and House and Senate journals.

The concept of the natural aristocrat was one of the most widely accepted notions in early social and political thinking about the creation of the American nation. Writing back in England, in the *Wealth of Nations* Adam Smith attributed the American struggle to the desire of "the leading men, the natural aristocracy" of the colonies to manage public affairs.[12] In America, this elite management, taken for granted by Smith, came under scrutiny during the efforts to design a governmental structure following independence. Even those who were most sympathetic to an English-style rank-ordering of society, who were often members of an elite based on birth, tended to accept an implicit and generally unexamined assumption of the situation later known as "equality of opportunity," in which personal virtues and talents, not advantages of birth, would be the primary sources of preeminence. On the other side, even egalitarian Anti-Federalists, such as Melancton Smith, "readily agreed that every society produces natural aristocrats, but he thought that 'We ought to guard against the government being placed in the hands of this class—They cannot have that sympathy with their constituents which is necessary to connect them closely to their interests.'"[13]

One of the most significant socioeconomic divisions behind the theoretical distinction of the free population into natural aristocrats and other categories in the early nation was the division between creditors and debtors. Many of the creditors were speculators in two sources of wealth: land and public securities. I have described land speculation earlier, identifying it as part of the real-estate boom that produced both the equality of independence and the inequality of fortunes among early Americans. Wealth in public securities was a by-product of the cost of war. As historian Woody Holton has pointed out, Congress and the states financed the war for independence from Britain primarily by issuing promissory notes, most of which were converted into bonds.[14] Soldiers in the Continental Army were among those paid in these IOUs. In the scarcity of hard currency that followed the war, soldiers and others were forced to sell their bonds to speculators at greatly depreciated values. The speculators needed a federal government with the power to cover both federal and state debts at full value in order to realize profits. One of the active and enthusiastic speculators in depreciated bonds was Abigail Adams. In contrast to her husband John, who preferred investment in land, Abigail insisted on directing the family funds toward the public securities; as such, Mr. and Mrs. Adams between them represented the two main forms of economic advantage in in the early republic: property and paper. This is particularly interesting because John Adams was one of the most intelligent and insightful commentators in the debate over the natural aristocracy, a debate largely focusing on the implications of economic stratification for American ideals of individual independence.

The general background of a society based on land settlement and an economically unequal but highly fluid situation resulting from speculation posed some of the problems to be resolved. If Americans valued independence, then what would debt and the possibility of the loss of farms to creditors mean for that kind of equality? If wealth could be inherited, then wouldn't people born into wealth tend to gain more power over their fellow citizens and gradually become like the aristocrats of England?

But Americans did not come to their times with blank slates to be written on by geography and current events. They also carried received traditions of political interpretation. The concept of balance of power was one of these received traditions. In English political theory, the balance of power was not between different wings of government with different functions, as modern Americans have come to understand this idea, but between different estates; notably, the commoners, the aristocracy, and the monarchy. When early Americans drew on the idea of balance of power to address their own issues of subordination and hierarchy, the concept of balancing the representation of estates or social classes existed along with the desire to limit the power of rising individuals and the goal of keeping individual "natural aristocrats" from becoming an estate of hereditary aristocrats.

Because American concerns were chiefly about hierarchy and dependence, arguments about unequal wealth and position in the early republic often concentrated on whether the most advantaged would employ power to subject others and become a true estate. A concentration of power could help to turn wealthier, more socially connected, and cleverer people into a European-style elite. This was the reason the debate over the Constitution became a debate over stratification. It was a debate that broadened and deepened American thinking about social classes and produced a range of views, but one that always stayed close to the issue of what a generally accepted socioeconomic inequality meant for relations of independence.

Many Federalists, as advocates of a stronger central government, saw the natural aristocracy as the obvious delegates and decision-makers of their new political system. "Hereditary aristocracy [in the Federalist view] was a bad thing but among every people there were 'natural aristocrats,' people with greater virtue, greater talent, and perhaps incidentally, greater wealth than their neighbors. It was they to whom the people should trust their government, for they would know what the people wanted better than the people themselves could."[15]

John Adams took a complicated view of the natural aristocracy, seeing its members as sources of both danger and national political advantage. To overcome the dangers of natural aristocrats to political equality, he proposed "to throw the rich and the proud into one group, in a separate assembley, and there tie their hands; if you give them scope with the people at large, or their representatives, *they will destroy all equality and liberty, with the consent and acclamation of the people themselves* [italics in the original]. They will have much more power mixed with the representatives, than separated from them. In the first case, if they unite, they will give the law, and govern all; if they differ, they will divide the state, and go to a decision by force. But placing them alone by themselves, the society avails itself of all their abilities and virtues; they become a solid check to the representatives themselves, as well as to the executive power, and you disarm them entirely of their power to do mischief"[16]. Behind Adams' political theory is a concept of stratification based on a categorization into the natural aristocrats and "the people at large."

Adams's argument about restraining the natural aristocracy was an ingenious use of a common Anti-Federalist argument for Federalist purposes because those opposed to a more centralized government often argued precisely that localized and diffused politics were needed to restrain the natural aristocrats. The author known as Cato, generally believed to have been Governor of New York George Clinton, wrote that "In every civilized community, even in those of the most democratic kind, there are principles which lead to an aristocracy—these are superior talents, fortunes, and public employments. But in free governments, the influence of the two former is resisted by equality of the laws, and the latter by the frequency of elections, and the chance that everyone has in sharing in public business; but when this natural and artificial eminence is assisted by principles interwoven in this government—when the senate, so important a branch of the legislature, is so far removed from the people, as to have little or no connexion with them; when their duration in office is such as to have the resemblance of perpetuity, when they are connected with the executive, by the appointment of all officers, and also to become a judiciary for the trial of officers of their own appointments, added to all this, when none but men of opulence will hold a seat, what is there left to hold and repel this host of influence and power."[17]

The idea of limiting the political power of an existing elite occurs repeatedly in the writings of the Anti-Federalists. The writer known as Philadelphiensis declared that "America under one purely democratical [government] would be rendered the happiest and most powerful nation in the universe; but under the proposed one, composed of an *elective king* and a standing army, officered by his sycophants, the starvelings of the Cincinnati, and an aristocratical Congress of the *well-born*, an iota of happiness, freedom or national strength cannot exist."[18] In this view, an aristocracy of birth already exists in the United States, in the sense that there is a class of the well-born. However, under highly localized government and without a standing army to enforce their will (one of the particular concerns of Philadelphiensis), the social elite will not be translated into a political aristocracy.

As noted previously, while the colonies that gave birth to the republic already contained significant variations in social class as well as a comparatively high level of mobility, people from different segments of the society took varying views on questions of power and independence. Several of the primary social positions of the new nation made up the Anti-Federalist opposition to the emerging Constitutional order. Saul Cornell observed that "Anti-Federalist support depended on three crucial groups in American society: back country farmers and artisans, the middling sort who dominated politics in the Middle Atlantic, and a small but highly influential group of elite politicians." [19]

The elite Anti-Federalists were, as one would expect, the least egalitarian of the three, pulled into an alliance with the other two only by their common opposition to centralized government. For the elite Anti-Federalists, such as George Mason, Mercy Otis Warren, Arthur Lee, and Richard Henry Lee, a truly natural aristocracy, ruling in harmony with the expressed interests of the many, would necessarily be highly localized in character. When Arthur Lee, writing as Cincinnatus, accused the Senate of setting up a "baneful aristocracy," he was not rejecting the idea of the natural aristocracy, but contrasting it with the oppressive form of the elite, characterized by its isolation from the multitude. "The analysis of society at the heart of elite Anti-Federalist constitutional theory was a mirror image of Federalist thought. For Federalists, the closer government was to the people, the greater the danger of corruption and demagoguery. Elite Anti-Federalists, by contrast, believed that it was vital to preserve the integrity of state and local government so that republican institutions could thrive. For these Anti-Federalists, the states provided models of the small republics in which liberty and virtue could flourish. In a properly constructed federal system, each state would function as a small republic, in which men of wisdom and virtue would naturally rise to positions of leadership while maintaining their ties to local communities."[20]

The desire to avoid political domination by elites as well as the inclination toward the balance of power theory led to some of the earliest efforts at describing American society in terms of social classes and interest groups. The Anti-Federalist writer who called himself Federal Farmer, for example, offered a three-class model of his society, consisting of the impoverished debtors, middling men, and aristocrats. Federal Farmer emphasized the role of middling men because as holders of property they had an interest in maintaining a republican form of government. The new constitution was problematic in Federal Farmer's view because it put too much power in the hands of the aristocracy, reversing a trend put in motion by the American Revolution. "The people of this country, in one sense, may all be democratic; but if we make the proper distinction between the few men of wealth and abilities, and consider them, as we ought, as the natural aristocracy of the country, and the great body of people, the middle and lower classes, as the democracy, this federal representative branch will have but very little democracy in it."[21] Federal Farmer saw the middling sort as possessing greater virtues than the natural aristocracy, who were tempted by their desire for immoderate wealth. However, he also saw his somewhat indistinct social classes as interest groups and argued for a variety of class-based interest group politics. Every social order should be represented because each had distinct interests. His criticism of the new Constitution, then, derived from his political sociology. The nation was composed of different social groups—the aristocratic elite, the middling sort, and the lower classes. A centralized national body, Congress would tend to be dominated by the first group. This would undermine republican government because it deprived the other two groups of the ability to express their interests and because it excluded the middle group, which had the greatest interest in maintaining a republic. One can see here one of the earliest expressions of the view that the stability of American democracy rests on the virtues of an independent, self-sufficient middle class.

The idea that different segments of government represented different estates in the society, found with Adams' arguments in favor of the Constitution, also occurred frequently in the writings of those opposing the Constitution. "The very term, representative," suggested the writer identified as Brutus, "implies, that the person or body chosen for this purpose, should represent those who appoint them ... They are the sign—the people are the thing signified"[22] The representatives should reflect the structure of society precisely because that society consists of different social groups with different interests. "In this assembly, the farmer, merchant, mecanick, and other various orders of people, ought to be represented according to their respective weight and numbers; and the representatives ought to be intimately acquainted with the wants, understand the interests of the several social orders in the society, and feel a proper sense and becoming zeal to promote their prosperity."[23] The wealth of the natural aristocracy gives its members influence, according to Brutus, and the members of the aristocracy have a natural interest in working together for their mutual benefit.

Brutus agreed with the widely held view that the activities of the senate "are designed to represent the aristocracy of the country," while the members of the House "represent the democracy."[24] Brutus asked for a rotation of the senate and limitation to single terms; otherwise, the rich and powerful individuals who would occupy senate seats would likely use their influence and connections to hold life-long office terms. Not only did the senate represent an aristocratic class, it would also, as Brutus feared, help to make the natural aristocracy of America a true aristocracy, closer to the lines of the noble class in Europe.

Along similar lines, A Federal Republican, writing in the *Pennsylvania Herald* on October 17, 1787, predicted that the scheme of state legislatures electing federal senators would allow an elite to rise out of an elective hierarchy. Comparing this system to the elective system of Venice that culminated in the doge as supreme leader, A Federal Republican asserted "that our boasted republic will ere long wear the face of an aristocracy may easily be seen."[25] The Anti-Federalists veered between arguing that the Constitution gave too much power to an existing natural aristocracy and that it would create an aristocracy.

It is interesting that the most important response to the Anti-Federalist objection to the Constitution, the Federalist Papers, contains no mention of the term "natural aristocracy." Nevertheless, the authors of the Federalist Papers were as much concerned to present the proposal for a more centralized government as a restraint on aristocracy as they were to present it as a more effective means of promoting the financial and political advancement of the new nation. In the Federalist #39, James Madison defined a republic in terms of its anti-aristocratic character. Madison pointed out that many different governments, including that of England, had been described in this way. For a true republic, though, he maintained that "it is ESSENTIAL to such a government that it be derived from the great body of the society, not from an inconsiderable proportion, or a favored class of it; otherwise a handful of tyrannical nobles, exercising their oppressions by a delegation of their powers, might aspire to the rank of republicans, and claim for their government the honorable title of republic." Further, in the Federalist #43, Madison asserted that that one of the purposes of the new Constitution was to protect the people in the various states "against aristocratic or monarchial innovations." By binding all the states together in a common dedication to republican principles, the Constitution would enable the individual states to check local efforts to institute systems of subordination.

With the successful adoption of the Constitution, the debate over the role of inequality in American life became less immediately relevant. But looking back at this debate reveals some of the assumptions and ideas about equality and inequality held by early Americans. Americans did not all agree on their opposition to rank-ordered subordination, nor were they always consistent in their views. The elite Anti-Federalists, in particular, often appeared to oppose centralization of governmental authority because they were inclined toward a kind of subordination, in which they imagined themselves, as local elites, better able than a distant authority to direct their own communities. This kind of anti-democratic localism would continue to be one stream in American social views, later appearing in the thought of John C. Calhoun and again among the

Southern Bourbons after Reconstruction. Alongside this regional elitism, though, the Jeffersonian image of independent White yeomen continued to hold imaginations in the South.

The most common opinion was a general acceptance of human inequality, combined with the goal of keeping that inequality from becoming permanently institutionalized as hereditary aristocracy and restraining it from becoming a system of subordination. Federalists maintained that their governmental plan would act as a balance for the power of the superior individuals. Anti-Federalists opposed the new Constitution because they feared that it would either provide insufficient protections against the powers of the natural aristocrats or would give those individuals mechanisms to exercise their powers.

Many of the participants in the debate reserved a special concern over those they called the "well born." Even John Adams was hazy about the extent to which being a natural aristocrat was a consequence of one's own talents and energy as opposed to a consequence of being born into an advantaged situation. The arguments of the late eighteenth century indicate that most writers of that time had not clearly formulated the question that haunts today's national discourse about socioeconomic status: to what extent is social position a matter of one's own abilities and efforts, and to what extent is it an accident of class position at birth? The vagueness on this issue was one of the reasons writers of the time often did not see that a traditional balance of power arrangement, based on the representation of estates, as inconsistent with a natural aristocracy of individual merit, in which constant mobility makes it difficult to identify the members of an estate. But the harping on the theme of the well-born indicates that a major political motivation of many Americans in the late eighteenth century was to prevent success from rigidifying into hereditary caste. Even as the phrase "natural aristocracy" began to slip into the past as a way of encapsulating national attitudes toward issues of social equality, many of its themes continued to shape those attitudes.

The last important discussion of the concept of the natural aristocracy took place as an epilogue to the old debate at the time of the Constitution, in the letters of Jefferson and Adams in the fall of 1813, the year after the two political rivals finally renewed their friendship. Writing on September 2, and commenting on a passage of Theognis, John Adams raised the question of who are the "aristoi." He translated this word, which means "the best" in Greek, as "aristocrats." "Philosophy may Answer 'the Wise and Good,'" Adams maintained, "But the World, Mankind, have by their practice always answered, 'the rich, the beautiful and well born.'"[26] Adams told Jefferson that "the five Pillars of Aristocracy are Beauty, Wealth, Birth, Genius and Virtues. Any one of the three first, can at any time over bear any one or both of the last two."[27]

John Adams, then, saw the inequality described by aristocracy as consisting of individual qualities, rather than inhering in social structure. Today, most commentators would probably classify being "well born," having an advantageous family situation, as a matter of the system of positions into which individuals are born. Adams, though, writing at a time before sociologically thinking permeated views of the world, considered advantages of birth, personal appearance, and financial situation all as individual qualities. Moreover, he argued that the social assets that individuals possess outweigh moral and intellectual capacities. Although Adams threw together different kinds of human inequalities, it is evident that Adams took a highly skeptical and critical view of social inequality, even while regarding it as inevitable. The things that make people "the best" in a society are usually not the most constructive traits. The suspicion of preeminence is consistent with the old Federalist's earlier concerns with setting up institutions that can control and direct the political influence of the supposedly best people.

Thomas Jefferson replied to these thoughts on October 28. He recognized that John Adams was lumping together different types of inequality as components of the aristocracy and then assuming that the least desirable components would receive the greatest emphasis. Jefferson responded by dividing the qualities identified by Adams into two categories: those belonging to the "artificial aristocracy" and those belonging to the "natural aristocracy." "The grounds of [the natural aristocracy]," according to Jefferson, "are virtue and talents." Bodily strength, he explained, was a primary ground of this natural preeminence, but modern weapons have rendered this obsolete. "[B]odily strength, like beauty, good humor, politeness, and other accomplishments, has become an auxiliary ground of distinction." Jefferson did not make it clear why these other accomplishments should have diminished along with strength, although presumably gunpowder did not displace beauty or politeness in the same way that it displaced physical prowess. The artificial aristocracy, in contrast, is "founded on wealth and birth, without either virtue or talents."[28]

As John Carson has pointed out, Jefferson distinguished between the fundamental political rights of White men, which were equal, and their opportunities for leadership, which the author of the Declaration of Independence believed should be distributed according to virtues and talents.[29] In addition, Carson argues that neither Thomas Jefferson nor John Adams was a social leveler. Both saw stratification as inevitable —and justifiable to the extent that it was the product of those virtues and talents. It is notable that Jefferson's optimism about the natural aristocracy was based on his differentiation of inequality based on "virtues and talents" and inequality based on "wealth and birth." We can see in Jefferson's interpretation some of the early traces of the "equality of opportunity" view that was gradually to emerge from the "equality of independence" perspective. The willingness to free the natural aristocrats from constraints came out of the belief that their superiority would be the expression of personal qualities. However, Jefferson also believed, as we have seen, that in a society of independent individual yeomen, even political leadership by people of superior talents would not subordinate the general citizenry.

Adams, true to his old dedication to restraining the natural aristocrats, was much more skeptical of inequality. While he combined different kinds of inequalities, he also made a point that many social scientists would accept today: that the advantages that modern commentators might describe as "ascribed status" influence and can outweigh the advantages of "achieved status." This did not lead him to argue for abolishing social inequality but rather to continue his long-held support for finding ways to restrain and direct those at the top.

In the years that have followed this interchange between the two founders, Americans have tended to lean toward the Jeffersonian approach when they have seen a wide opening for virtues and talents, especially as opportunity became a greater part of the national understanding of the meaning of equality. When they have become more conscious of threats to the efficacy of individual virtues and talents, as in the Progressive Era, they have tended to favor the Adams approach, although fostering opportunity for achievement became a more common rationale for constructing political means of constraint.

All of the early debates about equality came up against a major problem. While early American may have displayed unprecedented geographic and social mobility for much of its population, a prominent portion of the population had virtually no mobility of any sort, other than the involuntary mobility of being sold and transported from one part of the country to another. Slavery, and its historical consequences, would shape and challenge the nation's conversations on independence and opportunity.

SLAVERY AND THE BOUNDARIES OF EQUALITY

As we look back at the problem of slavery in American life and at the challenge this problem and its historical consequences posed for American ideals of equality, we should remember that slavery did not begin in the United States. The ownership of humans by other humans, deeply offensive to modern sensibilities, is an ancient practice. The race-based slavery as practiced in the Americas developed long before the political institutions or principles of the United States. The principles were not fully formed at the time of the creation of this country, nor did everyone agree on them. The society underlying the political institutions could not be redesigned according anyone's vision of justice and morality. Even those founders who deeply opposed slavery could not have abolished it. The colony of Virginia had attempted to ban the importation of slaves at the beginning of the eighteenth century before the institution had ingrained itself so deeply, but the British government blocked the effort. By the end of the century, some White Americans of the founding generation depended on slavery for their livelihoods or fortunes, while prejudice kept others from accepting the prospect of living alongside free Blacks, and still others worried how hundreds of thousands of landless, indigent, formerly dependent people could survive. Even the members of the founding generation who favored immediate abolition had to enter into agreements and compromises with advocates of more gradual emancipation and with proponents of continued bondage. White Americans of the founding generation could create a nation that in some way accepted slavery, or they could fail to create any nation at all. This does not mean, however, that it would be anachronistic to say that slavery contradicted early American ideals. Many in the late eighteenth century saw that bondage contrasted strangely with proclamations of independence and political equality.

Samuel Johnson, that friend to subordination and enemy of the American struggle against Britain, contemptuously dismissed American demands for freedom. "Why is it that we hear the loudest yelps for liberty from the drivers of Negroes?" he asked in his pamphlet *Taxation No Tyranny*.[30] Johnson's question might take on a special significance if we take "liberty" to mean the equality of independence, the state in which differences in which individuals can lead separate and distinct lives regardless of variations in wealth and property. Thomas Jefferson may have been able to imagine his poorer neighbors as self-sufficient yeomen.

Even with his capacity for intellectual and moral gymnastics, though, Jefferson certainly would not have been able to imagine his slaves as living in anything but the most complete state of subordinate dependence.

Johnson, of course, lived in London, far from the slave society of the American plantations. For him, excoriating the hypocrisy of Cousin Jonathan's attachment to the exploitation of the slaves came easy. Modern-day moral critics of the past might also do well to recognize that figuring out how to change a fundamental part of one's society without destroying the society itself is not an easy task.

Edmund Burke, also an opponent of slavery, sympathized with the Americans and suggested that it was precisely the institution of bondage that rendered the colonists so jealous of their perceived rights. The masters were constantly reminded of the state which they saw as the ultimate subjection.[31] Burke was correct in arguing that slavery shaped American political and social thinking. However, the influence was complicated. The yelpers were not all slaveholders in Virginia. Massachusetts, a center of opposition to slavery, was also one of the bastions of support for opposition to England.

Slavery was a reference point for American society in general, and not just for slaveholders or even people with direct experience of the institution. If equality meant the freedom of more or less self-reliant households from dependence on patronage, then slavery provided both a living example of what equality was not and a continual contradiction of the emerging American system of values. New lands made it possible for many Whites to settle on their own and produce their own crops. The continual geographic mobility of this restless population created job opportunities in urban areas, giving city dwellers control over their own lives and chances for economic mobility. Slaves were a constant reminder that people could be immobile and utterly dependent. At the same time, though, as Americans increasingly rejected not just their own subordination but the principle of subordination, slaves contradicted what was becoming the ideological foundation of the nation. In debates over the nature of the new government, both opponents and supporters of slavery pointed to this institution as what they wanted to avoid for citizens. At the same time, though, to avoid subverting the new polity, Americans had to place the enslaved people in brackets. Through euphemism, silence, and carefully directed attention, those constructing this polity placed slaves outside the discourse on independence and equality.

The line between the enslaved and the free was indeed the fundamental division of the early American republic and not just a demarcation of the society's bottom rank. People express the social distinctions that they consider meaningful by the ways in which they categorize those around them. The categories in the 1790 census illustrate the distinctions among people that were considered meaningful by the designers of the enumeration. For all states and territories, the first census counted "free white males of 16 years and upwards, including heads of families," "free white males under 16 years," "free white females, including heads of families," "all other free persons," and "slaves" (without distinction of age or gender).

In that first census, slaves were not only a category alongside the basic divisions of age and gender, they were also a substantial portion of the American population. Of the 3,893,635 people in the new United States, 694,280 (or just nearly one out of every five) were slaves. Only Massachusetts (including what was then the District of Maine) held no slaves because the state had abolished slavery in the 1780s. Vermont, with only sixteen slaves came close to being slaveless. Virginia had the largest number of slaves, with 292,627 people (or 39% of the total population held in bondage). Maryland and the two Carolinas each contained over 100,000 slaves; and slaves constituted 43% of the people in South Carolina. Despite the example of Maine, Massachusetts, and Vermont, though, slavery was by no means characteristically Southern in that first census year. New York held 21,324 slaves and neighboring New Jersey held 11,423. Even Pennsylvania, with its Quaker heritage, held 3,737 slaves.

Slavery should not be written off as an anomaly in the American dedication to equality. Indeed, the equality of yeoman farmers in regions with plantation economies rested on the institution of slavery. For, even if small farmers themselves owned few, if any, slaves, the holders of vast estates (such as Thomas Jefferson) could ascribe independence and theoretical equality to the poorer Whites precisely because the rural elite had access to nearly unlimited exploitation of slaves. Having slaves, members of the elite had little need to actively subordinate poorer Whites.

Nevertheless, by bringing the ideology of equality as the coexistence of independent citizens to heightened consciousness, the American Revolution did draw attention to the subversive character of slavery. As Ira Berlin has observed in looking at the historical attitudes of Black Americans, "the heady notions of universal human equality that justified American independence gave Black people a powerful weapon with which to attack chattel bondage."[32]

Slavery was also a weapon in debates among Whites over the form of the newly emerging state. Anti-Federalists frequently expressed the fear that a greater centralization of government would reduce less powerful citizens to slaves. Black slavery was often an explicit reference for these writers. Benjamin Workman, an immigrant from Ireland and a mathematics instructor at the University of Pennsylvania, who wrote under the name "Philadelphiensis" made repeated references to the perceived threat of slavery for White Americans and exclaimed in the pages of the *Independent Gazetteer*, "Strange indeed! That the professed enemies of *negro*, and every other species of *slavery*, should join themselves in the adoption of a constitution whose very basis is *despotism* and *slavery*.[33] Philadelphiensis repeatedly describes those aiming at the enslavement of the American people as the "well born."

In an interesting reference that suggests how Black slavery influenced arguments about democracy and aristocracy, Luther Martin said of the relationship between nine equal individuals and one more powerful with a vote equal to theirs, "to *him they* would be as *absolutely slaves* as *any negro* is to his *master*."[34] By extension, the states should each have an equal voice because unequal representation of states in any branch of government due to differences in population would make some states the masters of others.

On the question of counting slaves as part of the population for the purposes of unequal distribution of representation, Martin was particularly vehement. He argued that including slaves into the computation would encourage "that *infamous traffic*."[35] Slaves were not considered citizens but property, so including their numbers in reckoning representation was illogical, given that cattle and other forms of property could not be considered.

Throughout the debate over the more centralized government to be established by the Constitution, the Anti-Federalists portrayed greater centralization as an instrument of power and inequality as subjection to power, or slavery. "History exhibits this melancholy truth, that slavery has been the lot of nearly the whole of mankind in all ages, and, that the very small portion who have enjoyed the blessings of liberty, have soon been reduced to the common level of slavery and misery. The cause of this general vassalage may be traced to a principle of human nature, which is more powerful and operative than all the others combined: it is that lust of dominion which is inherent in every mind, in a greater or less degree; this is so universal and ever active a passion as to influence all our ancestors; the different situation and qualifications of men only modifies and varies the complexion and operation of it." [36]

The heavy-handed satire published in the *Independent Gazetteer* of Philadelphia as the "Address of John Humble" on October 29, 1787, presented the national Constitution as an instrument of class struggle by the "well-born" who intended to enslave the "low-born." John Humble, supposedly the "Secretary" of "three millions of low born American slaves" (i.e., lower-class Whites) sarcastically acknowledged on behalf of those three million that "we will allow and admit the said 600 *well born*, immediately to establish and confirm this most noble, most excellent, and truly divine constitution." [37]

While Black slavery was a reference point for Whites worried about their own equality of independence, it was also often seen as a genuine threat to this independence. The slaveless White yeoman might be in a position of political equality with the slaveholder, if slaves were taken out of the political equation. Admitting Black slaves as potential participants in the political equality of independent individuals would undermine the ideology of this kind of equality. Holding no land and being utterly subordinate to the will of their masters, the chattel would only fit into the ideology if they could be seen as mere property. But the Constitutional proposal to include them in the count for representation did more than just provide slaveholding states a representational advantage—it also recognized the slaves as persons, rather than property, at the same time that it increased the power of their owners.

The "Essays of Brutus" appeared in the *New York Journal* from October 1787 to April 1788. They are most often attributed to Robert Yates, but Herbert J. Storing questions this attribution.[38] Brutus objects to the three-fifths clause in the proposed constitution because this would apportion representation partly on the basis of the number of slaves in a state. While he expresses humanitarian opposition to slavery, he does not argue for abolition and inclusion of former slaves as citizens. Instead, he proclaims that "if this [the counting of slaves] be a just ground for representation, the horses in some of the states and the oxen in others, ought to be represented—for a great share in some of them, consists in these animals; and they have as much controul over their own actions, as these poor unhappy creatures, who are intended to be described in the above recited clause, by the words, 'all other persons.'" [39] Even opponents of slavery tended to take the view that slaves existed in a bracket outside the society to be represented in government.

Slavery in early America, then, presents a strange paradox in the emerging national ideology of equality. The institution was, as Burke realized, a vivid illustration of the condition of utter subjection and therefore a spur to the quest for liberty from dominion, at the national level and at the individual level. At the same time, it was also a living contradiction to the theoretical foundations of this quest and a concrete danger to its institutional realization. The three-quarters rule for counting slaves in the new governmental arrangement was a rather unsatisfactory compromise for the question of whether to deal with those in bondage as people in a hierarchical society or as possessions in a society of political equals.

In the "Essays of Brutus," as in most other statements on all sides of the Constitutional debate, the slaves, of course, had no voice of their own. They would either be counted, in some sense, or not be counted. Few actually imagined the slaves doing any counting of their own. In a society of political independents, the dependent had to be counted out. But what if they were to find a voice? James Madison at one point gave an interesting recognition of the need to place slaves outside of human society for the American project to work.

In Federalist No. 43, Madison argued in favor of the Constitution's guarantee of protection from domestic violence. A state may be endangered by alien residents, by adventurers coming in from elsewhere, or by others not holding citizenship, as well as by factions within in it. Madison, a slaveholder, included an evasive reference to another possible source of power during insurrection or partisan struggle: "I take no notice of an unhappy species of population abounding in some states, who during the calm of regular government are sunk below the level of men; but who in the tempestuous scenes of civil violence may emerge into the human character, and give a superiority of strength to any party with which they may associate themselves."[40] Madison, of course, was taking notice of the potential engagement of slaves in a clash. But his claim to "take no notice" is symptomatic of the early American need to avoid direct discussion of the racial caste system, as is his refusal to identify directly the "unhappy species." The attempt to pay no attention to the members of that species, to remove them from the conversation about construction of an egalitarian republic was based on the assertion that they have somehow "sunk below the level of men." But the attempt could not be entirely successful because Madison recognized that factional strife could free the slaves to take sides, allowing them to "emerge into the human character."

Joseph J. Ellis has remarked that Thomas Jefferson had a great gift for compartmentalization,[41] enabling this brilliant founder of the American republic to live as both an advocate of small government and a great extender of presidential power, as the philosopher of liberty and as an owner of the enslaved. Jefferson's ability to compartmentalize is, perhaps, simply a characteristic American trait carried to the extreme. I will argue throughout this book that our ability as Americans to overlook the contradictions in our ideals and practices has often depended on our ability to compartmentalize inconvenient and contradictory facts and views. Slavery and the problem of racial inequality that followed from slavery presented some of the most inconvenient facts in American life. Our ideals of equality changed over the course of the nation's history, but for a long time these ideals depended on the ability to bracket off these particular facts. When the racial caste system did emerge into awareness, it posed fundamental challenges to the ideals.

NOTES

1. Fischer, *Albion's Seed*, 6
2. Fischer, *Four British Folkways*, 36
3. Kornbluth and Murrin, "The Making and Unmaking of an American Ruling Class."
4. Ibid., 29.
5. US Census Bureau, 1990, CPH-3, Tables 2, 4.
6. Kagan, *Dangerous Nation*, 16
7. Main, "Social Mobility in Revolutionary America."
8. Quoted in Linklater, *The Fabric of America*, 29
9. Jefferson, "A Summary View of the Rights of British America."
10. Linklater, *The Fabric of America*, 47.
11. Taylor, *Inquiry into the Principles and Policy of the Government of the United States.*
12. Smith, *Wealth of Nations*, 118.
13. Quoted in Morgan, *The Genuine Article*, 231.
14. Holton, *Unruly Americans and the Origins of the Constitution.*
15. Morgan, *The Genuine Article*, 229.
16. Adams, "Letter XXXII," 4.
17. Storing, *The Complete Anti-Federalist*, "Letters of Cato" VI, 2.6.43, vol. 2, 122 .
18. Ibid., "Essays of Philadelphiensis" X, 3.9.76, vol. 3, 131.
19. Cornell, *The Other Founders*, 48.
20. Ibid., 73.
21. Quoted in Cornell, *The Other Founders*, 96.
22. Storing, *The Complete Anti-Federalist*, "Essays of Brutus" III, 2.9.42, vol. 2, 380.
23. Ibid.
24. Ibid., XVI, 2.9.200, vol. 2, 444.
25. Ibid., "A Review of the Constitution Proposed by the Late Convention by A Federal Republican, 3.6.38, vol. 3, 82.
26. John Adams, quoted in Cappon, *The Adams-Jefferson Letters*, 371.
27. Ibid.
28. Thomas Jefferson, quoted in Cappon, *The Adams-Jefferson Letters*, 388.
29. Carson, *The Measure of Merit.*
30. Johnson, *Taxation No Tyranny*, 89

CHAPTER 2

THE RISE OF THE SELF-MADE MAN

ECONOMIC EXPANSION, POPULAR POLITICS, AND MASS COMMUNICATION

THE IMAGE OF THE SELF-MADE MAN

Equality, defined as the independence of self-sufficient individuals, continued to be part of our national mindscape. This perspective on the ideal life condition of Americans carries the implication of self-making since those who do not depend on others are responsible for their own destinies. But independence can easily be a steady state, involving no improvement in station or even comparison with others. Ralph Waldo Emerson's 1841 essay "Self-Reliance" called for individualism in economic and social life, but it concentrated on encouraging readers to be true to their inner natures instead of being ruled and measured by external forces. Emerson's younger friend Henry David Thoreau became a posthumous American hero in his rejection of the ways and institutions of his contemporaries because he eloquently exemplified the equality of going one's own way without concern for self-improvement or rising in the esteem of others. Most Americans did not reject ambition, though. Instead, theirs became a nation of strivers. Thoreau's rejection of striving, moreover, was a self-conscious reaction against the currents of his day, and it is precisely as a reaction that it remains so appealing even down to the present.

In 1954, historian Irvin G. Wyllie declared that "the legendary hero of America is the self-made man."[1] As Wyllie recognized, the phrase "self-made man" only became common in public means of communication in the late 1820s, but Americans looked back into their history to connect a newly rising popular cult to a long tradition of striving. Benjamin Franklin, with his rise from humble origins and great success in so many fields of endeavor, offered an excellent model of the self-made man, but it was only in the Jacksonian era that Franklin's calls to self-improvement through industry and commerce became the basis of a widespread secular creed. Connecticut's Roger Sherman became another image of this type. "By 1830... in the great cities of the North and East, journalists, clergymen, lawyers, and other spokesmen began to lay the foundations for the powerful nineteenth century cult of the self-made man."[2]

Figure 2 shows numbers of times the phrases "self-made man" and "self-made men" (with and without the hyphen) occurred in newspapers in the database Archive of Americana. Part of the increase can be attributed to the sheer growth in numbers of newspapers; a development that I will argue next was linked to the spread of the self-made ideal. It is also notable, though, that the phrase seems to have come into common parlance in the period 1836 to 1855 and then become more frequently used throughout the nineteenth century.

Around the time of the Jacksonian period, Americans began to emphasize a new kind of unequal equality in their idealized visions of their nation. A form of what we now call equality of opportunity mixed increasingly with the older equality of independence. The concepts of equality were connected, and the newer one grew almost imperceptibly from the earlier. Both independence and self-creation emphasized the control of the individual over life circumstances, either to be free from the direction of those above or to move upward on a socioeconomic scale.

Figure 2. Mentions of "Self-Made Man" or "Self-Made Men" (With or Without Hyphen) in the Archive of Americana.

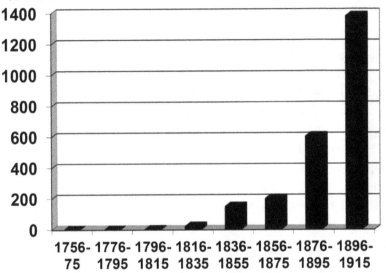

Source. Archive of Americana, Readax, https://infoweb-newsbank-com.

A perception of change and openness in American life encouraged the view that anyone could occupy any position. But the conditions that created this perception only helped to form the general background for a particular type of ideal of human equality. The rise of almost universal male suffrage made political leaders seek ways to proclaim their bonds with the greatest numbers of potential voters. Communication media, especially large-circulation newspapers, put these political leaders on display and began to establish a public arena, in which all elites would be on permanent display.

THE ECONOMIC AND SOCIAL SETTING OF THE EARLY NINETEENTH CENTURY

The extent to which the ideal of the self-made man may have been due to a real increase in the opportunities for upward mobility has been a point of debate among historians. For years, a number of social historians have questioned the perception of the time between the War of 1812 and the Civil War as a time of dramatic mobility and socioeconomic fluidity. Edward Pessen argued that the data from the period showed that actual mobility was quite limited, that antebellum society was highly stratified, and that most of the wealthy were actually from wealthy families.[3] Even before Pessen's work, Stuart Blumin looked at mobility in antebellum Philadelphia argued that low-status jobs in that city had actually become more common with the growth of manufacturing. At the same time, though, the resources of the wealthy increased with profits from the new economy.[4] Ironically, this inequality may have contributed to faith in equality of opportunity since some individuals did rise to be financially successful and those who were successful reached new heights of wealth.

Looking at a single city in the years 1850 to 1880, Stephan Thernstrom concluded that the image of America as an open society was largely illusory and that most the children of most laborers remained laborers and the children of most middle-class people remained middle class.[5] However, Thernstrom recognized opportunity as the essence of the ideology of the nation.

More recent research has suggested that social mobility may have been more common than previously thought and that available land and geographic mobility were still sources of potential opportunities. Steven Herscovici argued that many historians have underestimated economic and social mobility because of the convenience of studying only people who remained in place over time.[6] Herscovici compared men who migrated from Newburyport, Massachusetts, to those who remained in place. He found that the migrants were significantly more successful and suggested that overlooking migration had led historians to substantially underestimate the extent of economic opportunity in early nineteenth-century America.

However common measurable social and economic mobility may have been for Americans before the Civil War, the early nineteenth century was certainly a time of rapid change, marked by growth and fluidity. It was obviously a time of rapid territorial expansion. In 1800, before the Louisiana Purchase, the nation included 888,811 square miles. The Louisiana Purchase in 1803 added 827,192 miles to this, almost doubling the size of the country to 1,716,003 square miles. In another growth spurt, the 1819 treaty with Spain, also known as the Florida Purchase Treaty, brought another 72,003 square miles. Many Americans had already pushed into Spanish territory well before the treaty, so that this was largely a formal recognition of American settlement that had already occurred. Expansion in the West brought the nation to its modern contiguous continental boundaries, with Texas bringing in 390,143 square miles in 1845, Oregon adding 285,680 in 1846, the Mexican Cession contributing 529,017 in 1848, and the Gadsden Purchase adding 29,640 miles in 1853. Whether Americans settled these lands before or after their formal entry into the United States, the new spaces added many more opportunities to what was both an industrializing nation and one that was increasing its available farmland.

Reckoned in 1849 dollars, the total farm gross output of the United States expanded from $178 million in 1810 to $201 million a decade later (one dollar in 1849 would be equal to about $33.80 in 2020). By 1830, this had grown to $364 million, continuing to $631 million in 1840. In 1850, US farm output reached $904 million. While it may not have been true that all Americans were on their way to the path to riches, farm ownership was common. In 1850, a majority (54%) of adult White men living on farms were owners of real property. While there were regional variations in landownership, large proportions of farmers held some land of their own in all parts of the country, In New England, for example, 56 percent of adult White male farm dwellers were property owners. In the

Middle Atlantic division, this came to 52 percent and in the East North Central and West North Central divisions to 59 percent and 53 percent, respectively. Even in the South, under the shadow of plantations, the yeomen held their own. In the South Atlantic division, 51 percent of White male farm dwellers owned property; and in the East South Central division, 52 percent were property owners.[7] A White farmer, in other words, had a reasonably good chance of fulfilling something like the old dream of being an independent yeoman.

Even beyond extending the room for flow out of the eastern cities and raising opportunities for owning farmland, the spread of the United States (and of Americans to places such as West Florida and Texas ahead of the formation of the United States) perpetuated the great real estate boom. The United States Congress contributed to this boom when it passed the Preemption Act in September 1841. Under this law, those who squatted on western lands for at least fourteen months could purchase up to 160 acres for only $1.25 per acre (roughly $37 in 2020 values). As more settlers moved westward, the demand for land increased. Early settlers in a region could sell the land that they had acquired earlier at a profit and move forward, stretching out the frontier line. Ordinary Americans may not have been on the road to riches, but being on the road was at least giving many of them chances to get richer.

Meanwhile, the larger cities may have raised the problem of artisans sinking into an urban working class, but they were also home to another part of the expansive American economy. Between 1810 and 1860, the urban portion of the American population increased from 7 percent to 20 percent.[8] In 1810, employment in manufacturing accounted for only 3.2 percent of the American labor force. Thirty years later, manufacturing employees made up 9 percent of a labor force that was more than twice as large as in 1810[9]. During the 1840s, the value added by manufacturing increased from $187 million (in constant 1849 dollars (again, each 1849 dollar would be equal to about $34 at 2020 values) in 1839 to $447 million in 1849. In the following decade of the 1850s, the value added by manufacturing grew again to the equivalent of $755 million in 1849 dollars.

Entirely new cities sprang into existence as settlers pushed into the west and the south. Chicago, which began as a rude fort, had a population of only 4,470 people in 1840. Ten years later this number had grown to about 30,000, and by the time of the 1860 Republican Presidential Convention, where Abraham Lincoln won the nomination, the population of Chicago had swelled to over 112,000.[10]

Transportation systems spread out over the landscape, promoting geographic mobility as well as economic opportunity. The early nineteenth century was the heyday of canals. The Erie Canal project began in 1817, and the completion of the canal eight years later contributed to making New York one of the world's great cities. New roads, including the great Cumberland Road (also known as the National Road or National Turnpike)—the first national road funded by the federal government—which had begun in Maryland in 1811, moved freight and people along an elaborate network. The canal system slipped into obsolescence almost as quickly as it was built, when it was replaced by rail traffic. In 1830, the United States had only 23 miles of railroad. A decade later, this had grown to 2,818 miles, increasing to 9,021 miles by 1850 and then to 30,626 miles by 1860.

In his first book, *A Week on the Concord and Merrimack Rivers*, published in 1849, Thoreau reflected on a boating trip he had taken in 1839 with his brother. One of the book's numerous digressions recalls the changes on the river as a result of the railroad. "Since our voyage," Thoreau wrote, "the railroad on the bank has been extended and there is now but little boating on the Merrimack. All kinds of produce and stores were formerly conveyed by water, but now nothing is carried up the stream, and almost wood and bricks alone are carried down, and these are also carried on the railroad."[11]

Some individuals were certainly doing better than others in this expansive new economy. If we overemphasize the fact that those who came from advantaged backgrounds were more likely to garner the benefits of the expansion than those who came from disadvantaged backgrounds, or that many people experienced downward mobility, we may be missing an important part of the rise of the ideology of the self-made man. The fact that few people win at the lottery does not keep people from buying lottery tickets, nor does it necessarily lessen the appeal of a huge prize. In this situation, though, the lottery of American life did not just offer chances to the lucky. To establish a farm or to rise in manufacturing actually did depend on the efforts of individuals, even if it was undoubtedly an idealization to conclude that individuals controlled their own destinies.

The perception that America was in some sense an equal society was so widespread that prominent foreign visitors to this country perceived it as the nation's most obvious characteristic and saw equality as the most marked feature of the popular self-image of Americans. The type of equality that these visitors saw, moreover, was primarily an openness to self-creation for all men.

EQUALITY AND MOBILITY IN AMERICA: OBSERVERS FROM FRANCE AND ENGLAND

Two eminent foreign observers of the United States in the early nineteenth clearly saw some form of social equality, either in reality or in the minds of Americans, as a fundamental characteristic of the new nation. Both understood American equality at the time as Americans' faith in the possibility of individual self-creation.

Alexis de Tocqueville introduced his *Democracy in America* by declaring that "among the new things that attracted my attention during my stay in the United States, none struck me more forcefully than the equality of conditions."[12] Tocqueville explained that he "came to see the equality of conditions as the original fact from which each particular fact seemed to derive" *Democracy in America* was all about the nature and consequences of the social equality he found.

Another observer Frances "Fanny" Trollope apparently came to conclusions about the Americans that were somewhat different from those of her French contemporary. Mother of the novelist Anthony Trollope, she found almost nothing she liked during her travels through the United States. She did find that Americans were obsessed with notions of their own equality, but she dismissed any real equality among these "barbaric" people. Trollope preferred to associate with members of the social and cultural elite in the "barbaric" country, and she declared flatly "American citizens are not equal"[13]

Even Trollope, though, saw the unequal equality of social mobility in American life. After describing the progress in wealth of an industrious man she met in the village of Mohawk and telling of his ambition to make his son a lawyer, Trollope sniffed "I have little doubt that he will live to see him [the son] sit in Congress... This is the only feature in American society that I recognize as indicative of the equality they profess. Any man's son may become the equal of any other man's son."[14]

Trollope saw some positive qualities in this state of affairs, noting that "The consciousness [of chances to rise] is certainly a spur to exertion."[15] Still, unwilling to find anything good about the "barbarians," she dismissed the encouragement of ambition as promoting the familiarity of vulgar, low-class people with the refined higher classes. She did perceive a certain amount of equality of social condition, then, as well as equality through the ability to change conditions. The very fact that Americans believed they could change their stations on life encouraged those from humbler origins to put themselves on a level with those Trollope regarded as their betters.

Tocqueville's observations were similar to those of the English writer, but his discussion was more thoughtful and less snobbish. The French visitor saw also saw a high degree of ambition, and he maintained that Americans realized their ambitions within a certain amount of equality

of condition, which I would suggest was linked to the "familiarity" that
Trollope saw across social classes.

Chapter 19 of Volume II, Part III of *Democracy in America* dealt with
the ubiquity and limited scope of American ambition. "The first striking
thing about the United States" Tocqueville wrote, "is the huge number of
people bent on escaping their original condition. The second is the small
number of great ambitions that stand out amid this universal outpouring
of ambition. The desire to rise apparently gnaws at every American, yet
almost no one seems to nurse vast hopes or to aim very high." [16]

Tocqueville attributed the universal striving that he saw among Americans to the overturning of established barriers and the breaking of old
bonds, an explanation consistent with the rapid change and fluidity that
I have argued characterized the decades leading up to the Civil War.
He maintained, though, that although it had become relatively easy for
Americans to advance a little bit, to obtain their own land or to establish
a small enterprise, the very spreading of chances to advance tended to
limit the degrees of advancement. "But if equality of conditions gives all
citizens some resources," he argued, "it prevents anyone from amassing
very extensive amounts of them, and this necessarily imposes fairly
strict limits on desire."[17]

Most of the ambitions of the antebellum period do seem to have
been fairly limited (except perhaps among the quasi-Aristocratic large
slaveholders). Those described as self-made men in the first half of the
nineteenth century were generally sons of farmers who later became
professionals, such as lawyers and especially editors, or mechanics and
artisans. The political setting that I will look at more closely below also
tended to act as a brake on the open expression of overweening self-
aggrandizement. The tendency of popular opinion to promote advancement but discourage quests for glory was part of the conformity and
majority direction of thought that Tocqueville saw in American culture.

Efforts at personal advancement, limited though they may have been
from the French aristocrat's point of view, were part of a broader culture

of meliorism in many parts of the United States at the time. The experience of change and a belief in the constant mutability of positions helped to promote the idea that improvement, including the improvement of an individual's own life and station, could be achieved. One can see this idea in the flourishing of religious and social movements, many of them utopian in character, during the years from 1820 to 1850. The view that individuals can make their own lives better was nourished by the faith that life in general can be better. Along these lines, that astute observer Tocqueville argued that the democratic nature of American society helped to convince Americans of the perfectibility of human beings:

> When citizens are classed by rank, profession, or birth and when everyone is forced to follow the path chosen for him by chance, each individual thinks that the limits of human potential are not far off from wherever he happens to find himself, and no one tries to fight against a destiny that seems inevitable... As castes disappear; as classes come together, and change is evident in men subjected to tumultuous mixing as well as in usages, customs, and law; as new facts emerge and new truths are brought to light; as old opinions disappear and others take their place; the image of an ideal and always fleeting perfection presents itself to the human mind. Every man then becomes a witness to constant change. Some changes make his position worse, and he understands only too well that no nation or individual, no matter how enlightened, is ever infallible. Others improve his lot, and he concludes that man in general is endowed with an infinite capacity to improve his lot.[18]

Tocqueville did not identify economic expansion as the source of the relative classlessness that he saw among Americans and that many of them saw among themselves. From a modern perspective, though, we can see how a growing economy encouraged faith in a better state of affairs for individuals and for the world around them. The self-made man, though, was more than just an individual who had managed to improve himself by taking advantage of increasing opportunities. He was also a link between a humble origin and an elite destination, between the broad masses of people and the most successful.

Tocqueville observed that "[i]n the United States, the more opulent citizens take great care not to stand aloof from the people; on the contrary, they constantly keep on easy terms with the lower classes: they listen to them, they speak to them every day. They know that the rich in democracies always stand in need of the poor..."[19] The best way to avoid standing aloof from the common people was to emphasize that one truly was a common person and could therefore speak the same language and understand the thoughts of the people at large.

Trollope came to conclusions similar to those of Tocqueville, although the two differed greatly in their evaluations. "The assumption of equality," she wrote, "however empty, is sufficient to tincture the manners of the poor with brutal insolence, and subjects the rich to the paltry expediency of sanctioning the falsehood, how deep their conviction that it is such. It cannot, I think, be denied that the great men of America attain to power and to fame, by eternally uttering what they know to be untrue [about the equality of citizens]." [20]

Tocqueville and Trollope noted that the general equality of Americans came with a tendency toward sameness, with no one ranging too high or too low or differing too much from fellow citizens. American "conformity" would be a common criticism of the national character long afterward, not only among foreign observers (including D.H. Lawrence, in the early twentieth century) but also among Americans themselves. A decade and a half after Ralph Waldo Emerson's death, John Jay Chapman considered the great writer's life and work in a long essay in the *Atlantic Monthly*, observing that "Emerson represents a protest against the tyranny of democracy ... He expresses a form of belief in the importance of the individual which is independent of any personal relations he has with the world."[21] The pressure toward conforming or "vulgarity", derived from being part of a community of perceived equals, existed in tension with the individualism of self-authored, self-reliant strivers. This tension would encourage Americans, in politics and journalism, to continually attempt to stand out from their fellows, while also constantly stressing their common origins.

In their observations, the two European observers recognized the importance of a broad-based political system in American society and acknowledged, in their differing ways, the necessity of those in power to appeal continually to the greatest number of their fellows, a necessity that encouraged declarations of commonality. Tocqueville recognized such assertions as part of the culture of conformity that he saw as one of the negative sides of American culture. Trollope understood such proclamations of commonality as expressions of vulgarity by the Americans.

The fascination of the Americans with politics was intimately related to the prevalence of newspapers. Although Trollope, as might be expected, found the literary culture of Americans deplorable, she did note "the universal reading of newspapers."[22] Similarly, Tocqueville found that the sheer number of newspapers limited the power of any particular periodical, but that the press in general "wields enormous power in America. It carries the currents of political life into every section in this vast country." [23]

Electoral politics on a historically unprecedented scale and the sudden appearance of newspapers, the mass media of the nineteenth century, gave rise to the period often known as the Era of the Common Man, which I suggest can also be understood as the Era of the Self-Made Man. These two intertwined forces of the vote and the newspaper helped to take inherited ideas about equality and give these protean ideas a new shape that would become part of the national stock of preconceptions and assumptions.

VOTES AND SELF-MADE POLITICIANS

Economic growth provided the setting for the growth of the ideal of the self-made man. Within this setting, though, the ideal had two more immediate sources. These were the accomplishment of near-universal male suffrage and the development of mass communication. As early as 1802, Maryland abolished its property requirements for voting. Five years later, New Jersey did away with its limitation of the vote to owners of property. Other older states, such as Connecticut, Massachusetts, and New York, held conventions between 1817 and 1821 to lower requirements for property or to do away with it completely. The new states that entered the union by the early 1820s either had no property requirements at all or set these at very low levels. Only five states still required ownership of any property at all for a White man to qualify as a voter in 1824.

The native-born critics of American culture wryly observed the majoritarian power of widespread suffrage. Ralph Waldo Emerson was frequently disdainful of democracy and of voting because he saw elections as subjecting free-thinking individuals to the will of mere numbers. Emerson's protégé, Henry David Thoreau, lamented that "the practical reason why, when the power is once in the hands of the people, a majority are permitted, and for a long time continue, to rule is not because they are most likely to be right, nor because this seems the fairest to the minority, but because they are physically the strongest."[24] The perception that the majority were so strong and the very real need to appeal to popular support in elections provided a great stimulus for office seekers to emphasize their humble origins and their similarities to the voters.

Whether the period of the 1820s through the 1840s really was an Era of the Common Man, as it was frequently labeled, may be open to debate. But it was clearly a time when those running for political offices found it useful to describe themselves as common men, whatever their origins may have been. As the nation approached suffrage for all White men, political campaigns became the most common setting for the use of the term "self-made man" because the term emphasized both one's uncommon ability and continuing connections to the common people who made up a growing portion of the electorate.

Andrew Jackson's victory at the Battle of New Orleans in 1815 made Old Hickory a national hero. Although he lived the life of a wealthy gentleman on his plantation near Nashville, Jackson did rise from modest origins and this background combined with his military fame to make him an enormously popular figure with the small farmers and newly enfranchised segments of the electorate. Although Jefferson had engaged in democratizing symbolism, answering the presidential door in his slippers, Jackson took the symbolism to a new level by becoming the first president to invite the public to his inaugural ball. The riotous proceedings led his critics to label him "King Mob." Most of the presidents after him, though, would seek his kind of mob appeal.

Jackson's vice president and successor, Martin Van Buren, also came from a modest background, and Van Buren's backers sought to emphasize this personal history. In 1830, for example, the *City Gazette* of South Carolina expressed its support for Van Buren by extolling his rise from humble origins:

> His parents were poor; so much so that when a thirst after knowledge prompted him to employ his long winter evenings in reading books loaned to him by friends, they could not afford to furnish him with oil and candles, and he was forced to search the forest for pine knots, which he split up and used for that purpose. After acquiring enough of the rudiments of science to appreciate its value, and being (prevented by pecuniary circumstances from obtaining a public education, he commenced the study of law in his native village, and was admitted to the Bar at the age of 22. He subsequently practiced at Sandy Hill and at Albany, and has risen rapidly through the various grades of civil office to the distinguished situation which he now occupies. He is emphatically what has been said of Franklin, Rittenhouse, and Roger Sherman; a self-made man.[25]

The phrase "self-made man," and the identification with Benjamin Franklin and the other retrospectively identified self-made men of American history here occurred as part of the political effort to appeal to the new American voters. Again, in November 1836, the newspaper *The Age* hailed Van Buren as "The Self Made Man" and asked rhetorically "Who was the son of a poor but respectable farmer of Kinderhook, who acquired the rudiments of his education after the conclusion of his daily toils by the light of his father's fire – who [...] at the age of 18 years had already adopted the political principles of the Jeffersonian or Democratic party]...]?" [26]

By the 1830s, candidates for political office at all levels sought to exhibit simultaneously their superior abilities and their similarities to the great mass of voters by laying claim to the title of "self-made man." In the successful campaign of businessman and lawyer John Davis for governor of Massachusetts in 1833, a supporting article described him as "the son of an honest farmer [...] born to hard work and frugal fare [...] Until he was seventeen years old, he received no other instruction than what he was furnished by the town school. He then determined to go to College. His father was too poor to bear his expenses: John Davis went to work and himself earned money to defray the cost of preparation, and himself by his own exertions acquired the means to meet the expenses of his college life at New Haven. Knowledge is doubly valuable, when thus doubly acquired by a man's own industry. Mr. Davis is in every sense a self made man [...] [A]ll his habits, feelings, and sympathies [are] identified with those of the yeomanry."[27]

Claims of rising from lowly beginnings to eminence became part of the standard contest between the Democrats of Jackson and Van Buren and the Whigs of Webster. We can, in fact, see indistinct and shifting American ideas about the nature of equality in this second American party system, successor to the first party competition between the Jeffersonian Republican-Democrats and the Federalists. Part of the public appeal of the Democrats, personified in Andrew Jackson, was the claim to represent independent farmers. Thus, Jackson's opposition to a central bank that would presumably be controlled by an economic elite owed a good deal to the old worries about a natural aristocracy establishing a hierarchical order that would subordinate the yeomen-farmers and pioneer settlers. Whig support for tariffs to encourage industrial improvements and for federally financed industrial improvements, in contrast, was more consistent with the emerging antebellum economy that provided a setting for upward mobility. Both parties, however, drew on the same body of ideas about equality in their pursuit of political office.

Under the title "A Self Made Man," an 1837 newspaper portrait of the Virginia Whig politician Vincent Witcher proclaimed "he mauled rails until twenty-one, and his wife taught him to read [...] To have surmounted such difficulties, overcome the adversity of early circumstances, and by the force of native talent, honorable conduct, and self-directed energy, ranked himself with the distinguished men of his county, is a testimony of worth, to the wise and virtuous, which outweighs 'all the blood of the Howards.'" [28]

In this political environment, the term "aristocracy" lost the positive connotations that could be found in Jefferson's natural aristocracy and even the dangerous virtues that Adams ascribed to elites seemed to disappear from popular view. "Aristocracy" became a term of unmixed opprobrium. The self-made man from the second quarter of the nineteenth century on managed the feat of both rising above the common people and still being one of them. Defending the Jacksonian Democrat Amos Kendall, then serving as Postmaster General, against his critics, the *Daily Ohio Statesman* averred in 1837, "say what the opposition may, there is certainly a strong tincture of aristocracy in their composition." The reason for critics' attacks on Postmaster General Kendall "is to be found in the fact that he is a self made man. He cannot trace his descent through a long line of distinguished ancestors." [29]

In David "Davy" Crockett of Tennessee, the Whigs presented the politically advantageous combination of independence and upward mobility. Like Jackson, Colonel Crockett came to public attention through military exploits—in Crockett's case through fighting against the Creek Indians. Crockett was elected to Congress in 1827 and joined the Whig

Party in the 1830s after breaking with the Democrat administration. With the help of his new party, he packaged himself as a frontiersman and representative of the common people, most notably in the account he supposedly wrote of his own life and published in 1834.[30] This backwoods figure of independence rapidly became a spokesman for Whig projects of industrial improvement; touring the northeast and writing a glowing account of life in the Massachusetts factories.[31] Among Crockett's other literary endeavors, or works that were written for him, was a biography of President Martin Van Buren, which attacked the president, who really did have a legitimate claim to being self-made, as the undeserving, anointed successor of Andrew Jackson.[32]

Crockett's (or his ghostwriter's) attack on Van Buren was part of a Whig strategy that demonstrated how important it had become to be a self-made product of the common public. Coming from a privileged background, associating with an elite, or displaying any of the characteristics Americans now identified as "aristocratic" became, in the language used to defend Daniel Webster, a "vile calumny." Such a supposed calumny became central to the campaign against Van Buren for the 1840 presidency.

The *New York Spectator* in 1836 responded to a previous claim by the *New Orleans Bee* that "the great, the strong, the abiding claim of Martin Van Buren [...] is the fact of his being an *uncompromising opponent* of the would-be noblesse, the *aristocratical gentry* of the land." Calling this characterization of Van Buren a "precious bit of humbug," the *New York Spectator* quoted New York lawyer and former US Congressman Dudley Selden who protested against his own identification as an "aristocrat" by declaring that he had seen Van Buren

> [...] reclining in his splendid English coach, with a splendid pair of English horses, an English footman behind and an English coachman before dressed in splendid liveries, whirling by and splashing the mud on me, as I have been making my way on foot, through mud, wind, and rain in the Pennsylvania Avenue,

toward the Capitol, I have thought it strange, that I, the wind and weather-beaten pedestrian, should be called an aristocrat, and that he, master of that splendid gorgeous equipage, should be deemed the head of the great democratic family![33]

As the 1840 election approached, Van Buren the self-made man was transformed by his opponents into Van Buren the self-indulgent aristocrat, a term of opprobrium that politicians hurled at each other. Representative Charles Ogle of Pennsylvania assaulted the president's supposedly elegant way of life when Van Buren sought appropriations to repair the leaky and poorly outfitted White House. "Mr. Van Buren [...]," charged Ogle, "is fond of pomp and show, and the trappings of power [...] He dresses in the height of fashion, and his equipage is the most magnificent that dashes through the avenues of this magnificent city. His public dinner parties are also splendid beyond description." [34]

While Van Buren, who actually had risen from fairly common beginnings, was portrayed as an effete member of the ruling class, his Whig opponent, William Henry Harrison, who had been born into the Virginia aristocracy, became a log-cabin commoner. Following the path of Jackson and Crockett, Harrison had achieved renown as a military hero, while still retaining (or more accurately, assuming) the identity of a hard cider-drinking ordinary man. In the struggle between Tippecanoe, as Harrison became known after the battle where his forces defeated Chief Tecumseh's federation in 1811, and Van Buren, the greatest accusation of all became that of being an aristocrat, rather than a self-made man.

The example of Vincent Witcher shows us that the hard-working, self-taught, rail-splitting politician had become a recognized figure in public life before the rise of Abraham Lincoln. The legendary log cabin as a symbol of lowly origins and communion with the humble classes also dated back at least as far as the candidacy of William Henry Harrison, although Lincoln had actually lived in such a cabin as a child, while Harrison had only used one as the nineteenth-century equivalent of a photo op.

Richard Hofstedter's caustic claim that Lincoln opportunistically used the self-made man myth as a means of career promotion probably imposed a mid-twentieth century skepticism on a mid-nineteenth century commonplace idea.[35] By Lincoln's time, emphasizing humble origins had become normal among aspiring public figures. Lincoln became the apotheosis of the self-made man in public life only after the nation's bloody war and his assassination, but the figure he represented was well established by the 1860s.

NEWSPAPERS AND APPEALING TO THE COMMON READER

Ideas take form through communication, and forms of communication shape ideas. The mass-circulation newspaper was the most influential form of communication in American history before the invention of twentieth-century electronic media. The debates about the natural aristocracy that we saw in the previous chapter often took place in newspapers or in printed broadsheets aimed at wide circulation and quick consumption. In the same years that the vote spread across American society (at least among White males), the press flourished even more and became an essential part of the nation's popular culture.

The old flatbed press, essentially the same mechanism for printing with moveable type that Gutenberg had used, was a relatively slow mechanism that could print out sheets for distribution at coffee houses or other public places. By the beginning of the Jacksonian period, the steam-driven rotary press was making it possible to crank out thousands of pages rapidly at low prices. When James Gordon Bennett started publishing the *New York Herald* in 1835, his mass-circulation newspaper owed a great deal to the rotary press, but it also responded to a public demand for news already noted by Trollope and Tocqueville. With the invention and almost immediate spread of the telegraph in the 1840s, the United States became an information society that included almost all of the American White men, since estimates from census data show that over 92 percent of White males aged 21 or older were literate by 1850.

The growing mass-circulation newspapers were not as overtly partisan as the papers and broadsheets of the late eighteenth century had been. Nevertheless, the political and journalistic worlds were closely connected. This was not just because most of the news was political, then as now. Thoreau referred to the interweaving of press and politics in his dismissal of voting as a means of political reform. In an essay "Civil Disobedience," he wrote: "I hear of a convention to be held at Baltimore, or elsewhere, for the selection of a candidate for the Presidency, made up chiefly of editors and men who are politicians by profession." [36]

One can find numerous examples of individuals who moved back and forth between the professions of editor and politician. The life of political operative Thurlow Weed provides a vivid illustration of the inseparability of popular press and electoral politics in the early nineteenth century. According to the hefty two volumes of his autobiography, edited by his daughter Harriet Weed,[37] Thurlow Weed developed an interest in the party politics of the Republican-Democrats and Federalists and an ambition to work with newspapers while he was still a child. After a short time as a cabin boy on a sloop between Catskill and New York, Weed went to work at the office of the *Catskill Recorder* when he was about eleven years old. From there, Weed's political rise and his journalistic work were two parts of the same career.

Just as the cinematic media today celebrates people in the movie industry, the newspaper industry of the early nineteenth century often celebrated its members. While the politicians had a clear interest in offering themselves up to the public as exemplary because of their achievement and common in origins, those who were writing for the broad public also tended to portray themselves as models of public virtue.

A moral tale reprinted in various papers in 1840, variously known as "The Poor Printer and the Exclusives" or "The Journeyman and the Exclusives" told the story of Harriet Lee, who married the journeyman printer William Malcolm against the wishes of her haughty uncle and aunt, who wanted her to marry a lawyer or a merchant. Over the years, though, the lawyer ended up with a liquor habit and the merchant went to prison for forger. Malcom, through the hard work a diligent self-made man, became the successful, respected owner of the newspaper he had worked on, and the aristocratic uncle and aunt were forced to confess the error of their ways. It might be worth noting that the paragon of virtue lauded in this newspaper fiction was a newspaperman.

The early nineteenth century, then, saw the expansion of popular politics and the growth of the mass medium of newspapers. Those who sought public attention and those who sought to appeal for public support needed to emphasize their connections to the widest possible range of the people. Whether they came from humble origins, as Thurlow Weed did, or from the upper crust, as William Henry Harrison did, politicians and journalists alike had to place themselves on the same plane as their audiences. Building on the suspicion surrounding aristocracy and on the ideal of the independent individual, public men could establish their links to their fellow citizens by stressing their common origins. Whatever they had achieved was what everyone could achieve, or what would be possible for every individual in the rising generation through dedication, persistence, and virtue.

The equality of self-created common men reached a mystical pitch in Walt Whitman's *Leaves of Grass*, first published in 1855 and perhaps the most moving expression of democracy in the years before the Civil War. A printer and newspaper editor, Whitman lived and worked directly within that mass medium of journalism and his writing can be understood, at least in part, as a refinement and exaltation of the ethos of the self-created individual that permeated the popular publications of the times. In the work of this poet-journalist, the egalitarian celebration of self became a metaphysical principle, invoked in long lists of common men and women.

At the beginning of Book I of *Leaves of Grass* Whitman proclaimed:

> One's-self I sing, a simple separate person,
> Yet utter the word Democratic, the word En-Masse.

The poet-journalist resolved the tension between the self-reliant individual and the communitarian democrat by imagining all joined together but each living in a separate fullness. Whether this resolution could work outside of poetic enthusiasm is open to question. But the unrestrained cultivation of self within a commitment to egalitarianism perpetually recurred as a dream in the public imagination.

The ideal of the self-made man reached beyond the connected arenas of journalism and politics. When newspapers extolled men who had risen from nothing and when political leaders claimed to be such men, they played out their roles on popular stages. The agricultural and commercial expansion of the early nineteenth century made possible a relatively high degree of mobility by world historical standards. But economic conditions only create the conditions for popular concepts, which take hold and spread through communication and emulation. As newspaper readers and voters looked at their own lives, they interpreted their experiences and their ambitions for their children based on what they read and saw. During the second quarter of the nineteenth century, then, politics and journalism served as the main media for communicating a particular vision of individual upward mobility throughout much of American society.

SLAVES, YEOMEN, AND THE SLAVOCRACY

The ideal of the self-made man grew at the same time that there were more men (and women) who quite clearly had no opportunity for upward socioeconomic mobility. The US Census of 1800 reported that the nation had 894,452 slaves, including those residing in the Indiana and Mississippi territories and the territory northwest of the Ohio River. Forty years later, the Census of 1840 showed that the number of slaves had grown to 2,487,355. Many of the founders, including Jefferson, had hoped that if they would just ignore slavery it would eventually disappear by itself. Instead, in a nation that valued self-creation, more people than ever had not even the most minimal influence over their own destinies.

The territorial expansion of the United States in the early nineteenth century opened new opportunities for individuals, and it was a major part of the nation's economic expansion. The opening of new lands, together with new agricultural endeavors, though, introduced complications into the collective narrative of self-creation. As the old tobacco plantation economy of Virginia reached exhaustion, Eli Whitney's gin made vast fields of cotton profitable in the lower South. The revolution in Saint Domingue (Haiti) slashed sugar production on that island and sugar cane fields spread in the Lower Mississippi Valley. The lands of the South and Southwest that received American settlers offered opportunities for small farmers to make independent livings, but the big opportunities were in the plantation crops of cotton, sugar, and rice, which were dependent upon slave labor. The demand for slaves in the lower South tended to shift the older economy of Virginia away from producing tobacco and toward producing people for sale.

In the early nineteenth century, the South, especially the lower South, was a strange combination of class and caste systems. Some members of the elite in the new lower South did stem from long-established high-status families of the upper South. President Zachary Taylor, for example, was the descendant of Virginia landowners. He had used his inheritance to buy a large plantation in Louisiana. Other plantation owners, however, were children of immigrants with few claims to aristocratic status. Even John C. Calhoun, the South Carolina spokesman for the plantation way of life, was the son of a Scotch Irish immigrant who had settled first in Virginia and then moved to the back country of South Carolina. While Calhoun's father had become an eminent member of his community, he was hardly the scion of generations of Cavaliers.

While the expansion of opportunities in the South offered chances for upward mobility in the first decades of the nineteenth century, the same economic system that made that mobility possibility began to close down the window of opportunities in the early Jacksonian period. Economist John Majewski has argued that the antebellum southern economy faced two serious difficulties. The first was precisely the type of agriculture that made wealth possible for some Whites. Cash crops like cotton and tobacco exhausted the soil, so that they required large expanses of land, of which only small portions could be used, and they encouraged movement to new lands. Consequently, population densities tended to remain low. The second problem was the slave labor that worked those expanses of land. Slaves did not engage in entrepreneurship, and they consumed only limited amounts of goods. A scattered population with a large proportion of people who neither invested nor consumed did not create a dynamic economy.[38] The slave economy could only offer new chances to rise by providing new lands to settle, thus creating some of the pressures for the spread of slavery into the new lands acquired as a result of the Louisiana Purchase and the acquisition of Texas and the Western lands following the Mexican-American War.

Although mobility was rapidly closing down in the second quarter of the nineteenth century, we should remember that the Southern society that immediately preceded the Civil War had been a highly fluid one that was only beginning to solidify into an elite-dominated social hierarchy by the 1830s and 1840s. While it was a fairly open class system within the White race in the early part of the nineteenth century, it was still a closed caste system in terms of race. This introduced some odd elements into American thinking about the equality of people. Among Southern Whites, the existence of a subject race for a time provided chances for self-improvement and fueled the idea that the rich and powerful were the same as other people because other people could become rich and powerful. The plantation owner Andrew Jackson was not only a genuinely self-made man; he became a model for self-made men to the extent that the historical period around him has become known as "Jacksonian Democracy." Being a member of the slave-owning race also gave Whites a common claim to superiority, such that Whites could consider themselves equal because they all shared the same racial identity. When Tocqueville met with John Quincy Adams in Boston, the former president and newly elected congressman said that "every white man in the South is an equally privileged being, in that his lot is to make the Negroes work without working himself."[39]

Looking back at slavery today, our sole response as early twenty-first century Americans is one of moral repugnance. Many early Americans shared this repugnance and even slave holders often saw the institution as profoundly unjust in the first post-Revolutionary decades. However, as David Goldfield has recently pointed out, by the time America was entering the Jacksonian period Southerners often felt themselves to be utterly dependent upon this disturbing institution and unjustly condemned by other Americans who also benefitted from the agricultural economy of the South.[40]

Beyond mere economic concerns, many in the slave states worried about their own safety and that of their families if the slave population were to gain freedom. The Haitian Revolution (1791–1804) was an historic uprising against racial exploitation, but it was an extremely bloody conflict that entailed the mass slaughter of Whites, as well as the widespread torture and murder of insurgent slaves by French troops. The series of unsuccessful slave revolts in North America raised worries about whether a newly liberated population could result in similar violence in the United States. Thus, in writing to John Holmes on the Missouri question in 1820, the elderly Thomas Jefferson said of slavery that "we have the wolf by the ear, and we can neither hold him nor safely let him go. Justice is in one scale, and self preservation in the other."[41] Today, we might answer that worries about how freed slaves would react were exaggerated and that abolition would have been the best way to avoid conflict and to create a working market society in the South. But we see things from a different vantage point.

When justice is at odds with perceived self-preservation, people will seek ways to reconcile the two, and it is easier to change views of justice than perceptions of self-preservation. Slavery had been a source of opportunity and a basis for equal standing among White men. But even apart from the economic rigidity it began to introduce, justifying a caste system required interpreting society in terms of hierarchy, order, and stability. As the debate over slavery intensified from 1820 onward, opponents of slavery in the Northeast and West began to describe the South as a "slavocracy," and as the opposite of their egalitarianism and the chief threat to it. As often happens in a conflict, the accused revalued accusations as praise and created myths of the South as the ideal, ordered, aristocratic society.

By the eve of the Civil War, the term "slavocracy" had become a common term of opprobrium. At a meeting of German Republicans in Jersey City in 1856, one Mr. Wehle from Hoboken proclaimed, in speaking of the Kansas-Nebraska bill that "the Slavocracy was the most insufferable aristocracy that the world had ever seen [...] It was the natural result of slavery that White laborers would be slaves almost as much as the Black laborers to the slaveholders, and they should be regarded and treated by them as such."[42]

Outside the South and among the critics of slavery, the "slavocracy" contributed to the ideal of the self-made man by providing an opposite and contrast. When Frederick Douglass, a former slave and one of the most famous opponents of slavery, spoke at Shiloh Church in 1859, he devoted his lecture to the topic of "self-made men." According to a contemporary account in his own newspaper, Frederick Douglass "spoke of the qualities which distinguished the self-made man from all others, and of the great inducements which are offered to men in this country to rise to high positions by their own efforts [... and] of Slavery as the loathsome load which was dragging down the best energies of the country[...]"[43]

Contrasts between the slavocracy and the realm of self-made men brought both into sharp relief. Slavery was a living contradiction of equality as self-creation as it had been a contradiction of equality as independence. One way to resolve this contradiction would have been to continue the program of removing the peculiar institution from public discourse, as the framers of the Constitution had been forced to do in order to establish the nation. The gag rule that sought to prevent members of Congress from bringing up the issue of slavery sought to do just this. However, with the debate over the spread of slavery to the new territories, the issue of slavery became ever more difficult to avoid.

Unable to hide slavery or to take it out of public discourse, some of those who did not favor abolition rejected the egalitarianism of self-creation and adopted an explicit defense of a caste system. John C. Calhoun, that descendant of Scotch Irish immigrants, began to speak as a racial patrician, calling the old arguments for hierarchy and order into service to justify the system of human chattel of his own time and place. Calhoun went beyond simply asserting a racial exception to a general rule of autonomy and self-creation. He extended his argument historically and geographically. All civilized communities in the past, he maintained, have been unequally divided. According to Calhoun, in his day, not only were the societies of Europe unequal but those at the bottom of the European systems found themselves (according to Calhoun) in worse conditions than the slaves of the South. Calhoun may not have been the "Marx of the master class" of Richard Hofstedter's famous formulation, but the South Carolinian did describe a radically reactionary alternative to the individualistically egalitarian ideology of self-creation. This alternative was reactionary in the truest sense of the word, moreover, since it took shape as the reaction to a cultural rejection of the slaveholder's way of life.

By the middle of the nineteenth century, American social values took on a sharp dualism: an affirmation of hierarchy and stability voiced by articulate defenders of slavery, such as Calhoun, against a commitment to individualistic fluidity and personal responsibility. Polarization generally pushes opposed parties toward oversimplification of competing arguments. For his part, Calhoun, as a spokesman for the new planter class, dismissed the suffering of slaves and the highly individualistic, striving origins of many members of the class. As a political thinker, though, Calhoun also raised important questions ignored by the proponents of egalitarian individualism. If a society rests on stable institutions, what happens when those institutions, however unfair, dissolve into a mass of competing individuals? How can unprepared and widely unaccepted groups of people suddenly enter a competitive labor market and expect to rise to any satisfactory condition? When national numerical majorities make political decisions, who protects regional interests? Today, of course, few Americans would accept Calhoun's answers. But we also fail to give the questions serious consideration because we associate them with an institution that we find morally repugnant and with the side that lost the war.

While we are heirs to the doctrine of individual self-creation, we also need to remember that the doctrine has changed over time. For devotees of the self-made man, including Douglass, equality did not require that the state regulate society to ensure equal opportunity for every man. Equality required only that no legal institution maintain a caste system and prevent individuals from distinguishing themselves from others. This type of unequal equality had a great deal in common with the ideal of the equality of independent individuals: both free yeomen on their lands and self-made men enjoyed procedural equalities of negative freedom. No aristocracy, slavocracy, or governing body imposed a status. The argument that everyone should have exactly the same opportunities in life would have seemed strange to most early Americans. In fact, the distinguishing characteristic of self-made men was precisely that they had enjoyed fewer chances than others, and this was what made their success admirable.

SELF-MADE WOMEN?

The contemporary reader may well have noticed the absence of women, aside from the traveler Frances Trollope, in this chapter. This absence is not an oversight, although unconscious bias is always a potential problem in social historical analysis, but rather because the discussion thus far represents an effort to understand early American public values on their own terms. In looking at politics and journalism as helping to make a stage for the role of the self-made man, I have stressed that this was a part played in the nation's emerging public life. Most Americans did not see the household as belonging in public life, and most men and women tended to allocate women to the household. Women would only gradually begin to participate in the shifting conversation about equality and inequality over the course of many decades.

The debate over slavery did spark some of the earliest assertions that women should be free to define themselves. By throwing into stark relief the distinction between "slavocracy" and self-creation, the debate challenged even widely accepted household hierarchies. It also stiffened support for slavery as an established social institution. As Christine Stansell observes, "the association of women's rights with the preeminent issue of the day pushed it into proslavery discourse as well. Women's rights reformers would turn into Exhibit A for the slaveholders' case that abolition was an insult to the God-given order of master governing slave, husband governing wife."[44]

Even for many of the staunchest opponents of slavery, though, the emancipation of women was too extreme and radical in the early nineteenth century. The view that a woman should create her own life and identity outside the home would have been considered bizarre not only by most men but also by most women in the antebellum era. Catherine E. Beecher's response to the abolitionist Angelina E. Grimke's linking of women's public participation and abolitionism represents a common response among even women who intensely opposed slavery. Deeply committed to the domestic role of women, Beecher wrote to Grimke in 1837 regarding their differing social ideas. On relations between the sexes, Beecher argued that "Heaven has appointed to one sex the superior to the other the subordinated station, and this without any reference to the character or conduct of either. It is therefore as much for the dignity as for the interest of females, in all respects to conform to the duties of this relation."[45]

In the public sphere of action, of jobs, politics and newspapers, position was the consequence of individual self-making; however, in the domestic sphere of marital relations, established hierarchy still reigned. For people to be equal in their capacity to attain positions, there must be a distinction between the person and the position. Those who are identical with some established place in a society cannot readily move among positions. In the early nineteenth century, men and women were identical with their socially determined gender roles. Participating in a market society, White men did not ultimately define themselves as farmers, artisans, or merchants because in theory someone who occupied one place at one point in time might later occupy another one. The debate over the condition of Black men concerned whether Black men would participate in that fluid market system. If not, they would be wholly circumscribed by positions in a racial caste hierarchy. The widely accepted separation between the domestic and the public identified women so closely with their social roles that the question of the political and economic equality of women simply could not be taken seriously by most Americans. The effort to seek the kinds of access to public life for men and women would come only as people became less likely to define themselves according to the traditional gender roles of the time. and to define themselves instead as abstract individuals in the public world outside of a restricted domestic sphere. As social and economic change weakened the boundaries between the public and the domestic, the conditions and opportunities available to women, like the conditions and opportunities available to non-Whites, would pose fundamental challenges for these early American notions of equality.

NOTES

1. Wyllie *The Self-Made Man in America*, 7
2. Ibid., 13
3. Pessen, *Three Centuries of Social Mobility in America*.
4. Blumin, "The Historical Study of Vertical Mobility."
5. Thernstrom, *Poverty and Progress*.
6. Herscovici, "Migration and Mobility," 58.
7. Author's calculations from census data
8. US Census. 1990 Census of Population and Housing, "1990 Population and Housing Unit Counts: United States," table 4.
9. Gibson and Jung, *Historical Census Statistics*, 167–181
10. Gibson and Jung, *Historical Census Statistics*.
11. Thoreau, *A Week on the Concord and Merrimack Rivers*, 264.
12. Tocqueville *Democracy in America*, 3.
13. Trollope, *Domestic Manners of the Americans*, vol. 2, 160.
14. Ibid., vol. 1, 171
15. Ibid.
16. Tocqueville, *Democracy in America*, 738.
17. Ibid., 740.
18. Ibid., 514–515.
19. Ibid., 127.
20. Trollope, *Domestic Manners of the Americans*, vol. 2, 159–160.
21. Chapman, "Emerson," 601.
22. Trollope, *Domestic Manners of the Americans*, vol. 1, 128.
23. Tocqueville, *Democracy in America*, 212.
24. Thoreau, "Civil Disobedience," 6.
25. "Mr. Van Buren," *Salem Gazette*, October 25, 1853, 1.
26. "Democratic Candidates for President, Martin Van Buren, the Self-Made Man," *The Age*, November 2, 1836, 3.
27. "Mr. Davis," *Salem Gazette*, October 2, 1833, 2.
28. "A Self Made Man," *Hampshire Gazette*, February 22, 1837, 2.
29. "Amos Kendall," *Ohio Daily Statesman*, November 6, 1837, 1.
30. Crockett, *A Narrative of the Life of David Crockett*.
31. See Crockett, *An Account of Col. Crockett's Tour*.
32. Crockett, *The Life of Martin Van Buren*.
33. Selden, "Who are the Aristocrats?," 3.

34. Quoted in "See How the People's Money Goes, The Gold Spoon Story," *The Vermont Phoenix,* August 7, 1840, 2.
35. Hofstedter. "Abraham Lincoln and the Self-Made Myth."
36. Thoreau, "Civil Disobedience," 14–15.
37. Weed, *Autobiography of Thurlow Weed.*
38. Majewksi, *Modernizing a Slave Economy.*
39. Quoted in Damrosch, *Tocqueville's Discovery of America,* 100.
40. Goldfield, *America Aflame.*
41. Jefferson, "Letter to John Holmes," 159.
42. "Jersey City German Republicans," *New York Herald Tribune,* September 9, 1856, 5.
43. "Frederick Douglass," *Frederick Douglass' Paper,* January 14, 1859, 3.
44. Stansell, *The Feminist Promise,* 43.
45. Beecher, "An Essay on Slavery and Abolition Addressed to Miss A.E. Grimke," 207.

CHAPTER 3

THE SELF-MADE MAN AND THE CITIZEN IN A SEGREGATED, CORPORATE SOCIETY

IDEOLOGY AND SOCIAL CHANGE

People in every era interpret their environments with concepts received from the past. As social environments inevitably change, though, the interpreters have to rework their received concepts to make sense of the present. In this chapter, I identify the main features of American society in the late nineteenth century as the emergence of a large-scale corporate, city-based economy fueled by immigrants seeking and generally finding opportunities for themselves and their children and as the replacement of slavery by segregation.

By the end of the Civil War, the ideology of the self-made man, the common individual rising through life by his own efforts, had become deeply entrenched in the shared worldview of Americans. The traditional, ordered social hierarchy called up not only images of European aristocracy but also the newly defeated slave powers. While slavery had been largely discredited, racial castes continued to be a fact of life in much of the United States. While the continuation of a caste society posed one challenge to the ideal of the self-made man, the rise of a new type of class society produced another. The market economy of the United States underwent a dramatic transformation to a system of corporate mass production, entailing rapid urbanization and the growth of formal organizations. Americans faced the dilemma of how to adapt their social values to account, on the one hand, for the continuation of racial castes and, on the other, for the sudden appearance of vast, impersonal bureaucratic institutions.

The period that immediately followed the war saw some attempt at reordering the society of the former slave states along lines more consistent with the ideals of independence and self-creation. Historian Eric Foner has argued that the Reconstruction era was an "unfinished revolution" because its efforts at redesigning the social, political, and economic order created by slavery proved half-hearted and ultimately left the racial caste system in place. Foner's argument may labor under the usual burdens of counterfactual history. Present-day historians, looking back from the vantage of the post–Civil Rights era, may see clearly what the American government should have done in the 1860s and 1870s. The view was probably murkier for those who were living during those times.

Whatever alternative paths we may imagine and prefer for our own past, the actual past was one in which the reality of a racial caste system had to somehow be reconciled with the idea that each individual should be equal in the ability to control his own destiny, an idea with roots in older popular notions of autonomy. One way to reconcile the contradiction was to continue to place questions of race outside the national conversation, by ignoring these questions altogether or by asserting racism as a way of making a special exception to the general rule. Another way was to imagine the races as somehow equal within separate spheres. Part of the attraction of Booker T. Washington's public program, for both Black and White Americans, was that it offered a way of seeing the option of becoming a self-made man for Black Americans within a segregated society.

While racial inequality posed a challenge to ideals of equality as individual self-direction, new demographic trends gave these ideals a boost. The period from the Civil War to World War I was the time of the first great immigration wave in American history. People incline most toward the acceptance of hierarchy, order, and stability when they stay in one place and when they do the things their parents and grandparents have done before them. Those who are on the move look for better chances, for greater opportunities. Previously, I identified geographic mobility within America as a stimulant to real social mobility and as an even stronger stimulant to belief in social mobility. The population movement from the Old World to the New World at this time brought in so many people who were seeking opportunities, boosting the "land of opportunity" image of American society.

The land the immigrants reached differed from the pre–Civil War agricultural society. The new arrivals often remained in urban locations and found their opportunities, however limited at first, in an industrializing setting rapidly consolidating into large corporate organizations. Many Americans responded to this emerging corporate setting with ambivalence. The concept of the equality of individuals retained commitments to the ideal of independent yeomen and to that of freely competing self-made men. These commitments came into conflict with the structured environment fostered by the factory and the corporate bureaucracy. However, this environment also provided increased chances for upward mobility. Corporate society at once intensified allegiance to older views of individualistic competitive equality by offering challenges to those views and built new and more formalized channels for individual competition.

The turn-of-the century movement known as progressivism is sometimes characterized as a reaction against the displacement of older ways of life, especially the displacement of the self-employed middle class. I suggest in the following section that this characterization has substantial basis in fact but oversimplifies progressivism, which involved a debate about how to reconcile traditional images of American life with the corporate setting. Some currents of the progressive movement attempted to limit the corporatization of life, while others sought to embrace this trend. This ambivalence is evident in public attitudes toward formal education as an increasingly important means for individual upward mobility in a bureaucratic society. Competing pressures to reject and to embrace a formalized bureaucratic society also, however, brought a new version of equality into American life along with the equality of independence and the equality of self-creation. This was the equality of citizens in extensive, articulated, and often intrusive economic and political organizations.

CITIZENS OF A CORPORATE SOCIETY: PROGRESSIVISM AND THE RISE OF BUREAUCRATIC EQUALITY

The expansion of federal authority required for the prosecution of the Civil War, as well as the fact that the war had been fought by the victors in the name of a union, stimulated political consolidation and a larger, more centralized government. The political consolidation of the United States was accompanied by economic consolidation, stimulated by war spending that promoted the development of railroads, the steel industry, and big finance. During the decades from the Civil War to the end of World War, the United States changed from a mainly agricultural nation to a major industrial producer.

The railroads drove a simultaneous transportation and organizational revolution. By greatly extending the geographical scope of the market-place, railroads made it possible to produce goods in one part of the country and sell them in another, creating demand for the vast fields and stock yielded by the West. That 1869 linking of the railroad tracks connecting the East Coast to the West Coast helped bind the nation into a single market that spurred the expansion of the firms, as well as created needs for a vast army of workers from domestic and international places of origin.

Locomotives also pulled the financing for the new corporate society. Railroads were the first publicly traded stock in the United States. The need for coordinating train schedules over wide expanses of territory led to more elaborate and efficient organizational forms under supervisory hierarchies and highly specialized job descriptions. Railroads even brought a new and more systematic way of thinking about time; the time zones that we now use across the continent initially came into existence by railroad decree.

The total output of coal in the United States grew from 8.4 million short tons in 1850 to 40 million in 1870. By 1890 the United States had outstripped the leading industrial nations of Europe to become the world's foremost producer of manufactured goods. Although we often think about this period as the heyday of the laissez-faire economy, it was, in fact, a time of close collaboration between business and government. The corporate nation, the dominance of big business, big labor, and big government became evident in the United States over the course of the decades following the Civil War. According to the 1930 US Census, from 1914 to 1927, wage earners employed in factories producing products valued at $5,000 or more grew in number from 6,895,000 to 8,350,000, and the value added by manufacturing nearly tripled, from $9,708,000 to $27,585,000. Carol Nackenoff has observed that "The number of production workers nearly quadrupled from the eve of the Civil War to the end of the century. In this same period, the number of manufacturing establishments in the United States expanded more than three and a half times; two-fifths of all US industrial establishments were factories by 1899. Employment in transportation, public utilities, trade, finance, and real estate increased over six fold in these four decades."[1]

The consolidation and institutionalization were clear to contemporary commentators. In his 1905 study of the development of the corporations of his time, John P. Davis noted that "the most important and conspicuous feature of the development of society in Europe and America on its formal or institutional side during the past century (and particularly during the second half of it) has been the growth of corporations. The movement has been most noticeable in the domain of industry, but has by no means been confined to it; only less influential has it been in religion, in the promotion of science, the arts and literature, in amusements, and in the satisfaction of the social-fraternal impulses of mankind. So rapidly have the industrial corporations increased in numbers and wealth in the United States that they are counted by the thousands in the several States and are estimated to own from one fourth to four fifths of all the property in the nation."[2] The self-made tycoon John D. Rockefeller, more succinctly, declared "The day of the combination is here to stay. Individualism has gone, never to return."[3]

The industrial society of the time was increasingly urban. Factories and businesses concentrated the American population in the cities. Figure 3 shows that within a single generation, from 1870 to 1920, the United States went through the transformation from a land in which three-quarters of the people lived in rural areas to one in which the majority lived in cities.

The question of how to respond to the rise of big corporations and to attendant urbanization ran through the political and social debates of the end of the nineteenth century and the beginning of the twentieth. The complex interweaving of reformist thinking known as "progressivism" came out of various attempts to answer this question. Turn-of-the-century progressivism, like most social movements, entailed different and sometimes contradictory strands. Historian Richard Hofstadter oversimplified the movement when he argued that it was essentially a middle-class reaction to the rise of new money, although this reaction was certainly a part of the movement.[4]

Figure 3. Proportions of American Workers in Rural and Urban Locations, 1870–1910.

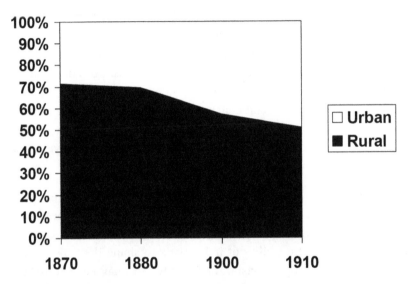

Source. Steven Ruggles, Sarah Flood, Ronald Goeken, Josiah Grover, Erin Meyer, Jose Pacas and Matthew Sobek.2020. IPUMS USA: Version 10.0 [dataset]. Minneapolis, MN: IPUMS, 2020. https://doi.org/10.18128/D010.V10.0

At the risk of engaging in simplification myself, I suggest that one can find two major trends in progressivism, both of which were efforts to identify an appropriate political reaction to the rise of large-scale corporations. What might be termed "regulatory progressivism" perceived society as ideally composed of autonomous individuals engaged in competitive market activities. Regulatory progressivism saw the role of government as limiting the size and influence of business corporations through strategic regulations. What we can call "corporatist progressivism" tended to see public and private corporate collectives as new essential structures in American society. The corporatist progressives believed in close cooperation between big business and an emerging big government, with government controlling and directing or even absorbing large-scale business activities.

In the 1912 Presidential election, these two streams of progressivism flowed as Woodrow Wilson's New Freedom and Theodore Roosevelt's New Nationalism. "For Roosevelt," a biographer of Wilson observed, "the government needed to oversee a mature economy, manage a distribution of power that was not likely to change, and ensure that people affected by that power—workers and consumers—were protected from abuses. For Wilson, government had to reopen the market-place to fresh players, intervene to restore competition, and ensure that smaller players and their workers got a fair shot at getting ahead."[5]

The New Nationalism's progressivism cast government as the ultimate coordinating unit in a regulated, incorporated society. The New Freedom's progressivism sought to limit the power of economic corporations in order to maintain the ability of individuals to shape their own lives. Early Wilsonian progressivism, then, tended to imagine that a state of competition among individuals, conducive to a society of self-made men, could be sustained by political restraint of anticompetitive forces. Ironically, though, President Wilson presided over a vast extension of corporate government following the entry of the United States into World War I. His administration enacted a military draft much more far-reaching than the compulsory military service of the Civil War. Wilson's war administration also became a more active participant in the American economy than any previous federal government had been, and it created close collaborations between big business and big government. As the leftist historian Gabriel Kolko has pointed out "by July 1917 the Wilson administration created the War Industries Board under the domination of men largely from finance and industry [...] Railroad executives ran the Railroad Administration and an oil engineer and entrepreneur ran the Fuel Administration. Advocates of business-government cooperation were predominant, including those who had for some time urged national regulations which would have permitted industry-wide price and output agreements to attain stabilization."[6]

While one strand of political progressivism entailed an individualist reaction, one can also find a general tendency toward institutional control and coordination running across the lines of progressive thought. How did individuals fit into the pattern of growing corporatism and institutionalization? In accordance with the idea of reform as making institutions more responsive to individuals, one trend was to support the equality of all individuals in their relationship to government, especially the federal government. In a centralized state, each citizen would, in theory, have exactly the same relationship to government, which would maintain equality among all. This represented an emerging type of bureaucratic equality, defined by membership and participation in the institution of the state. A second trend, though, moved toward institutionalization as hierarchical efficiency. Each person would have a distinct place and set of duties in the corporate polity, similar to corporate business.

President Theodore Roosevelt, Wilson's most serious rival in the three-way election of 1912, embodied the explicitly statist, corporatist strand of progressivism. Roosevelt summed up in his person the complications and contradictions of shifting images of equality and social position in American society. A scion of the upper crust east coast, Roosevelt's background could serve as an illustration of John Adams' argument that the natural aristocracy of the republic would tend to concentrate power and wealth in families. But Roosevelt also owed a great deal to the kind of public appeal to the everyman that had become common with the expanding influence of the press and the interweaving of press and politics. Although born to privilege, Roosevelt found his own equivalent of the log cabin in the ranch that enabled him to publicize himself as a rugged, self-reliant individual. In a real sense, Roosevelt was indeed a self-made man: he created his own public persona. This highly individualistic character became the most visible advocate of the corporate state.

Herbert Croly, a devoted adherent of Theodore Roosevelt, wrote a key text of strong government progressivism. Croly's *The Promise of American Life* recognized the institutionalization of American society and made an argument for an institutional response. Croly maintained that in the pre–Civil War period, the United States offered a chance to start anew by crossing the Atlantic and to create an independent and abundant life through access to the vast forests and lands of the frontier. [7] However, the promise of liberty and self-sufficiency held out by the earlier nation was becoming a thing of the past. By Croly's time, the frontier had already been settled. Even more importantly, large, highly specialized organizations now dominated the economic, social, and political character of the nation.

The nationalist vision of equality proposed by Croly was markedly different from the competitive equality of self-made men. From Croly's perspective, citizens were equal because each had the same relationship to the corporate state. This rising bureaucratic version of equality appears even more clearly in Edward Bellamy's 1888 utopian novel *Looking Backward,* which extended the logic of this strand of progressive ideals into a hoped-for future, in which membership in a centralized corporate polity results in both the perfect equality of citizens and a completely efficient organization of society. Bellamy, of course, wrote before Theodore Roosevelt ascended to power and before Herbert Croly's intellectual formulation of Rooseveltian progressivism. Still, it makes sense to read Bellamy's fantasy as carrying the national corporatist thinking that Roosevelt and Croly would take up to an ultimate conclusion.

In Bellamy's novel, the hero awakes in a distant future, in which the consolidation and coordination of business and labor have resulted in utopia by reaching the final point of a completely coordinated society under public management. Dr. Leete, the protagonist's guide to the wonderful world of the future explains the benevolent evolution:

> Early in the last century the evolution was completed by the final consolidation of the entire capital of the nation. The industry and

commerce of the country, ceasing to be conducted by a set of irresponsible corporations and syndicates of private persons at their caprice and for their profit, were intrusted to a single syndicate representing the people, to be conducted in the common interest for the common profit. The nation, that is to say, organized as the one great business corporation in which all other corporations were absorbed; it became the one capitalist in the place of all other capitalists, the sole employer, the final monopoly in which all previous and lesser monopolies were swallowed up, a monopoly in the profits and economies of which all citizens shared. The epoch of trusts had ended in The Great Trust.[8]

In Bellamy's vision of the Great Trust, the citizens accept universal military service as a matter of course. They purchase their goods with credit cards that give them each the same share of the national goods. Revealingly, the sequel to *Looking Backward*, which never achieved the same popularity as the first book, bore the title *Equality*.

Edward Bellamy offered a much more extreme version of the bureaucratic reshaping of America than the Croly wing of progressivism ever would. Still, precisely because it is an extreme version, it gives us a clear example of the new goal of equality introduced by the increasingly coordinated and organized character of American society. Dramatically different from the equality of independence, it entailed each person's participation in a large-scale, unitary state and dependence on the state.

A society of nation-wide formal organizations can promote substantial upward mobility through productivity and by creating new managerial positions. The land of opportunity for immigrants that I discussed earlier was largely the product of industrial organization. For this reason, it encouraged a shift in thinking about the self-made man, from the autonomous individual to the one who rises through the established ranks. At the same time, though, the corporate rationalization of a society also promoted the competing idea of equality, seen in the Bellamy-Croly version of progressivism, in which the equality of individuals meant their participation in some sort of great trust. Efforts to achieve the

Great Trust could be participatory, yielding direct election of senators and popular referenda in order to involve citizens in the coordination of public affairs. But these efforts also had authoritarian implications precisely because they sought to make organizations, especially state organizations, more actively involved in the lives of citizens and such involvement could only come about by force of regulation. With the growth of bureaucratic corporatism came a tendency to make citizens equal as anonymous, abstract entities subject to an impersonal system of direction and distribution.

As sociologist Max Weber recognized, bureaucracies are inherently unequal because they are organized for efficiency. The rationalization of American society encouraged a view of Americans as equal, in the sense that each citizen would be a unit within organizational structures, but also unequal, in the sense that the state itself and the vast businesses would be staffed by individuals occupying hierarchical positions within bureaucracies. This latter sense, though, would entail a type of equal inequality because the placement of individuals would, in theory, depend on the abilities of office holders to perform tasks.

This bureaucratic "equal inequality" may be clearest in the New Nationalism strain of progressivism. However, one can also see it running through all progressive reform efforts, including the early Wilsonian variety. If government were going to be a disinterested, professional-ized regulator, government would have to be redesigned to serve the public interest. Thus, Woodrow Wilson, in both his academic and polit-ical careers, had advocated the creation of an efficient bureaucracy in government.[9]

Progressivism's drive for efficiency found its expression in "Taylorism," after Frederick Winslow Taylor, who pioneered the new field of scientific management. In addition to his famous time studies of the most efficient ways to carry out tasks, Taylor championed a top-down, hierarchical division of labor. He argued for a clear separation of management from labor, with trained engineers and managers making all the decisions on production goals, objectives, and methods.[10] The Jeffersonian ideal of independent individuals lived on in the minds of many Americans, but it existed alongside plans for a society of interdependent, specialized actors, planned and managed by experts.

From progressivism, then, Americans developed three different and often opposing interpretations of equality and inequality in a bureaucratic society. First, as members of a corporate state all individuals were abstract units who were the same and apart from primary groups such as families and communities. Second, because the corporate society was bureaucratically organized, they were also unequal because they had to fit in to specialized, hierarchical positions. Third, because social planning became a way of organizing the society, the supposedly equal citizens were all subject to expert direction and control.

CLERKS, CITIZENS, AND FINANCIERS

The Bellamy-Croly embrace of social and political incorporation was far from the only response to institutional consolidation. How should people who saw the world as consisting of autonomous individuals respond to the new business bureaucracies? The cult of success and the popular literature on the self-made man displayed the tension between older concepts of self-reliance and self-improvement and the world of rationalized mass production. Judy Hilkey observed that "in the years between 1870 and 1910, a special, new type of book became commonplace in millions of homes across America. These new books were typically large, elaborately bound, and illustrated volumes boasting such titles as *The Way to Win, Pushing to the Front, The Royal Path of Life,* and *Onward to Fame and Fortune* [...]. They were marketed with a rural and small-town market in mind and addressed to an audience of native-born Protestants of moderate means and modest education."[11] Hilkey stressed the uncertainty of the period, arguing that this was the time when a new industrial order came into existence. In a nation moving toward incorporation, readers of self-help manuals tended to be members of the self-employed old middle-class. Self-help manuals were mass-marketed commodities, peddled by door-to-door salesmen and by subscription.

In his examination of the abundant success literature of the era, Richard Weiss has described the tension between the changing American socioeconomic environment and ideals received from the pre–Civil War period by distinguishing between the "dream "and the "myth" in inspirational writing. "The 'dream,'" according to Weiss," grew out of the new possibilities for wealth and power that industrialization brought in its wake [...] The 'myth' [...] reflected the values of a merchant-agrarian society, religious, moderate, and simple in tone." [12]

The "dream" of financial success retained the humble beginnings. During the thirty years before the Civil War, according to the classic study by Irvin G. Wyllie, the up-from-poverty theme had already captured the imaginations of young men in the nation's developing cities.[13] It was not, as Wyllie makes clear, a delusion. Although starting out wealthy may have been a common and more assured route to success, examples of extraordinarily successful men with poor origins abounded. John Jacob Astor and Thomas Mellon were only two of many examples. This emphasis on poor beginnings necessarily entailed what Wyllie called the "glorification of poverty" because the rise to riches depended on moral qualities developed in rags.

While examples of self-made men continued to begin in poverty and to proceed by industry and virtue, the ultimate goal became defined more and more in terms of finance. Riches, in the quickly developing economy of the time, became the most critical part of being "made." Of the late nineteenth century in America, Richard Weiss noted "the popular conception of this period is formed by the image of the millionaire."[14]

Obituaries of the times abounded in hagiographic accounts of men born to deprivation who amassed wealth by industry and perspicacity. Samuel Warren's 1888 obituary in *Harper's Weekly* offered a paradigm of the life course valued and praised in the time:

Mr. Samuel D. Warren, the paper manufacturer, who died in Boston a few days ago, furnished in his business and social life one of the best examples that could be given of that much-abused term, a self-made man. At the age of fourteen he was compelled by the death of his father to leave his home at Grafton, Massachusetts, and not only earn his own living, but assisting the support of the family.....After seven years of service with the firm of Grant & Daniell, paper dealers, of Boston, he was admitted as partner in the firm, and exhibited from the first that comprehension of broad mercantile principles, soundness of judgment, and aggressiveness of action which were characteristic of his whole business career, and which were the secrets of his financial success. In building up the trade of the paper-mills at Pepperill, Massachusetts, and West-brook, Yarmouth, and Gardiner, in Maine, Mr. *Warren* invariably sought out and introduced every improvement in manufacture which seemed calculated to lessen the cost or improve the quality of his products. He was in this respect exceptionally progressive, taking risks that few of his associates in business would care to encounter. Thus he was the first American paper-manufac-turer who comprehended sufficiently to give practical purpose to the thought the advantage to be gained by importing rags from southern Europe and Egypt—a business which, since he began it, has developed into very large proportions. In his dealings with the mercantile world Mr. *Warren* won a high and well-deserved reputation, not only for inflexible honesty, but also for a kindly consideration of the welfare of others. Fully aware, apparently, of his ability to succeed in the competitive struggles of trade, he was not in the least jealous of the successes won by others, and was ever ready to extend a generous recognition to those who performed good work both in and out of his office. While the daily demands of business did not give him the time for thor-ough intellectual cultivation, he was, for a non-professional man, exceptionally well informed on a wide range of subjects—a mental possession which, with his readiness of speech and keen humor, served to make him a remarkably agreeable companion. In the charitable and public-spirited work of Boston he took a prominent part, which makes his death an occasion for sorrow to a very large number of people, as he was a man sought for to act upon the boards of directors of those benevolent institutions where the burden of contribution chiefly falls upon the directors. Mr. *Warren* was married, at the age of thirty, to Miss *Susan Clarke*, daughter of Rev. *Dorus Clarke*, D.D., and had six children, five of whom, four sons and one daughter, are now living. **Taking his career as that of a typical American merchant**, it was one of which our people have every reason to be proud.[15]

Clearly, the self-made man was not fiction. Mr. Warren did exist; presumably he did begin his life having to take care of his family, and he did evidently succeed in the competitive world of business. We have no way of knowing, of course, whether his character was as saintly as presented. Two decades after Mr. Warren's death, in the wake of the scandalous murder of the aristocratic New York architect Stanford White, a *Harper's Weekly* writer qualified the magazine's stereotyping: "The fact is that drawing indictments against classes is as insane and illogical as drawing indictments against nations," proclaimed Rupert Hughes, "[...] there are rich men who overwork, and poor men lazy enough to beg; there are millionaires' sons who are normal and athletic, and self- made men who are degenerates [...]"[16] But the very fact that the writer needed to make this objection illustrates the common tendency to idealize those who began poor and were not lazy and made something of themselves, while retaining a suspicion of the "millionaires' sons." One notes that Samuel Warren worked his way up through a combination of industry, astute business practices, and daring, while retaining admirable civic virtues. Moreover, in the phrase I emphasized in bold, the saintly Warren was "a typical American merchant."

By 1880, the tale of rising to financial heights had become so commonplace that a writer in the *Oregon State Journal* declared that "all of these stories about self-made men and the amount of property that they have succeeded in accumulating are getting to be rather monotonous."[17] However, as Wyllie and other commentators on the topic have long recognized, the accumulation of vast property also posed challenges for an ethic of egalitarian self-creation. Rapid urbanization brought new opportunities, but it also created fears of the new way of life. By imbuing success with a moral character, Americans could interpret their emerging dreams in terms of their existing myths and bring together their ambitions and their values. The success gospel of the self-made man in the time between the Civil War and World War I became a way of imposing a backward moral discipline on forward-looking practices.

The best-known exponent of the rise from rags to riches was Horatio Alger. Although the vast riches available in the new American economy came from the nation's industrial complexes, Alger's work conspicuously avoided the realm of modern industry. Nackenoff has observed that "Alger's world is filled with small shopkeepers, mercantile establishments, and white-collar workers."[18] Factories were oddly missing from this literary land of opportunity. Mr. Warren, whose obituary was mentioned earlier, extended his paper manufacturing business around the world, importing rags from distant lands. Despite the huge scale of his business and his openness to technological innovation, though, this man cited as a typical American merchant retained, in this account of his life, the character of a self-employed tradesman writ large.

The post–Civil War self-made man, then, was a complicated amalgam of the old self-reliant merchant, the prominent man of affairs, and the successful corporate executive. These different ideas about competitive equality existed in uneasy tension, coalescing in different ways. The "gospel of wealth" of Andrew Carnegie portrayed the millionaire titan as the ultimate product of the self-reliant individual. Ultimately, the millionaire's administration of his vast wealth would contribute to public well-being through philanthropy.[19] The early Wilsonian progressive public man, the elected representative of the people, and the spiritual descendant of the leader from the log cabin would control and limit the world of high finance for the sake of the small-shop keepers, independent merchants, and self-employed white-collar workers. The big government progressive, incarnated to different degrees in Edward Bellamy, Herbert Croly, and Theodore Roosevelt, would enable the representative to use the machinery of the bureaucratic state to harness bureaucratic business oligopolies.

Nostalgia for a lost era of civic virtue and autonomous individuals was no more realistic than human dreams of a golden past. But writing this off as a romanticized reactionary response to an urbanizing and industrializing past is too simple. Ideals of humble men rising to prominence came out of a century of efforts to interpret the experience of Americans in a world that had broken down Old World hierarchies and then offered ever-changing opportunities. In adapting these ideals to understand an increasingly formal and organized setting, Americans never abandoned received concepts, but they had to work with new variations on the theme of human equality and to struggle with contradictions within the contradictions produced by these new variations.

Among the institutions produced by the Gilded Age and the Progressive Era, the modern public school stands alongside the business corporation in importance. The two institutions were closely connected. The systematic mass production of goods shapes and encourages the systematic mass preparation of people. How would Americans fit factory-style schooling into the national conversation about citizenship, self-reliance, and autonomy?

EDUCATION: INSTITUTIONALIZATION, SELF-ADVANCEMENT, AND PRIVILEGE

The political and economic consolidation of the industrializing nation produced a new system of mass socialization: universal, compulsory schooling. Stephen Caldas and I have argued, in a social history of public education in the United States, that the Civil War gave a huge boost to this development by stimulating a more active central government as well as by accelerating the growth of an urban, corporate economy.[20] Reconstruction encouraged a heightened emphasis on education and promoted the extension of public schooling to new population groups under the expanded authority of the federal government. Proponents of social change in the South identified education with the enforced creation of a new society and a new democracy. Articles in the press at the time frequently portrayed the education of freedmen, in particular, as a first step in redesigning the whole of Southern society through the missionary efforts of schools.[21] In 1867, these efforts to spread education through the South inspired the establishment of the Department of Education. Although this department was downgraded to the Bureau of Education as Reconstruction came to an end, the Bellamy-Croly style of using education as an instrument for planning social and economic relations continued.

In his advocacy of organizational responses to America's newly institutionalized character, Croly placed special emphasis on formal education as a way of creating a new and better citizenry for his democracy of control and coordination. Croly wrote, "The real vehicle of improvement is education. It is by education that the American is trained for such democracy as he possesses; and it is by better education that he proposes to better his democracy. Men are uplifted by education much more surely than they are by any tinkering with laws and institutions, because the work of education leavens the actual social substance. It helps to give the individual himself those qualities without which no institutions, however excellent, are of any use, and with which even bad institutions and laws can be made vehicles of grace."[22]

The turn of the century saw the growth of a nation-wide system of public schooling along with corporate industry. In the introduction to the Progressive Era volume of his documentary history of American education, Sol Cohen notes that "by 1918 elementary education was virtually universal" and that "high schools, in 1890 confined largely to the cities and more affluent rural areas, were by 1918 a well-accepted part of American education."[23]

Progressivism, especially in its Theodore Roosevelt variety, tended to substitute the bureaucratic shaping of citizens for the self-creation of individuals. Early educational theorists repeatedly sounded themes similar to those of Edward Bellamy's two books. In 1896, pioneer sociologist Albion W. Small spoke to the National Education Society about the educational approach required by sociology. Approaching the issue from what he saw as the perspective of the social sciences, Small spoke in visionary and almost millennial terms. He expressed his view of teaching as a means to the radical reconstruction of society: "sociology demands of educators, finally, that they shall not rate themselves as leaders of children, but as makers of society. Sociology knows no means for the amelioration or reform of society more radical than those of which teachers hold the leverage."[24] In that same year, John Dewey established the Laboratory School at the University of Chicago in 1896. Through the school, Dewey intended to create a model community in order to shape individuals and socialize them to become elements of a better American society. As Sol Cohen has observed, "Dewey looked to the schools to provide the necessary social discipline and cohesion necessary to national unity." [25]

Mandatory public schooling in the United States was largely the creation of progressivism.[26] Educational historian Lawrence A. Cremin describes in detail how the progressive movement shaped schooling in America. He maintains that the movement began to grow in the decades right after the Civil War. By 1900, in his account, the movement had acquired wide appeal among intellectuals. It gathered momentum around World War I and subsequently dominated the educational profession.[27]

The bureaucratic shaping of citizens by government through public schools found its ultimate form in the school plan of Gary, Indiana. Described by journalist and progressive visionary Randolph Bourne in 1916 as the "most complete and admirable application" of John Dewey's philosophy of education.[28]. The Gary Plan was largely the work of a single administrator/social experimenter, Gary School Superintendent William Wirt, who completely redesigned the system of Gary schools and organized each school as a community. Wirt's "platoon system," an idea adopted by many other school districts, involved rotating students among classrooms, workshops, and other facilities. While Wirt's plan to extend the school year to the full twelve months did not spread widely, the Gary Plan was greatly admired by progressive educators and elements of it did take root in American school administration [29] While the Gary schools did not set a pattern that all schools would adhere to in the following years, they did demonstrate the kind of social order that would be pursued through public education. It would be an order pursued through the socialization of students according to the blueprints of educational experts operating as social engineers.

Unease about upward mobility through schooling stemmed partly from the association of advanced study with inherited social advantage and partly from the connection of growing educational institutionalization with the corporate, industrial environment. By the middle of the twentieth century, as will be argued later in this book, advanced formal education became a mass phenomenon. This encouraged seeing the bureaucratic setting of the educational institution as a setting for self-advancement, producing a convergence of progressive-style corporatism and commitment to self-reliance. At the earlier turn of the century, though, higher education often still retained the taint of aristocratic privilege, even though industrialization and bureaucratization were changing the nature of status attainment in the United States. Wyllie's classic work notes the expanding role of higher education in placing people in the nation's occupational hierarchy: "In the fall of 1903, when the Mosely Educational Commission came from Great Britain to study the relationship of education to prosperity in the United States, businessmen told the investigators that whereas few employers had been willing to hire college graduates in 1890, many had developed a preference for them by 1900 [...] The central fact behind this tendency was the coming of age of the American economic system. The pioneer merchantile, industrial, and financial operations of the post-Civil-War years had been handled by practical, strong-willed men who were more distinguished for ruggedness of character than for refinement of intellect [...] At century's close, however, businessmen were less concerned with pioneering than with the expansion and maintenance of their complex empires."[30]

While advanced levels of schooling became more important for the society and for occupational mobility, the success literature of the times tended to emphasize life outside of the schools. Hilkey has identified the social order of the success manuals as a hierarchical but permeable one consisting of "'mechanics' and 'masters,' 'clerks, and 'proprietary merchants.'"[31] The emphasis on work and inexperience in the realm of self-employment often led to a contrast between the self-made man and the college graduate. This resulted in defensiveness about higher education by its advocates that sounds somewhat peculiar to readers today. For example, writing of commencement addresses, *Harper's Weekly* complained in 1885, "The number of college graduates in this country every year is not very large, but the space which the newspapers devote to the Commencement exercises shows a just consciousness of the importance of the college in our national system. One of the tendencies most to be deprecated is the disposition to sneer at college-bred men as necessarily effeminate, priggish, and unpractical, and to hold that the only genuine American is 'the self- made man,' as if educated men were not quite as much self- made as ignorant men."[32]

Formal education was an external source of position in the society. Individuals who had attained their positions through schooling were deemed not to have struggled upward through their own efforts. Moreover, a high level of formal education was generally closely linked to inherited wealth and position. More importantly, the popular tendency to contrast self-made men with college graduates suggested that Americans of the Gilded Age tended to see educational credentials as placing people in desirable social positions, whereas those who occupied those positions because of work or self-training were regarded as having achieved their places by themselves.

Sneering at the nation's oldest and most prestigious institutions of higher education has been a long-standing national tradition. Even those of us in the university business who teach at places below such institutions have been known to engage in this practice. It is precisely because the Cambridge college is so venerable and prestigious that the sneering has always come so naturally. Heirs to contempt for aristocracy, we still see long-standing prestige as a symptom of privilege, even as the top Ivy League schools have become more meritocratic than they were in the past. In the America of over a century ago, Harvard was much more closely connected to inherited privilege than it is today. No college graduate could be more readily contrasted with the self-made man than the graduates of the elite colleges. *Harper's Weekly*, again coming to the defense of the institutional elite acknowledged this contrast:

> Harvard College is the permanent symbol of one of the chief forces which have made this country. The college everywhere has the same great distinction. At the time of the Revolution, Columbia College, in New York, had graduated hardly a hundred students. But among them were leaders of the Revolution; individual men multiplied, as it were, by thousands. The disposition to sneer at college-bred men, and to hold that what are called self- made men are the only valuable practical citizens, is curiously offset by the simple facts of college annals [33]

In the growing importance of education for the institutionalized environment of American society, then, one can see two sources of tension with the image of the self-made man. First, although schooling as a basic form of preparation for citizens was well-established in parts of the country, particularly in the northeast, schooling as a means of acquiring position in a formalized setting was new and it was part of the corporate rationalization of American life. Thus, the success manuals and the literature on self-improvement tended to touch on diligence in school only as the childhood display of virtuous character and to emphasize activities outside the school as the true means of self-making. Second, advanced levels of schooling were still linked to privileges of birth.

The type of education generally available in America's elite institutions intensified the tension between the image of the college-educated individual and that of the self-made man. The liberal arts, classics-based curricula of the old prestigious schools had been historically associated with aristocratic culture. As mass education at lower levels began to move away from the old part-time, one-room schools, though, even higher education began to take on a new character. On July 2, 1862, even as the Civil War raged, Congress passed what was then known primarily as the Agricultural College Act and has gone down in history as the first Morrill Act (after Vermont Representative Justin Morrill, its primary sponsor in the House) or as the first Land Grant College Act. The intent of the act, as described by the *New York Herald-Tribune* in the days leading up to its passage, was to educate the nation's young people in "agriculture and mechanic arts." The legislation clearly addressed a population of farmers and artisans even as it planned for more institutionalized training and for greater governmental involvement in economic activities. With it, Congress offered grants of public lands within the states and funds to the states for the establishment of colleges.[34]

Immediately after the war, Congress amended the act to extend its benefits to the former Confederate States. A second Morrill Act, passed in 1890, provided monetary benefits in place of land and required all states to either extend admission without regard to race or to open separate colleges for non-Whites. The Land Grant Colleges based on the two Morrill Acts, then, displayed interesting combinations of ideas about equality and individual autonomy. Even though higher education often retained the stigma of privilege and passive reception of social and economic position, education at all levels was beginning to become a path for mobility. Popular ideas of self-made men tended to distinguish them from college men, but the distinction was already blurring due to the extension of formal schooling. This extension was the consequence of the still limited but increasing authority and reach of the federal government. It was no accident that the initial bill passed during the Civil War, a time of rapid political centralization, and that its implementation came during the postwar years. The Land Grant colleges should be seen as part of the institutionalization of American society during the years between the Civil War and World War I. In a manner analogous to the self-help manuals of the period, the Land Grant schools were consciously designated to improve the skills of a nation of farmers and mechanics, but it in fact channeled graduates into the emerging urban, corporate economy.

While Americans struggled with the question of the connection between institutionalization and traditional ideas of individual self-reliance in higher education, they came to see education at the lower levels as an instrument for incorporating the new population groups drawn to the United States by industrialization. Among the native born, schools provided a bureaucratic approach to teaching a generation growing up off the farm and away from apprenticeships. Accordingly, finishing ever more years of school became a precursor to rising through the corporate ranks. But American schools were also charged with acculturating the children of immigrants, so that schooling became part of the new ideal of individual opportunity growing out of the interplay between concepts of self-reliance and upward mobility through institutions.

IMMIGRATION AND OPPORTUNITY

Outside of the South, which was still recovering from the Civil War, an American industrial revolution provided opportunities that drew immigrants from around the world. The war caused disruption, but it also stimulated production in the North and ultimately created a more politically and economically unified nation. The completion of the railroad across the continent in 1869 meant not only that people could travel relatively quickly from the East Coast to the West Coast but also that goods from one part of the country could be shipped and sold to other parts of the country. This completion of the transportation infrastructure spurred rapid industrialization in the decades following the Civil War. By 1890 the United States had outstripped the leading industrial nations of Europe to become the world's foremost producer of manufactured goods.[35] The quickly developing industrial economy required workers, and the availability of jobs drew immigrants to American shores in unprecedented numbers.

Transportation systems not only linked the United States from within, but they also made it easier to reach North America from Europe. Train systems in Europe by the late nineteenth century enabled Europeans to reach their own coastal cities. The replacement of sailing ships by steamships cut travel time over the ocean from one to three months in the 1850s to ten days by the 1870s. Between 1891 and 1900, 350,000 newcomers reached the United States. In the decade after, from 1901 to 1910, this more than doubled to 800,000 new arrivals. Although the absolute number of foreign-born people was greater at the end of the twentieth century, immigrants made up a larger proportion of the American population in the late nineteenth and early twentieth century, when fifteen percent of Americans were immigrants. Moreover, due to continuing immigration, another fifteen percent of native-born Americans were children of two immigrant parents by 1910, and seven percent of native-born Americans had at least one immigrant parent. By 1910, immigrants and children of immigrants made up over one-third of the US population.

The large immigrant population of the United States came from places that had sent few people in earlier years. America's population at its beginning consisted mainly of people from Northern and Western Europe and people of African heritage, and newcomers in the first century of the nation's existence continued to come primarily from northern and western Europe. In 1882, 87 percent of immigrants came from the northern and western European countries. By the end of the century, though, economic hardship in southern Europe and political oppression combined with poverty in Eastern Europe, together with the improved transportation, led to a geographic shift. By 1907, 81 percent of immigrants to the United States came from southern and eastern Europe. According to the statistics of the Dillingham Commission, set up by Congress in 1907 to study the new immigration, of the 1,285,349 foreign-born people who arrived in the United States in 1907; 285,943 (22%) came from the

Russian Empire and 338,452 (26%) came from the Empire of Austria-Hungary. Eastern European Jews, fleeing persecution in the two empires, made up many of these arrivals. That same year, 285,731 Italians also arrived, most of them coming from impoverished southern Italy, and they made up 22% of total immigrants.[36]

The arrival of these newcomers into an industrializing nation contributed to an elaborate system of ethnic stratification on top of the racial stratification that followed slavery. As a result of the flow of workers from abroad, the nation's new industrial working class rapidly became disproportionately foreign born. The Dillingham Commission looked at twenty-one industries and found that 58% of the workers in these industries were immigrants. The commission found that immigrants were particularly predominant in construction work, railroads, textiles, coal mining, and meat packing.[37] My analysis of census data shows that in 1870, 37 percent of the foreign-born in the American labor force were employed as craftsmen or operatives. Fifty years later, this had increased to 42 percent. By contrast, only 20 percent of native-born Americans were in craft or operative jobs in 1870, growing to 28 percent by 1920. Immigration scholars Charles Hirschman and Elizabeth Mogford have described immigrants as the mainstay of the turn-of-the-century American industrial workforce, observing that "immigrants and their children comprised over half of manufacturing workers in 1920, and if the third generation (the grandchildren of immigrants) are included, then more than two-thirds of workers in the manufacturing sector were of recent immigrant stock."[38]

The analysis by Hirschman and Mogford indicates that immigrants did more than find places in the American economy. Their provision of abundant and relatively inexpensive labor helped to create the large-scale corporate industrial system of the United States. The inexpensive labor and the highly differentiated economy meant that immigration was also associated with an expansion of inequality of condition along ethnic lines. The Duncan Socioeconomic Index score is a widely used measure of social position, composed by calculating an individual's occupational prestige, level of education, and income. This score did not exist at the beginning of the twentieth century, but we can apply it to workers back then to obtain a rough measure of their standing in the status hierarchy. Immigrants from northern Europe ranked fairly high in this hierarchy: People in the labor force born in England, Scotland, and Germany, for example, show socioeconomic scores of 28.27, 29.16, and 25.02, respectively. By contrast, people from places in southern and eastern Europe were clearly much lower on the social scale. Italians, perhaps the largest of the late nineteenth-century and early twentieth-century southern European immigrant groups, show a socioeconomic score of only 17.63. The average scores for Hungarians and Portuguese, respectively, can be calculated at 16.53 and 14.47 (these figures come from my analysis of census data). These numbers indicate that there were clear variations in social positions among immigrants from different locations.

The emerging ethnic stratification scale may have been driven to some extent by existing prejudices and preconceptions among Old Stock Americans and among the immigrants themselves, but it seems to have also been due to skill differences among the various immigrant groups. Of the skill differences between immigrants and natives, economist George J. Borjas has written, "immigrants were [...] less skilled than natives. One quarter of the immigrants present in the United States in 1910 (and over a third of those in the 1900–1910 wave) were laborers, compared to only 11% of White natives employed outside agriculture. In addition, 96% of natives were literate (knew how to read and write "any" language, meaning at least one language, although not necessarily English), but only 87% of immigrants, and 77% of the immigrants in the 1900–1910 wave, were literate."[39] The skill differences between immigrants and natives, as opposed to those among the immigrant groups, were offset somewhat by the fact that most natives (and especially most children of natives) still made up the rural yeomen of the nation, while immigrants and their families resided in the cities, places of high inequality but also relatively high chances for some mobility.

Although industrialization and immigration worked together to increase inequalities of condition in the United States, we should remember that the ideal of equality as self-creation was entirely compatible with this. Self-made men did not live in a world in which people enjoyed the same standards of living, but one in which individuals could rise and could look forward to better futures. The massive tide of international migration, then, reshaped the story of the self-made man, recasting America as the land of opportunity, in which individuals would start from a common point and move forward.

The "land of opportunity" narrative was not a fable. Instead, it was an episode in the experience of structural mobility that would mold how Americans thought about equality and inequality. Immigrants are people who move from one place to another looking for better lives. Generally, they did find better lives. Studying census data from 1900 and 1910, economic historian Chris Minns found that immigrants in the early twentieth century were both earning relatively high wages and showing high degrees of upward mobility.[40]

A summary examination of socioeconomic scores from the turn of the century indicates that immigrants and their families on average did experience improvement in their lives. Figure 4 shows that the foreign-born as well as the children of both foreign-born and native-born Americans enjoyed steadily rising socioeconomic statuses from 1900 to 1930. Even more notable is that native-born Americans with two immigrant parents not only experienced rising occupational and social positions, but they also tended to have higher socioeconomic standings than the children of native-born Americans. For all the problems that may have afflicted early twentieth-century America, its image as a land of opportunity for immigrant families was solidly based in reality.

Figure 4. Average Socioeconomic Index Scores of Immigrants, Children, and Native-Born, 1900–1930.

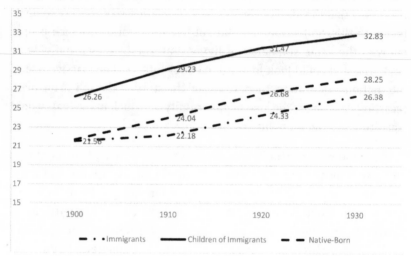

Source. Steven Ruggles, Sarah Flood, Ronald Goeken, Josiah Grover, Erin Meyer, Jose Pacas, and Matthew Sobek. 2020. IPUMS USA: Version 10.0 [dataset]. Minneapolis, MN: IPUMS, 2020. https://doi.org/10.18128/D010.V10.0

The mobility of immigrants resulted in part from the rapidly expanding economy. Even if the benefits went disproportionately to those at the top and even if many immigrants lived in conditions of urban poverty that shocked reformers of the era, general abundance meant more chances to move ahead. In addition, fresh immigration, as part of this expanding economy, tended to push each decade of arrivals ahead. Nancy Landale and Avery Guest reported general economic progress on the part of immigrants and that "both inter- and intragenerational socioeconomic gains between 1880 and 1900 were greatest among men living in counties with a relatively high concentration of new immigrants, suggesting that the new immigrants entered low-status positions, effectively boosting the standing of the old immigrants."[41]

The era of mass immigration recast the ideal of the self-made man into the vision of individuals rising in the promised land of opportunity.

This vision owed much to the older yeoman image of independence from the hierarchies of the Old World. For example, Mary Antin's 1912 portrayal of America in her popular book, *The Promised Land,* was a paean of liberation. Antin was born in the Jewish Pale in Russia, and her family suffered the hardships and persecutions of Jews in the anti-Semitic Czarist empire. Her father managed to scrape together enough for passage to America, where the family would find a better life, especially for the children. "With the children, he argued," Antin wrote of her father, "every year in Russia was a year lost. They should be spending the precious years in school, in learning English, in becoming Americans." For her part, Antin responded to her father's decision with an emotion that can only be described as ecstasy: "So at last I was going to America! Really, really going, at last! The boundaries burst. The arch of heaven soared. A million suns shone out for every star. The winds rushed in from outer space, roaring in my ears, 'America! America!'"[42]

While we can assume that many immigrants lacked Antin's retrospective enthusiasm, the evidence indicates that they did generally find better lives in their destination and that their lives improved over time. In their own eyes and in the eyes of Americans in general, the immigrant story became a new version of the story of the self-made man, gradually becoming a mainstream part of the narratives of equality and opportunity. In 1918, the *Baltimore Sun* proclaimed:

> Today there are in every large city successful Americans for whom Ellis Island was the gateway to opportunity. Their names are painted over the doors of mercantile houses; they write for our mercantile journals; they entertain large audiences from the concert stage. Yet many of them can recall vividly the day when they were among a strange-looking, homesick crowd, sitting forlornly on their lumpy baggage in the immigrant depot.[43]

While Old Stock Americans often felt uncomfortable with the new immigrant waves, especially those coming from eastern and southern Europe, they also began to share in the perception that immigrant origin was a part of the American success story. This success story, moreover, was increasingly urban in character. The phrase "in every large city" in the passage from the *Baltimore Sun* reflects the fact that immigrants settled heavily in urban areas. Their realization of the ideal of individual accomplishment depended on success in a nation of cities, factories, and big companies.

If immigrant success came from participation in the corporate society, the mobility of the children of immigrants depended heavily on that critical governmental corporate bureaucracy, the public school. The progressive educators, in the spirit of Herbert Croly, saw schools as the means for incorporating immigrant children into the emerging American nation, "Americanizing" them, in the term of the era. "Education," in the words of a pre–World War I high school principal in New York, "will solve every problem of our national life, even that of assimilating our foreign element."[44] For immigrant families, educational advancement was one of the greatest opportunities available in the new society. Much of Mary Antin's book on America as the promised land can best be described as a paean to American schooling, which gave her the chance to rise, an opportunity that she would never have had back in the Russian Empire. Through schools, the immigrant experience helped to produce a new version of the old idea of the self-made man, which involved upward movement through an established organization more than autonomous self-reliance.

UP FROM SLAVERY (AND INTO SEPARATION)

While immigration helped to create a new form of equality of opportunity, the opportunities of many Americans remained severely constrained. Racial subordination was deeply entrenched in the United States by the end of the Civil War; particularly in the Southern states where over 90 percent of Black Americans lived. Although slavery ended with the war and federal troops made some initial efforts to enforce Black political equality, the real economic power remained in the hands of Whites. The defeated Whites of the South attempted to control the freed slaves, and to force them to continue doing plantation labor through laws known as "Black Codes." The first states to pass Black Codes, in 1865, were Mississippi and South Carolina. Under the Mississippi law, all Blacks were required to show proof of employment for the coming year each January. Blacks were forbidden to leave their jobs before the end of a contract. Those who were unemployed or judged to be "disorderly" could be prosecuted for vagrancy. The South Carolina law forbade Blacks to hold any job except as a farmer or a servant, and it required them to sign annual contracts and to work from sunup until sundown. As was the case in Mississippi, unemployed Blacks were considered guilty of vagrancy. Almost all the states of the former Confederacy enacted similar laws.

The Southern states were forced to repeal the Black Codes by the end of 1866 because of opposition from the North and the Civil Rights Act of 1866. Still, most Southern states, including Louisiana, retained strict vagrancy laws that were based on the Black Codes, and these were enforced almost exclusively against Blacks. By these kinds of legal strategies, the former slaves were retained as cheap agricultural labor, even after the formal end of slavery. Reestablishing the status of the Black population as a source of labor subordinate to Whites as a group became a primary goal of White Southern Redeemers, and the Southern Democratic Party became the chief legitimate vehicle for achieving this goal. Either Whites would rule, in this view, or Blacks would rule—and Black rule was to be opposed by all possible means.

In the US Congress, during the years just after the end of the war, Radical Republicans such as Thaddeus Stevens and Charles Sumner, who had long fought to eliminate slavery and to recognize the rights of Blacks, achieved increasing influence. The need to establish the status of the former slaves and the rising power of the Radical Republicans pushed even relatively conservative politicians toward legislation that would protect Black rights. Lyman Trumbull, a moderate Republican, introduced the first Civil Rights Act. Much of the language of the Civil

Rights Act of 1866 was incorporated into the Fourteenth Amendment to the Constitution.

Congress required the southern states that had attempted to secede to guarantee the voting rights of Blacks and to ratify the Fourteenth Amendment in order to gain readmission into the union. By July 1868, the thirty states needed to pass a Constitutional amendment had ratified the Fourteenth Amendment. This established the citizenship of all those born or naturalized in the United States, and it provided penalties for states that violated civil rights and gave the US government the power to enforce its provisions. The Equal Protection clause of the Fourteenth Amendment, guaranteeing equal protection of the law to every citizen, would later become the basis of all legal challenges to race-based separation and racial differences in conditions or opportunities.

In March 1875, Congress passed an even more thorough Civil Rights Act. The Civil Rights Act of 1875 guaranteed equal rights to Blacks in all public accommodations, such as theaters, inns, public amusements, and means of transportation. The act also prohibited the exclusion of Blacks from jury duty. In 1883, however, as the country increasingly turned away from the enforcement of civil rights, the Civil Rights Act of 1875 was declared unconstitutional by the US Supreme Court.[45]

If Reconstruction was an "unfinished revolution," to use Foner's phrase, it involved a version of the paradox of liberal democracy often seen in revolutionary societies. Individual autonomy, one of the premises of liberal democracy and a dominant version of equality in the developing American republic, requires that the state leave people alone to pursue their own interests. When people are members of dominant and subordinate groups, though, leaving people alone allows the dominant to assert their will. When a central state or occupying power attempts to act on behalf of people in subordinate groups, it necessarily imposes equality by force, undercutting individual autonomy. This creates an identity of interests between the central state or occupying power and the locally disadvantaged, and it also tends to replace liberal democracy with a more authoritarian and bureaucratic version of egalitarianism, in which a central state enforces some version of equality among citizens.

As discussed earlier, some ideas of bureaucratic egalitarianism did begin to appear in the late nineteenth century in the statist versions of progressivism. Reconstruction was a harbinger of these versions of progressivism in many ways. The effort to reform the society of the South promoted the use of formal systems of schooling to socialize citizens of a centralized state. The employment of federal power to reorganize unequal social relations in local communities presaged the reformist political philosophy of many progressives. As in the different streams of thought about equality in the rest of American society later in the century, though, the efforts at reconstruction carried forward older ideas of equality as autonomy along with newer ideas of equality as identical bureaucratically accomplished rights and opportunities. In a typical expression of this mixture of ideas, the *New York Times* in 1870 described the schooling of freedmen as a way of training them in "independence and the capacity for self control."[46] Paradoxically, the recently freed slaves would be made autonomous and readied for directing their own destinies by official intervention and resocialization. This paradox would appear again much later in American history. However, the nation turned its attention away from reshaping the defeated South, and a federally enforced version of civic equality only began to respond to the racial caste system about a hundred years after the Civil War.

We may date the end of Reconstruction from the 1876 election in Louisiana in which the Democrat and former Confederate general Francis T. Nicholls ran for governor against Republican Stephen B. Packard. Results of the Nicholls-Packard contest followed the racial distribution of the state's population. In parishes with Black-majority Black populations, Packard was victorious. In parishes with White-majority populations, Nicholls was the clear winner. Although Packard won and initially took office, the Republican administration crumbled with the withdrawal of Federal troops. Nicholls and the Democrats came to power.[47]

The Ku Klux Klan and similar organizations emerged during Recon-struction as the terrorist wing of the Democratic Party, sharing the Democrats' dedication to White people as a group with objective interests that were in conflict with the interests of Blacks. The division of the political universe according to skin color was codified during the Jim Crow period of the late nineteenth and early twentieth centuries. Legally, the division was maintained by segregation and by laws forbidding miscegenation. Illegally, it was maintained by lynching and other forms of violence.[48]

Life and politics in the South were driven by the perception of the world as divided into mutually incompatible interest groups along lines of race. By 1877, when President Rutherford B. Hayes withdrew all remaining federal troops from the Southern states, the racial subordination of slavery was replaced by the racial subordination of segregation. Whites in the Southern states saw the world as divided into Black and White, and they saw Black public involvement as a permanent threat to White interests. Property and educational qualifications, poll taxes, grandfather clauses, and other means of restricting voting practically eliminated Blacks from voting in Mississippi by 1890, in South Carolina by 1895, and in Louisiana by 1898. These laws also often had the effect of limiting participation by poorer Whites. Mississippi, for example, cut back the total number of voters in the state by about 70% between the end of Reconstruction and the early 1890s. In 1897, Louisiana had 130,000 registered Black voters and 164,000 registered White voters. By 1904, there were only a little over 1,000 registered Black Louisianans and 92,000 registered White voters. In this manifestation of the paradox of democracy, the end of authoritarian rule by an occupying military force and the restoration of local control meant restriction of suffrage and the recrudescence of a racial caste system.

In 1896, the exclusion of Blacks from participation in public life achieved legal acceptance on a national scale. In that year, the US Supreme Court ruled that a Louisiana law requiring the racial segregation of railroad cars was constitutional, establishing the "separate-but-equal" doctrine. Today, we recognize "separate-but-equal" as a discredited fiction, but it was also an interesting attempt to reconcile the practice of subordination with the principle of equality as the opportunity to make oneself. In theory, Blacks and Whites could inhabit distinct social spheres within which each would live in a manner consistent with the norms of American life. This supposed equality extended beyond procedural equality under the law to the egalitarianism of the self-made man. Booker T. Washington's autobiography, *Up from Slavery*, offers one of the best illustrations of this self-creation carried out on a separate track.

SELF-MADE MEN ON A SEPARATE TRACK

Like the earlier stories of self-made public men, Washington's book was as much a political appeal as it was an account of his life. It addressed the sentiments of the White financial backers of his educational and economic programs as well as those of potential Black supporters. In this book, being born in slavery appeared to be the Black version of being born in a log cabin. The humble origins removed all advantages of birth, so that every accomplishment of the author could be attributed only to his own efforts and virtues. Washington's birth in slavery gave him the chance for the most extreme form of self-creation. He recounted how, when he started school, he did not even know the second name of "Taliaferro" his mother had given him, so he christened himself "Washington" when the teacher asked him for a last name.

As in the tales of log-cabin politicians and diligent journalists, the efforts of self-creation produced the virtues. In his second chapter, Washington told how he was embarrassed by the fact that he was the only pupil in his school who had no cap. When he complained to his mother, she responded that they had no money for a store-bought hat, and she made him a cap out of two pieces of homespun. Washington wrote that he took this as a lesson in self-reliance and strength of character. He noted that later in life some of his schoolmates with store-bought hats ended up in the penitentiary, clearly having failed to develop strength of character as a consequence of their early sartorial privileges.

When Washington wrote of working in a coal mine after the early school days, his greatest objection to this kind of work was neither its dangers nor its difficulty. Rather, he observed that the labors in the mines often stunted the ambitions of the young miners. For Washington, the drive to rise through one's own struggles was always the greatest of qualities.

Of course, Washington recognized that being Black was a severe disadvantage in late nineteenth-century America. Although, probably as a deft, if disingenuous, reassurance to his White supporters, he relegated the Ku Klux Klan and the more extreme forms of oppression to the unsettled time of Reconstruction, he never claimed that the one born in slave quarters had the same life chances as the White child of a log cabin. Instead, he made an argument that applied the self-made man ideal to Black Americans, while simultaneously accepting segregation. He asserted the common claims for the virtues of humble origins, while accepting a distinct path of advancement for Blacks:

> In later years, I confess that I do not envy the white boy as I once did. I have learned that success is to be measured not so much by the position that one has reached in life as by the obstacles which he has overcome while trying to succeed. Looked at from this standpoint, I almost reached the conclusion that often the Negro boy's birth and connection with an unpopular race is an advantage, so far as real life is concerned. With few exceptions, the Negro youth must work harder and must perform his tasks even better than a white youth in order to secure recognition. But out of the hard and unusual struggle through which he is compelled to pass, he gets a strength, a confidence, that one misses whose pathway is comparatively smooth by reason of birth and race.[49]

Self-making always involved some reversal of the valuation of life chances. The more limited one's chances at the beginning, the better one's moral character and—because success that was truly worthwhile depended on moral character—the greater one's opportunity for ultimate success. In Washington's narrative, starting out as a slave became, in a sense, the best opportunity of all. This was clearly a comforting view for Whites in post-bellum America. It was comforting not only because it cleared the moral books on slavery but also because it rationalized a serious contradiction in one of the fundamental sociopolitical values of the nation. In the *Up from Slavery* account, slavery became a log-cabin story and segregation became separate but equal spheres of endeavor for autonomous individuals.

We should be cautious not to dismiss Washington's romanticism of disadvantage too lightly. Other Americans shared this inclination to attribute moral superiority to deprivation. As argued in later chapters, this inclination is still strong among us today, shaping, among other things, some of our college-admission policies. But looking back at this older version of our social romanticism, we can see the paradoxical nature of the self-made man concept of equality. All individuals are equal because each has control over personal destiny. However, those who start with the least are really the best because their destinies are most obviously due to nothing but their own efforts. Further, starting out with little or nothing means that one overcomes more challenges, challenges build character, and character creates success.

Readers might also be skeptical of how much the romanticism of disadvantage actually reflects reality, whether during the post–Civil War era or today. Later in life, Booker T. Washington stirred up a minor scandal in some quarters when President Theodore Roosevelt invited him to the White House. Roosevelt did not notably lack confidence or success, although he reportedly enjoyed store-bought hats and a few other privileges as a child.

Whatever the soundness and validity of the worldview of *Up from Slavery*, its separate-but-equal approach to personal autonomy provided the basis for Washington's earlier speech at the Atlanta Exposition, perhaps the most influential public pronouncement of a Black leader in an America that was still inhabited by millions of former slaves.

The separate-track concept of self-made men also existed alongside a separate-track ambivalence about education and privilege. The second Morrill Act in 1890, by establishing separate Black land-grant colleges, created the same distinction between those who advanced through the land grants, and could be seen as Black self-made men, and Black men who were products of elite institutions. When Roscoe Conkling Bruce went to the Tuskegee Institute in 1902 to work with Booker T. Washington, *Harper's Weekly* remarked that "It will be an interesting and inspiring spectacle to see Mr. Washington, the self- made graduate of Hampton Institute, and Mr. Bruce, the carefully reared graduate of Harvard, working side by side as a Moses and Joshua for the elevation of their race."[50]

Founded by missionaries in 1868, Hampton Institute received a charter as a land-grant college in 1870. Working his way through the new kind of college, then, was part of Washington's pulling himself up from slavery. Within this separate racial track, as within the majority track in American society, formal education was becoming part of the trajectory of self-propelled mobility. The contrast of the Black self-made man with the Black Harvard man also displays the same distinction between autonomous virtue and institutionally bestowed prestige found in the dominant society of the time. The collaboration of the two men is as revealing as the contrast, given how it suggests how the traditional elite seats of learning and the emerging factories of construction could become part of the same formally organized system of status attainment within the separate track as well as within the dominant society.

WOMEN'S RIGHTS: ABSTRACT INDIVIDUALS IN THE CORPORATE SOCIETY

In the previous chapter, I argued that most men and women in the United States before the middle of the nineteenth century did not ask whether women should be equal to men because men and women occupied separate social realms and because most people entirely defined themselves and others according to the gender roles of the time. Specifically, these roles associated men with activities outside the home and women with domestic activities. A long-standing division of labor supported this distinction. Although farm work often required all available hands, especially during planting and harvest, in general the sheer amount of work required specialization in cooking, sewing, and cleaning within the home and in plowing and taking care of animals outside the home.

Large farm families further encouraged specialization according to gender. Women were (and remain) the primary caregivers for children; the larger the family, the greater the work required for the rearing of children and the closer the identification of women with motherhood. On family farms, children at very early ages became useful workers. One can see this reflected in the family sizes of the time. According to my analyses of census date, as the nation urbanized, average family sizes decreased steadily, from 5.43 people per family in 1870 to 4.89 in 1920. Families living on farms, logically, were the largest, with an average of 5.99 in 1870 and 5.75 per farm family in 1920. By contrast, nonfarm city-dwelling families decreased from 4.87 to 4.46 during that period. In other words, family sizes in general were going down, but much of the decrease was linked to the movement off farms, out of the countryside, and into cities.

Entry into the labor force further loosened the separation of women into a separate domestic sphere. Only 15 percent of women aged 16 and older participated in the American labor force in 1870, but this grew to just over a quarter of American women by 1910. The urban setting of the new industrial America, shrinking families, and movement into the public sphere of the market economy meant that the complete identification of women with traditional roles began to weaken. In the minds of a growing number of Americans, women were becoming abstract individuals, citizens whose rights and social roles entailed participation in an impersonal, rationalized society.

The growing presence of women in the industrial, non-domestic work force made the employment of women an area of concern for social reform by organizations and the bureaucratic state. In 1903, progressive activists founded the National Women's Trade Union League (NWTUL). The issues of the NWTUL "included protectionist legislation for female workers, a minimum working wage, and suffrage" as well as education, especially vocational education.[51] As women shifted from being considered as essentially members of households within face-to-face communities and toward being recognized as individuals within an impersonal industrial labor market, they moved toward forming political interest groups aimed at state intervention on their behalf. While joining the market made them more abstract individuals, separate from immediate and direct social relations, it also encouraged them to link up with others who shared their interests and to form relationships with a powerful, protective government.

Many women began to identify themselves not primarily by their roles within households but as members of a category of citizens. Gayle Gullet observed that "the suffragists belonged to a loose network bound by a sense of identity called 'organized womanhood.'"[52] The goal of political equality for women involved two important developments in American concepts of equality. On the one hand, equality was a matter of individual people as social units in the public sphere, distinguished from ascribed statuses within homes. On the other hand, since traditional ascribed statuses did still affect those individuals, they constituted a categorical interest group.

Those who opposed the change in gender roles emphasized what they saw as the fundamental nature of gender specialization in society. The eminent historian Francis Parkman, for example, arguing against women's suffrage, maintained that "from the earliest records of mankind down to this moment, in every race and every form or degree of civilization or barbarism, the relative positions of the sexes has been the same, with exceptions so feeble, rare, and transient that they only prove the rule. Such permanence in the foundation of society, while all that has passed upon it has passed from change to change, is proof in itself that this foundation lies deep in the essential nature of things."[53]

Parkman explicitly connected his traditionalism on the question of women's political participation to a belief in the organic nature of politics. "Government by abstract right," he wrote, "of which the French Revolution set the example and bore the fruits, involves enormous danger and injustice. No political right is absolute and of universal application."[54]

Parkman's advocacy of the exclusion of women from full civic participation is difficult for us to understand today, from the perspective of the twenty-first century. I am certainly not adopting his point of view here. Instead, I am suggesting that comprehending why this argument made sense to him and to others at the opening of the twentieth century and why this was an embattled position involves considering how competing ideas about the equal rights of individuals in the abstract, regardless of gender, were responses to the transformation of American society through urbanization and corporatization. When Thomas Jefferson wrote that all men are created equal, he probably did not ask himself whether he was talking about "men" defined as "human beings" or "men" defined as "male human beings." The political realm, in which people were equal, was in the public sphere, where male human beings were the chief actors in Jefferson's day, and women moved mainly in the private sphere of households.

The entry of women into public activity involved two trends, analogous to the two strains of progressivism. As abstract individuals, women would seek the same political rights as their male counterparts. They would expect to be treated simply as individuals holding the rights of all other individuals, and the role of government would be to secure and protect these rights. As members of a category, political institutions would protect and promote their particular concerns as citizens. This second trend lay behind the interests of social reformers in "women's issues," and in finding answers through schemes for social efficiency and scientific management to problems such as difficult work conditions for low-wage female employees or family conflict.

The achievement of the right to vote by women was only a step, albeit a major step, toward the redefinition of the statuses of women from a separate private sphere of the household to the public sphere of government and business. The massive entry of women into the labor force, much later in the twentieth century, would be an even bigger step. The more that men and women occupied the same area of activity, the more evident became the problem of gender inequality for American sociopolitical culture.

NOTES

1. Nackenoff, *The Fictional Republic*, 80.
2. Davis, *Corporations*.
3. Quoted in Nevins, *Study in Power*, vol. 1, 402.
4. Hofstedter, *The Age of Reform*.
5. Cooper, *Woodrow Wilson*.
6. Kolko, *Main Currents in American History*, 18.
7. Croly, *The Promise of American Life*.
8. Bellamy, *Looking Backward*, 33.
9. See, for example, Wilson, "The Study of Administration."
10. Taylor, *The Principles of Scientific Management*.
11. Hilkey, *Character is Capital*, 1.
12. Weiss, *The American Myth of Success*, 91.
13. Wyllie, *The Self-Made Man in America*.
14. Weiss, *The American Myth of Success*, 48.
15. "Samuel D. Warren," 380–381 (my emphasis).
16. Hughes, "The Vice of Generalizing," 1168.
17. "A Self Made Man,' *Hampshire Gazette*, February 22, 1837.
18. Nackenoff, *The Fictional Republic*, 6
19. See Cawelti, *Apostles of the Self-Made Man*, 192–193.
20. Bankston and Caldas, *Public Education, America's Civil Religion*.
21. Ibid., 41–42.
22. Croly, *The Promise of American Life*, 400.
23. Cohen, *Education in the United States*, ii.
24. Quoted in Cohen, *Education in the United States*, vol. IV, 2188.
25. Cohen, *Education in the United States*, vol. 4, xiii.
26. Bankston and Caldas, *Public Education, America's Civil Religion*.
27. Cremin, *The Transformation of the School*.
28. Bourne, *The Gary Schools*, 144.
29. See Dewey and Dewey, *The Schools of Tomorrow*; and Strayer and Bachman, *The Gary Public Schools* for contemporary views of the Gary system.
30. Wyllie, *The Self-Made Man in America*, 107.
31. Hilkey, *Character is Capital*, 25.
32. "The College Commencement Season," *Harper's Weekly*, June 27, 1885, 402.

33. "Harvard's Two Hundred and Fiftieth Birthday," *Harper's Weekly,* August 21, 1886, 531.
34. "The Agricultural College Act," *New York Herald Tribune,* June 21, 1862, 4.
35. Jaycox, *The Progressive Era,* 9.
36. Jenks and Lauck, *The Immigration Problem.*
37. Jones, *American Immigration,* 186.
38. Hirschman and Mogford, "Immigration and the American Industrial Revolution from 1880 to 1920," 897.
39. Borjas, "The Long-run Convergence of Ethnic Skills Differentials," 555
40. Minns, "Income, Cohort Effects, and Occupational Mobility.
41. Landale and Guest, "Generation, Ethnicity, and Occupational Mobility in Late 19th Century America," 294.
42. Antin, *The Promised Land,* 162.
43. "The Gates of Opportunity in America Open to Immigrants," *The Baltimore Sun,* July 14, 1918, 2B.
44. Quoted in Crawford, *Hold Your Tongue,* 83.
45. Foner, *Reconstruction.*
46. "The Freemen's Great Want," *New York Times,* April 1, 1870, 4.
47. Tunnell, *Crucible of Reconstruction.*
48. Foner, *Reconstruction.*
49. Washington, *Up from Slavery,* 39.
50. "A Distinguished Young Colored Man" 1902, 1209b.
51. Powers, *The "Girl Question" in Education,* 52.
52. Gullet, "Women Progressives and the Politics of Americanization in California,1915–1920," 71.
53. Parkman, *Some of the Reasons Against Woman* Suffrage, 8.
54. Ibid., 9

CHAPTER 4

THE NEW DEAL AND THE TRANSFORMATION OF CITIZENSHIP

BUREAUCRACY AND THE EQUALITY OF CITIZENS

The political and economic environment of the United States in the first half of the twentieth century differed greatly from that of a hundred years earlier. Following the Civil War, a system of railroads had tied the country into a single economy, in which goods produced in one location could be readily shipped to others. Along with the growth of a nationwide economy, major corporations began to dominate banking, the steel industry, and extractive activities. The US government also gradually began to take on a more centralized and corporate form. As discussed in the previous chapter, the federal government became more involved in the nation and in the lives of its citizens during the Progressive Era and World War I. But the greatest expansion of the centralized state took place in the major shift of the New Deal.

During the decade before World War II, both business corporations and government became recognizable as large-scale organizational entities, or bureaucracies. Although the word "bureaucracy" generally carries negative connotations in popular use, it also implies professionalization and relative efficiency. The sociological theorist Max Weber identified the rise of bureaucracy as essential to the rationalization of human endeavors, in government and in business. A bureaucracy in the Weberian sense is a hierarchy organized according to systematic processes, with specialized duties attached to offices held by individuals appointed through rule-based accreditation, rather than to personal loyalties to the powerful or to popular favor.

From one point of view, a bureaucracy is antithetical to equality. Bureaucracies are, after all, hierarchically organized. But in the American context, centralized organizational bureaucracies produced subtle redefinitions of older ideas of equality. One of these redefinitions is the equality of consumers. Buyers, in this view, are in theory equal in the opportunity to purchase goods and services. This equality of purchase was not fully realized, of course, as long as buying and selling were not completely impersonal. A seller could always refuse to do business, based on personal prejudice or preference. This set up a tension that would become more obvious in decades following the New Deal, during the Civil Rights era.

The equality of citizens before a government that takes its mission as ensuring public well-being and providing goods and services is a variant of consumer equality. Government is no longer limited to respecting the independence of individuals, but actively intervenes in society on behalf of citizens who, again in theory, all have an equal claim on government protection and resources. Government bureaucracies, like business bureaucracies, may have hierarchical structures but their justification is that they serve consumer-citizens. Under this justification, citizenship became more than the right to vote and run for office. It became a claim on benefits to be provided and guaranteed to each by the state.

Another way in which bureaucracy and equality could be recognized was through a version of equality of opportunity that had begun in the period between the Civil War and World War I, but that became even more deep-seated during the years following World War I. The hierarchical character of bureaucracies, once again in theory, was entirely consistent with a kind of competitive equality. An individual could rise within an organizational hierarchy, and the competition to do so would be equal as long as outcomes depended on the efforts and abilities of that person. The corporate setting of business and government of the New Deal era, then, laid much of the framework for the type of competitive equality that would become known as "meritocracy" in later decades.

Finally, the corporate environment of organized labor and business promoted a new role for government, stimulated by the economic challenges of the thirties. The federal government took on the role of overseer and mediator between these two major blocs. As a number of influential figures in the New Deal explicitly state, promoting an equality of bargaining power between the blocs and negotiating agreements and compromises became a mission of the central state.

A RACIALLY BRACKETED NEW DEAL

Throughout most of US history, Americans maintained their evolving ideals of equality by bracketing out the greatest and most obvious form of inequality—that of race. This was also partly true of the social citizenship of the New Deal. Neither the promotion of equality of opportunity through the political provision of goods and services nor governmental promotion of categorical equality in many situations applied to African Americans throughout the 1930s.

African Americans made up a large segment of the poor during the Great Depression, and they were among the poorest people in American society. In 1935 over three-fourths of the African Americans in the United States lived in the South, and the overwhelming majority of this group still worked as sharecroppers or in other low-wage agricultural jobs or as domestic servants. The White political leadership of the South opposed extending New Deal assistance to Black citizens for the same reason the earlier White leadership had opposed programs to help freed slaves during the period following the Civil War. Economic help to Black workers would mean the end of a cheap Southern workforce, and it could make it possible for Blacks in the South to disrupt the established political order.

President Franklin D. Roosevelt (FDR) needed the support of the Southern congressmen to ensure passage of the New Deal programs. Given this, agricultural workers and domestic servants, the two occupational categories mostly filled by Black workers, were specifically excluded from most of the programs of the Social Security Act. The Federal Housing Administration (FHA) allowed banks to refuse to loan money in neighborhoods considered financially risky, and these included most Black neighborhoods. The FHA also encouraged White neighborhoods to use restrictive covenants, agreements banning Black homeowners because these agreements were believed to protect property prices. Consequently, Black citizens were largely ineligible for the main forms of federal public assistance until the late twentieth century.

Although racial equality may not have been part of the consciousness of many Americans during the New Deal, it was certainly a matter of concern to African Americans. Harlem activist Benjamin Jefferson Davis bitterly criticized the New Deal for excluding Black Americans. In the *New York Amsterdam News* in 1935, Davis denounced the National Recovery Administration as a "white monopoly," proclaiming that "the white man has a monopoly on all relief projects [...] No Negro is permitted to supervise any relief project [...] The question of social equality in all places operated by the government for the accommodation of public officials [...] has been lost sight of."[1]

However, while recognizing that the New Deal in general followed the historic pattern of bracketing out racial inequality, there were some instances in which African Americans were, to a limited extent, included in governmental programs and especially among the early New Dealers there were those who sought to use political intervention in order to promote racial equality, such as Secretary of the Interior Harold Ickes, who had previously been president of the Chicago chapter of the National Association for the Advancement of Colored People (NAACP). In a 1936 speech given to the NAACP, Secretary Ickes claimed that the New Deal could be particularly beneficial for African Americans because they "preeminently [belong] to the class that the new democracy is designed especially to aid."[2]

Two of the New Deal programs that did make some effort to use governmental intervention to improve the situations of African Americans, if not to aggressively seek racial equality, were the Public Works Administration (PWA), under Ickes, and the Works Progress Administration (WPA), under the direction of Harry Hopkins, one of FDR's most trusted advisers. The PWA required the hiring of Black laborers, both skilled and unskilled. The WPA actively enrolled Black participants, although with only limited success in the South, and it extended educational programs to Black families.[3]

While acknowledging the largely racially bracketed character of the New Deal, then, one should also recognize that more than any other group in American society, Black citizens were connected directly to Washington, DC. This created a close association between racial minority status and centralized big government. Although racially discriminatory policies of agencies such as the FHA helped to maintain and intensify residential segregation, the New Deal also contained the seeds of what would in the late twentieth century become a new version of the American ideal of equality—the pursuit of equalization of racial categories through political action.

FROM PROGRESSIVISM TO THE NEW DEAL

Historian Jason Scott Smith has pointed out that the programs of the
FDR era owed much to the Progressive Era plans for governmental
intervention in economic life and to practices of governmental economic
direction during World War I.[4] In adopting "New Deal" as the slogan for
his administration Franklin Roosevelt apparently intended to echo the
"Square Deal" promised by his much-admired distant cousin, Theodore
Roosevelt, whose corporatist progressivism prefigured much of FDR's
general approach.

One of the early uses of the phrase "new deal" to describe a project for a
corporate statist strategy, though, came from the engineer and economist
Stuart Chase. In its obituary for Chase, the *New York Times* credited him
with coining this term.[5] Chase participated in the corporatist wing of
progressivism, writing for the magazine *The New Republic*, which was
closely associated with Herbert Croly. Chase's 1932 book *A New Deal*,
published the year before Franklin Roosevelt assumed office, made an
argument that would have appealed to Edward Bellamy. The underlying
question of the book was "what is an economy for?" This question
assumed that an economy is not a product of the interactions of market
actors, but an intentionally designed system with an overall purpose.

Chase divided the American economy of his day into three sectors,
which he termed the sectors of government collectivism, nongovern-
ment collectivism, and competition. The first consisted of government
employment, regulation, aids to business, and public banking by means
of organizations such as the Federal Reserve and Federal Land Banks for
farmers. The second consisted of great corporations and their interlocking
associations and restrictive agreements, labor unions, and producers' and
consumers' cooperatives. Competition, according to Chase, only existed
in some retail activities, wholesaling and jobbing, and in the manufacture
of novelties and new commodities. This third sector was steadily being
crowded out by the other two, though.

Similar to Bellamy's vision, Chase believed that the collective activities of the second sector should be encompassed and absorbed by the first, which had the power to organize all activities rationally. While Chase saw government collectives as similar to others, he also saw government as the ultimate controller, above and outside the society it manages. For example, in arguing for the ability of government to increase its spending, he dismissed concerns about public debt. Regarding balanced budgets and the government economy, Chase declared, "You and I, when the cycle begins lopping off our incomes, have to cut expenses. Business houses, even great corporations, have to do the same [...] But [...] the government [...] is in a *totally different category*. The government is *not* held to the money medium; it is above them, for it *makes* the money medium."[6]

Chase argued that greater social control of economic activities was not simply desirable but inevitable. He described three "roads" toward this greater control. The first was socialist revolution. The second was the seizing of political and economic power by a small group of businessmen and bankers, or fascist revolution. Although Chase sympathized with the Soviet Union, he advocated the third road for the United States. On this third road, "an aroused citizenship forces its government to revise much of its business law, to institute certain powers and controls, which will attack the problem of distribution at its source, intelligently, not too violently, and with increasing thoroughness."[7]

Chase's description of the third road had significant implications for ideas about human equality from the perspective of what had become the corporatist progressive tradition by 1932. The first implication concerns the political dimension of social citizenship. In the third type of corporate state, as in the other two, people are primarily members of a centralized political system and they act on the world around them (and on each other) through political action. The second implication is that determining distribution is an essential function of government. People act through government, but they also receive goods and services through government. They are equal, then, in their direct relationship to the state and in their dependence on the state.

Rebecca E. Zietlow has referred to this equality of citizens through their relationship to the state, first hinted at in Reconstruction and developed more extensively during the New Deal as "social citizenship."[8] Social citizenship conceived of citizens as members of a centrally organized polity. While it drew on the tradition of individual rights, it reconceived these rights as claims on the federal government, rather than as independence from governmental interference. Although the New Deal was not primarily concerned with racial issues, it revived the Reconstruction idea of political equality as federal intervention to protect individuals in their relations with other individuals and corporate actors. During Reconstruction, this had involved the use of federal power on behalf of the newly freed population against other citizens and state and local governments. Under legislation such as the Wagner Act of the New Deal, the federal government exercised its power on behalf of workers in their relations with management. While Reconstruction and the New Deal shared the commitment to federal intervention and protection, the shift from the Civil Rights Act of 1866 to the Wagner Act also involved a major change in the kinds of protection promised by Washington. The first had been intervention to enforce the exercise of political liberty and was therefore closely connected to the old idea of equality as independence, only it was an independence that was paradoxically dependent on an authority. The second was also a dependent kind of equality, but it involved the extension of central political power into economic relations.

CORPORATIZATION: BIG BUSINESS AND BIG GOVERNMENT

Although the push for a greater role for the federal government in national life was most immediately a response to the Great Depression, it grew out of earlier developments. The previous chapter discussed the role of the corporatization of American society in pushing American concepts of equality in new directions. This corporatization proceeded apace up to and through the Great Depression.

By the end of the First World War, the United States had been largely transformed from a republic of farmers to one of city dwellers who lived and worked in a corporate industrial setting. The 1920 census was the first in American history to show a majority of Americans living in urban areas, rather than rural areas[9]. From 1914 to 1927, wage earners employed in factories producing products valued at $5,000 or more grew in number from 6,895,000 to 8,350,000, and the value added by manufacturing nearly tripled from $9,708,000 to $27,585,000.[10] By 1937, nearly 14% of all wage earners in manufacturing were working in establishments that employed more than 2,500 workers, and three-quarters of American manufacturing wage earners were employed by businesses with more than 100 workers. [11]

The automobile industry had become central to the American economy by the end of the 1920s. This industry was already a centralized oligopoly by 1929. Ford, General Motors, and Chrysler employed vast numbers of workers on its assembly lines. By then, an estimated one in nine nonfarm workers worked in jobs connected with building, selling, or servicing the 30,000,000 automobiles and trucks that were transporting people and goods each day. The major automobile companies were operating extensive networks for advertising and extending credit.[12] Automobiles were not just items of consumption; they were means of expanding an economy of mass consumption and integrating mass consumption into an interlocked corporate system. The vehicles could transport goods to even wider markets than the railroad system had. With cars, purchasers could go shopping in supermarket chains such as A&P that had spread rapidly following the First World War.

In his 1905 study *Corporations,* John P. Davis pointed out the dominance of large corporations in the American economy. In 1932, the year before Franklin Roosevelt took office, two Columbia University professors, Adolf Berle and Gardiner C. Means, published an analysis of trends in corporate development. They maintained that apart from size and scope of activities, modern corporations were also distinguished by the separation of control from ownership, noting that "the property owner who invests in a modern corporation so far surrenders his wealth to those in control of the corporations [the managers or directors] that he has exchanged the position of independent owner for one in which he may become merely recipient of the wages of capital."[13] From this, Berle and Means derived a normative argument about the communitarian role of privately held companies. Because the owners of "passive property" had given up control and responsibility over their active property, they claimed, the owners had also given up the right to have the company run in their sole interests and surrendered some of their property rights. Thus, from the view of Berle and Means, property rights in corporations had to yield before the larger interests of society. Ultimately, Berle and Means suggested that "the 'control' of the great corporations should develop into a purely neutral technocracy, balancing a variety of claims by various groups in the community and assigning to each a portion of the income stream on the basis of public policy rather than private cupidity."[14]

This control of corporations as a neutral instrument of public policy would fall to government. Many of the experts the Roosevelt administration brought to Washington were committed to the goal of reshaping American society through federal government intervention. Frances Perkins, the new Secretary of Labor, and Harry Hopkins, administrator of relief efforts, were both former social workers. Perkins played an important part in creating federal labor policy, promoting the passage of the Wagner Act, the Fair Labor Standards Act, and the Social Security Act by Congress. Hopkins ran the federal relief act of 1933–1934. The members of Franklin Roosevelt's "brains trust" were overwhelmingly advocates of big, active central government that would intervene directly in the society and in the lives of citizens. Columbia University political scientist Raymond Moley espoused coordination between corporations and the federal government for the sake of social planning. Columbia economist Rexford Tugwell believed in a centrally planned collectivist economy[15].

Although Tugwell was more radical than the others, together the social workers and economic engineers of the early Roosevelt administration seemed to embody a concept similar to Edward Bellamy's dream of the nation's future. After the recession of 1937, a new generation of New Deal experts began to employ antimonopoly rhetoric, sounding more like the early Wilsonian progressives than the Bellamy-Croly variety[16]. These regulatory statists, though, shared the goal of a more far-reaching and intrusive federal government with the first generation of New Dealers.

Speaking to graduates of Washington and Jefferson College in June 1933, Secretary of the Interior Harold Ickes linked the new ideas of government intervention for the sake of social citizenship to older ideas of equality of opportunity. Arguing against the "rugged individualism" of earlier eras, Ickes proclaimed that "all we asked from government [in earlier times] was negation." In what he called the "social revolution" of his own day, he noted, "we must adhere to the policy of protecting the weak against the strong, of curbing overreaching and ruthless power, of assuring to all, both weak and strong, the equality of opportunity which is the cornerstone of our American civilization."[17]

The pursuit of this type of social citizenship entailed a greatly enlarged role for the central government. Regarding the National Recovery Administration, a centerpiece of the early New Deal, Ira Katznelson writes, "nothing like this comprehensive restructuring of market capitalism by a national state had ever been tried before in a constitutional democracy [...] it combined tools of planning and corporatism borrowed from those regimes [i.e., German and Italian dictatorships] with American progressive ideas about the regulation of business and the rights of labor."[18]

Economist Gene Smiley identifies the New Deal as the origin of the vast regulatory welfare state, noting: "The 1930s saw a huge expansion of the regulatory activities and powers of the federal government. The door to this expansion had been opened with the passage of the Interstate Commerce Act of 1887 to regulate railroads. But its full flowering did not occur until the 1930s when federal regulation was extended to interstate activities in trucking, busing, airlines, radio, power generation and transmission, oil and gas pipelines, securities exchanges, coal mining, agriculture, and other sectors."[19] Whether one sees this expansion as an unwarranted encroachment by the federal power or as a desirable response to economic complexity, there is no question that during the New Deal, Washington, DC, began to influence the lives of citizens more extensively and more directly than ever before. This influence included new federal responsibilities for the social well-being of individual citizens, in addition to greater coordination of the economy. Smiley observes that "one of the most striking changes to emerge from the Great Depression decade was the rise of a set of government-sponsored social welfare programs [...] Whether all of these social welfare programs were desirable can be debated. What is not debatable is the fact that the way we live, work, and retire was dramatically changed as a result of these New Deal social welfare programs."[20]

Government Intervention, the Market, and Social Welfare

Critics of the New Deal, at the time and in the following decades, often accused the Great Depression's transformation of the relationship among government, business, and citizens of introducing elements of socialism into American life. Whether this is true or not depends on how socialism is defined. If it is defined as any government involvement in the economy, this characterization is true virtually as a tautology. However, if one defines socialism as government ownership of the means of production or the attempt to replace market forces of supply and demand with setting production and prices by mandate, then the "socialistic" activities of the New Deal and of the governmental programs that followed it were extremely limited.

Self-identified socialists did not consider the interventions of the New Deal to be socialism. In a June 1933 editorial, socialist leader and former presidential candidate Norman Thomas argued that "what Mr. Roosevelt has done has been to lay the foundations for an immense structure of State capitalism" and that "socialism would capture the power of the political state and use it to establish the cooperative commonwealth. State capitalism would use the power of the political state to bring order out of our present chaos and stabilize it."[21] One does not need to accept Thomas' views on the desirability and feasibility of socialism to recognize that he had a strong argument. The New Deal was less concerned with creating the kind of relative equality of condition generally associated with socialism than it was with attempting to provide stability to the corporate market economy by cushioning extremes in inequality of condition and trying to influence the supply of market-produced goods and the demand for them.

The Tennessee Valley Authority (TVA), early in the New Deal, was probably the most outstanding instance of government ownership of a means of production. The publicly owned and managed dam in the Tennessee River Valley that would supply electricity throughout the region was opposed by businessmen associated with the private utilities industry, most notably future presidential candidate Wendell Wilkie, as a Soviet-style project that would take over an industry and wipe out the value of investments in private utilities. The consequence of this apparently socialist project, though, was not to destroy private business, but to create a new kind of partnership between the federal government and profit-seeking corporations. The new source essentially boosted the supply of electricity, lowered its costs, and created a demand for privately produced goods. As Michael Hiltzik notes:

> Across the Southeast, rates fell so sharply that residents and businesses began thinking up new ways to use electricity [...] New electric appliances appeared in homes—refrigerators, washing machines, water heaters—due in part to a TVA program subsidizing their purchase. Ownership of electric appliances tripled overall.[22]

Even in this clearest example of government ownership, the federal government was influencing the market, rather than replacing it. Instead of fixing prices, the Franklin Roosevelt administration was trying to affect prices by influencing supply and demand. In the case of the TVA, this resulted in equalizing the condition of citizen-consumers by giving the relatively disadvantaged more access to a resource. It also boosted the profits of businesses by increasing effective demand for their goods.

This consumer orientation was not present in every New Deal program. The Agricultural Adjustment Administration (AAA) became notorious for its efforts to restrict production. Farmers had experienced falling prices in the early 1930s, arguably because of overproduction. Critics of the AAA objected to the organization's attempts to boost prices by controlling farmers' activities. The drastic early interventions to bring down supply by slaughtering hogs and plowing under fields seemed particularly egregious. A large part of this problem of overproduction may have been that although agribusiness was becoming a force in the 1930s, much of the agricultural economy lagged behind other sectors in corporatization. The Jeffersonian independent family farms remained ideologically important for Americans, but the plethora of small farms could not respond to shifts in prices as readily as large corporations could, nor could they reach economies of scale that could make food cheaper while maintaining high profits. Eventually, the American farm sector would be saved by corporate concentration, government subsidies, and expanding overseas markets.

Some of the most long-lasting New Deal programs, however, were clearly consumer oriented. The Social Security Act of 1935, for example, put spending power in the hands of consumers not only by providing a basic retirement income for the elderly but also by creating Aid to Dependent Children (later called Aid to Families with Dependent Children) for widows with minor dependents, and Supplementary Security Income for the elderly who did not qualify for regular Social Security, the blind, and the disabled. This type of public assistance benefit was an attempt to raise the bottom economic levels of American society, thereby contributing to the market by increasing demand for products. It was also an indirect way of doing something somewhat similar to what the AAA had attempted: increasing the wages of workers by reducing the supply of workers, through getting people aged 65 and older out of the labor force.

SETTING THE STAGE FOR THE GREAT COMPRESSION

The middle of the twentieth century is often called the Great Compression because it was a time of general income equalization. Although most authors date this as the end of World War II,[23] the origins of this equalization can clearly be traced back to the 1930s.

Figure 5. Household Income Inequality (Gini Coefficients) and Net Share of Wealth Held by the Top 1% of Households, 1929–1945.

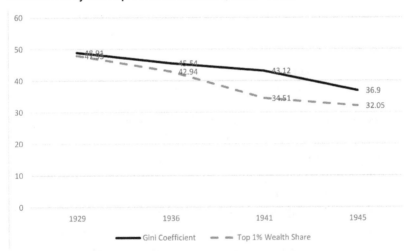

Source. The Chartbook of Economic Inequality, "Economic Inequality in USA," https://www.chartbookofeconomicinequality.com/inequality-by-country/usa/.

Figure 5 gives two key indicators, in the form of the Gini coefficient, a measure of economic inequality, and the total share of wealth held by the top one percent of families in the United States. Simply explained, the Gini coefficient displays wealth or income between 0 and 1 or between 0 and

100. The lower the coefficient, the more economic inequality approaches complete equality of distribution; and the higher the coefficient, the more economic resources approach complete concentration.

Economic inequality, as indicated by these two measures, declined from 1929 to 1936 and then went down further as the United States entered World War II. Sociologist Douglas Massey has attributed the Great Compression to the initiation of the New Deal, followed by the postwar Fair Deal by President Harry S. Truman, tracing the sources of this relative equalization to the welfare state policies and governmental support for organized labor that began with the Franklin Roosevelt administration.[24] Determining causation in history is always difficult, and it is hard to say to what extent the regulation and social supports that began with the Roosevelt administration produced this equalizing and to what extent the demands of the corporate economy contributed to this trend. As the next chapter will point out, some economists have argued that the continued equalizing in the years that followed the New Deal was less a consequence of policies than of demand for labor.

Whether the US government helped to end the Great Depression or actually prolonged it through raising labor costs and interfering with the efficient allocation of labor also remains a matter of debate.[25] Whatever position one may take on this, it seems evident that a broad trend of equalizing, whether at the cost of economic growth or not, began during a time characterized by central government intervention, centralized corporate bureaucracies, and increasingly organized labor operating with mediation from the former and in negotiation with the latter. The consequence for ideas of equality was a resetting of expectations. A relative rising in the standard of living among Americans in general became more a part of an expected future, for individuals and for the society in general. An active role by government in promoting this rising standard of living became gradually more accepted.

CITIZENS AS CONSUMERS

As the nation intensified mass production and distribution of goods through large-scale business and labor, mediated and subsidized by government, Americans tended to redefine citizenship. Being an American began to mean consuming products. Again, this was not a sudden break with the past during the New Deal but grew out of the corporatization of American society. Ronald Edsforth has pointed out that although we now look back on President Herbert Hoover as a "conservative," Hoover in fact shared much in common with his successor, including the idea that the purpose of America as a nation was to deliver the goods to its citizens. Edsforth has observed that far from looking backward, Hoover's Republicanism was imbued with the culture of mass consumption, noting, "Like Hoover, most Americans accepted the constantly advertised message that the New Era economy would eventually bring almost everyone better homes and health, as well as cars, electricity, frozen foods, mass entertainment, and annual vacations. By the late 1920s, this vision of the future amounted to the modern 'American Dream' that leading figures in both major political parties embraced as the proper goal of federal government policies."[26]

The main difference between the consumerism of the Hoover administration and that of Franklin Roosevelt concerned how the nation could best deliver the goods. In what would come to be called a "demand side" approach to political economy, the New Dealers saw government's direct provision of jobs, services, and products to consumers as an indirect way of subsidizing businesses. Thus, in his 1935 account of the creation of the PWA, Harold Ickes justified the public works program as a way to put more money into circulation in order to restore the health of the economy.[27] The New Dealers saw the role of government in subsidizing demand as a major redesign of the relationship between government and society, and not just as a pragmatic strategy. Writing in the same year as Ickes in *The New York Times* on August 18, Labor Secretary Frances Perkins reiterated the idea that the economy required government to channel funds to those at the bottom: "If we are to maintain a healthy economy and thriving production, we need to maintain the standard of living of the low-income groups in our population, who constitute 90 percent of our purchasing power." The Social Security Act's redistribution, in her view, was "a milestone in our progress toward a better-ordered society."[28]

Although it has often been suggested that Franklin Roosevelt was an experimenter, seeking solutions to the challenges of the Great Depression without ideological guidelines, the perspectives of Ickes and Perkins that the changed conditions required rejecting individualistic ideas of equality for a governmentally subsidized version of equality of opportunity appears to have been a viewpoint held by Roosevelt even before he entered the presidency. In his book on the New Deal as the origin of later American political history, Ira Katznelson recounts:

> In a hallmark address to San Francisco's Commonwealth Club on September 23, 1932, he [Franklin Roosevelt] lamented how "equality of opportunity as we have known it no longer exists," and he sought to explain why "we are approaching a drab living for our own people." That speech offered a structural analysis. It identified a closed frontier, a built-up industrial structure and "a steady course toward economic oligarchy as the Depression's culprits. Needed in such circumstances were "new terms of the old social contract [...] a new "economic constitutional order "in which our "our government would restrict the operations of the speculator, the manipulator, even the financier. To check competitive markets and the reach of business power, FDR announced, would require plans in the public interest.[29]

As the new program of social citizenship took shape, it soon moved beyond regulatory control of business activities, and to the provision of economic benefits to citizens. Perhaps the most significant and far-reaching program of benefits came in the form of the Social Security Act, which the president signed into law on August 14, 1935, creating a federal pension for the elderly and an unemployment insurance. The core of the Social Security system was a program to collect money from workers and employers in order to pay the workers when they later retired or became disabled. However, the act also contained provisions for public assistance in addition to this retirement plan. The 1935 act designated three categories of people who would receive direct federal payments: children in families without a parent capable of working, who could receive assistance under the Aid to Dependent Children (ADC) program; the blind and disabled, who were eligible for the Aid to the Blind (AB) and Aid to the Disabled (AD) programs; and the elderly who were not eligible for regular Social Security payments, who qualified for the Aid to the Aged (AA) program.

While enacting social security entailed some debate about the proper role of government in the lives of citizens, it became one of the most widely supported federal programs in the population at large. Even when some of its products, notably Aid to Families of Dependent Children (AFDC, a later version of ADC) became controversial in later decades, social security itself was extremely popular because nearly all Americans were potential beneficiaries. Social security also played a large part in redefining the relationship between individual citizens and the government. Being a citizen meant having a claim on government benefits and services, and the equality of citizens became more of an equality of consumers in the relationship to a provider.

In addition to the pensions and other kinds of public assistance created by social security, the federal government also took on the mission of expanding access to homeownership. In the hard year of 1933, foreclosures of homes had become widespread. In response, early in Franklin Roosevelt's first term, his administration sent to Congress a bill to create the Home Owners Loan Corporation (HOLC). The HOLC made direct low-interest, long-term loans to homeowners who were in default or in danger of default. In 1934, HOLC issued three-quarters of all the home mortgages in the nation.

In 1934 the newly established Federal Housing Administration (FHA) began issuing mortgage insurance. By 1944, nearly half of all new mortgages were secured by FHA insurance. Both HOLC and FHA made mortgage lending less risky and homeownership more secure. In the long run, these programs essentially subsidized entering and remaining in the middle class by expanding access to mortgages and homeownership. Economic opportunity took place through resources provided by government, so that equality of opportunity became a situation structured by government and by the relationship of citizens to government. These new housing programs are especially important for later developments in American ideas of equal opportunity because widening access to mortgages would over the decades become one of the principal ways in which the federal government attempted to broaden upward mobility through subsidies.

The Jeffersonian independent householder ideal twisted in a new direction as the federal government took on the responsibility of subsidizing homeownership. As foreclosure threatened thousands of homeowners in the difficult spring of 1933, the Franklin Roosevelt administration sent to Congress a bill to authorize the Home Owners Loan Corporation (HOLC), creating an agency that made low-interest, long-term direct mortgage loans to homeowners in default or in danger of default. During 1934, this agency made three-fourths of all the home mortgage loans in the country.[30]

The redefinition of citizens as consumers of federal resources became deeply rooted. Anthony J. Badger noted that "the New Deal welfare programs provided direct assistance to perhaps as many as 35 percent of the population. It bequeathed a commitment to a minimum level of social welfare from which successive governments have never been entirely able to escape." [31]

THE MASS COMMUNICATION STATE

In discussing the ideal of the self-made man as a form of egalitarianism, I emphasized the cultural centrality of newspapers in the nineteenth century. Print journalism continued to shape American society, but its influence began to diminish in the twenty-first century under pressure of competition from the internet. Alongside newspapers, though, from the 1920s into the middle of the twentieth century a new form of mass electronic communication contributed to the centralization of American society. This was the radio.

Bruce Lenthall's 2007 study, *Radio's America: The Great Depression and the Rise of Modern Mass Culture*, may have overstated the extent to which radio homogenized American society and absorbed individuals into a system of mass communication. Local communities and diversity of geographic cultures did not disappear into the empire of the radio. Moreover, this was not the only form of mass communication. National magazines were also influential throughout this period. Nevertheless, the presence of a radio in nearly every home, broadcasting the same programs to all, unquestionably worked a huge change in American culture.

Jason Loviglio has argued that the ubiquitous voices of the radio blurred the boundaries between the public and the private realms of life.[32] Through broadcasts such as Franklin Roosevelt's "fireside chats," national politics and the president himself became an everyday part of the home, drawing individuals into the life of the nation. The first of these radio addresses by the new president took place on Sunday, March 12, 1934, at the very beginning of the New Deal, as banks were starting to reopen. The Roosevelt administration saw radio as crucial to the president's program. "With the success of the New Deal's opening initiative hanging on the address," Michael Hiltzik writes, "Roosevelt and his advisors took exceptional care with the text."[33] By nearly all accounts, this first chat, with the president speaking directly and informally to each citizen, was enormously successful in garnering public support.

Thereafter, these radio talks would continue to announce and promote each new strategy of the federal government for the New Deal.

Franklin Roosevelt was not the only figure on the political landscape to realize the potential of the new medium of communication. Father Charles Coughlin, a Catholic parish priest in Detroit, began broadcasting his sermons in 1926. By the time Roosevelt entered office, Coughlin had become a prominent presence throughout the nation, commenting on political and economic, as well as religious issues. Coughlin's radio broadcasts directly addressed, and attacked, the corporate centralization of his era, with broadsides against Wall Street, big banks, and the power of concentrated finance.[34]

This absorption of people into a national sphere made their linkage to the bureaucratic state a direct, if almost entirely one-way, relationship between each citizen and the national center, tending to replace civic participation through social network connections. At the same time, radio, through its advertisements promoted similar direct lines of association between consumers and corporate purveyors of mass-produced goods.

The intimate connection of radio to the corporate concentration of business activities during the 1930s is evident in the phrase "soap opera," a term that continues to be used to refer to broadcasted melodramas. This type of radio entertainment dates from about 1930, and the reference to "soap" is a consequence of the sponsorship of Proctor & Gamble, which used these programs as vehicles for advertising its goods. Listeners to soap operas stood in essentially the same relationship to corporate producers as they did to national political figures.

CITIZENS AS CATEGORIES

While the corporate state and corporate business redefined citizens as consumers with direct, individual links to providers of goods and services, the political and economic environment of the interwar years also encouraged a tendency to think of social relations in terms of abstract blocs or categories. Equality could be understood as the equality of categories of citizens, represented by large-scale organizations.

Although the New Deal was not primarily concerned with either questions of race or gender, it revived Reconstruction and Progressive Era ideas of political equality because of the federal intervention to protect categories of individuals in their relations with other individuals and corporate actors. During Reconstruction, this involved the use of federal power on behalf of the newly freed population against other citizens and state and local governments. In the Progressive Era, one part of the push for women's suffrage had been the redefinition of women as abstract individuals. Another part, though, had come from a perception of "women's issues" as matters to be addressed by a corporate state, or women as a distinct category in the public sphere with distinct interests to be addressed through political participation. Under the legislation of the New Deal, the federal government exercised its power on behalf of workers in their relations with management. While Reconstruction and the New Deal shared the commitment to federal intervention and protection, the shift from the Civil Rights Act of 1866 to the Wagner Act also involved a major change in the kinds of protection promised by the government. The first had been intervention to enforce the exercise of political liberty and was therefore closely connected to the old idea of equality as independence, only it was an independence that was paradoxically dependent on an authority. The second was also a dependent kind of equality, but it involved the extension of central political power into economic relations.

The Wagner Act, formally known as the National Labor Relations Act, signed into law on July 5, 1935, was the most important legislative foundation of the developing idea of the equality of categories of actors, promoted and supported by the federal government. As stated by Ira Katznelson, "Crucially, this bill aimed, as it stated, 'to promote equality of bargaining between employers and employees.'"[35] This language of governmental intervention through legislation to establish a corporate form of equality was common among the New Dealers. For example, in a statement at the end of 1936, Secretary of Labor Frances Perkins wrote: "There should also be cooperation during 1937 between workers and employers in terms of honorable and competent bargaining between groups of equal influence and responsibility [...] But real and effective cooperation requires terms of equal bargaining power which results from organization and recognition of equality between the two parties."[36]

SCHOOLING AND SOCIAL CITIZENSHIP

In our study of the social history of American public education, Stephen J. Caldas and I pointed out that schooling has been central to American ideals of citizenship and to shifting American views of the relationship between individuals and the government.[37] During the period of the New Deal, prominent educational social reconstructionists presented schooling as a means of reshaping American society into a more egalitarian form. In his pamphlet, *The Schools Can Teach Democracy*, initially delivered as an address before the Progressive Education Association on Washington's Birthday in 1939, George S. Counts argued that the proper business of schools was to create a democratic society through cultivating "democratic habits, dispositions, and loyalties," as well as relevant political knowledge in students.[38] Through schooling, "the entire nation would be subjected to the most critical examination for the purpose of revealing submerged and exploited regions, occupational groups, and racial, national, and religious minorities."[39] Counts maintained that educational programs should not simply reflect the social order—they should direct the social order.

Counts' colleague, Harold Rugg, showed a similar cast of thought. The 1939 volume *Democracy and the Curriculum*, written by ten progressive educational thinkers, including Counts, and edited by Rugg argued for an approach to curriculum design that amounted to a redesign of American society. Rugg said of the curriculum designer that "not only must he be a sociologist and statesman, philosopher and educational technician; he must also be a competent student of individual physiology and psychology."[40] While Rugg acknowledged that this was a difficult challenge, he declared that he and his colleagues were ready to undertake it, "heartened and guided by the conviction that, with the creative resources within our grasp, we can bring into existence on the North American continent a golden age of abundance [...] democratic behavior [...] and integrity of expression."[41] The Great Depression, Rugg argued, gave an impetus to social planning, and he maintained that "in the decade after 1929 the *social engineering mind* was given a conspicuous role in government."[42]

As Caldas and I note, conservative and progressive educational commentators largely agreed on schools as ways to shape the citizenry because "for both, [the society of the future] was corporate and bureaucratic in character."[43] Ideological disagreements largely concerned whether schools should train young people to fit into this corporate society (the conservative view) or reshape the minds of students in order to reshape the society along more egalitarian lines (the progressive view). The idea of education as a primary way of promoting equality of opportunity and upward mobility tended to be relatively limited in the years before World War II. As education, especially higher education, later became a primary avenue for mobility, the view that public education was a way to shape citizens could fit easily into seeing schooling as the process by which public policy would shape individuals to take advantage of economic opportunities.

Elementary and secondary education, offering preparation for the blue-collar jobs that were the most widely available, had become widespread in the early twentieth century. By 1920, over 60 percent of Whites and about half of Blacks aged 5 to 19 were enrolled in schools. Between 1930 and 1940, this rose from 65 percent of Whites in that age group and 55 percent of Blacks to over 70 percent and over 65 percent, respectively.[44] Mass education had become a reality by the prewar years. Higher education, though, was still not a common avenue for mobility, in theory or in practice. Percentages of adults (25 years and older) with college educations rose from 3.9 percent in 1930 to 4.6 percent in 1940. Even by 1960, despite a postwar college boom (see the following chapter), only 7.7 percent of Americans had graduated from college, as a result of the rarity of higher education in earlier years.[45] Education had become a way of equalizing citizens by incorporating them into a mass society, but the goal of everyone having a chance to move upward through higher education would come at a later time.

CONTESTED IDEALS OF EQUALITY

Many aspects of the social citizenship of the New Deal coexisted uneasily with older ideals of equality, such as the equality of independent citizens or the self-made man. The centralized state character of social citizenship often seemed particularly inconsistent with some cultural traditions of independence and self-creation, as well as with decentralized concepts of authority. During the first half of the New Deal, the Supreme Court consistently ruled the efforts of the Franklin Roosevelt administration unconstitutional.

Mississippi Senator Theodore Bilbo advocated the abolition of the WPA. "If we keep the WPA much longer," Bilbo declared in 1937, "we will create a nation of mendicants [...] It is not the government's business to support its citizens, but it is the business of citizens to support the government. The only duty of the government is to have such laws and economic conditions that citizens will have an equal opportunity to make a living."[46]

Along similar lines, the *Hartford Courant*, commenting on President Franklin Roosevelt's legislative agenda in early 1935, opined, "[n]o political system can possibly guarantee either a national economic security or an individual standard of living. Government can guarantee no man a job or a livelihood, but it can do a great deal to provide equality of opportunity."[47]

It is notable that both Bilbo and the *Hartford Courant* ascribe to government the ability and obligation to provide equality of opportunity for individuals, without specifying how government is to do this. Because these views were expressed before the time of government intervention to prevent discriminatory treatment on the basis of categorical identities, we can safely assume that this was not how they saw government creating equality of opportunity. Most likely, they believed that this kind of equality would naturally occur if government pursued a policy of noninterference in business, which would create more opportunities for which individuals could compete.

While some critics of the New Deal objected to governmental intervention for the sake of social security, economic regulation, redistribution, and equalization, others believed the Franklin Roosevelt administration did not take these efforts far enough. Louisiana Governor Huey Long figured prominently among the latter group. Proposing a 100% income tax on incomes above $1 million and a guaranteed income of over $2,000, Long promoted his redistribution programs through "Share Our Wealth" clubs. Revealingly, his campaign song was "Every Man a King." Implicit in this slogan was a new version of the old equality of independence. With a security created by political redistribution, rather than by possession of a plot of farmland, every individual could be sovereign.

The "radio priest" Father Charles Coughlin at the start of the New Deal supported Franklin Roosevelt but also became critical of the Roosevelt program for not taking governmental intervention into society and economy far enough. Coughlin also helped to popularize a term that would become identified with later versions of politically subsidized egalitarianism: social justice. Derived from Catholic social theology derived from the philosophy of Thomas Aquinas, Catholic social justice essentially referred to the conception of society as a divinely ordained, interdependent whole, with all having rights and obligations within it. Writing in the Catholic magazine *Commonweal* in February 1936, Vigil Michel wrote that "we can [...] define social justice as that virtue by which individuals and groups contribute their positive share to the maintenance of the common good and moreover regulate all their actions in proper relation to the common good."

Father Coughlin applied this term to a political program of redistribution through monetary inflation, government control of banks and major industries, and setting wages and incomes. In 1936, he sought to advance this program by launching the newspaper *Social Justice* and by organizing the National Union for Social Justice. While Coughlin's version of social justice remained linked to his religious beliefs, he had pushed the term into a distinctly secular direction, with the idea that reordering society for the benefit of the relatively disadvantaged was an absolute moral imperative for the federal government.

For roughly three decades following the implementation of the New Deal, the voices of its critics were muted. The demands of World War II tended to encourage national unity behind an active federal government and draw attention away from social policy. The booming economy and expanding socioeconomic opportunities following the war encouraged broad agreement on social issues, even if undercurrents of dissent stirred beneath the surface. However, contradictions in ideas about the equality of independent individuals and the desired equality of previously excluded categories of people, about competitive equality and the expectation of universal upward mobility, and about individual energies and talents and political efforts to equalize outcomes would become more difficult to reconcile as economic opportunities later contracted and as the society began to fragment into identity groups.

NOTES

1. Davis, *Corporations*, A2
2. Quoted in Sklaroff, *Black Culture and the New Deal*, 22.
3. Sklaroff, *Black Culture and the New Deal*.
4. Smith, *A Concise History of the New Deal.*
5. "Stuart Chase, 97," *New York Times,* November 7, 1985, sec. 1, 44.
6. Chase, *A New Deal*, 141 (emphasis in the original).
7. Ibid., 155.
8. Zietlow, *Enforcing Equality.*
9. US Census Bureau, *Census of Population and Housing, 1990*, Table 4, 5.
10. US Census Bureau, *Census of Population and Housing, 1930*, Table 802. 791.
11. US Census Bureau, *Census of Population and Housing, 1940*, Table 827, 803.
12. Edsforth, *The New Deal.*
13. Berle and Means, *The Modern Corporation and Private Property*, 3.
14. Ibid., 356
15. Smiley, *Rethinking the Great Depression.*
16. Brinkley, "The New Deal and the Idea of the State."
17. "Ickes Portrays New Social Order," *New York Times,* June 4, 1833, N1.
18. Katznelson, *Fear Itself,* 231.
19. Smiley, *Rethinking the Great Depression*, 151–152.
20. Ibid., 153–154
21. Thomas, "Is the New Deal Socialism?," XX3.
22. Hiltzik, *The New Deal,* 77
23. See, for example, Bronstein, *Two Nations, Indivisible*; and Goldin and Margo, "The Great Compression."
24. Massey, *Categorically Unequal.*
25. See Kaufman, "Wage Theory, New Deal Labor Policy, and the Great Depression" for a statement of this debate that argues in favor of New Deal policies
26. Edsforth, *The New Deal*, 13
27. Ickes, *Back to Work.*
28. Perkins, "Social Security: The Foundation," , SM1.
29. Katznelson, *Fear Itself,* 249.
30. Edsforth, *The New Deal.*

31. Badger, *The New Deal*, 301.
32. Loviglio, *Radio's Intimate Public*.
33. Hiltzik, *The New Deal*, 50.
34. Tull, *Father Coughlin & the New Deal*.
35. Katznelson, *Fear Itself*, 257.
36. Quoted in "Miss Perkins Urges Job Security Plans," *New York Times*, January 1, 1937, 11.
37. Bankston and Caldas, *Public Education, America's Civil Religion*.
38. Counts, *The Schools Can Teach Democracy*, 22.
39. Ibid., 36.
40. Rugg, *Democracy and the Curriculum*, 12.
41. Ibid.
42. Rugg, *Foundations for American Education*, 578 (emphasis in the original).
43. Bankston and Caldas, *Public Education, America's Civil Religion*, 74.
44. Snyder, *120 Years of American Education*.
45. National Center for Education Statistics, *Digest of Education Statistics*, Table 104.10.
46. Quoted in "WPA Makes Beggars, Bilbo Asserts," *Atlanta* Constitution, February 21, 1937, 7A.
47. Reprinted in "Editorial Views: Welfare Limitations," *New York Times*, January 27, E8.

CHAPTER 5

THE UPWARDLY MOBILE SOCIETY

POST- WORLD WAR II AMERICA

LIFE CHANCES AND EXPECTATIONS

In the years following World War II, three trends promoted shifting attitudes among the American people toward their own life opportunities. First, Americans in general experienced structural upward mobility. Desirable, relatively high-prestige jobs became increasingly available. Consequently, much of the American population moved up on the socioeconomic scale. While success continued to be understood as a result of individual effort and individual efforts were indeed usually necessary for success, the chances of getting ahead were more widely available than ever before. Second, the years after the war saw the US government expand programs that would subsidize upward mobility. Specifically, the postwar years saw increased government support for homeownership and education. The latter, moreover, tended to be the type of higher education oriented toward white-collar, professional employment, which had previously been the domain of small elite groups in American society. The third trend was the growing association of the concept of equal opportunity with a large segment of the nation that had been shut out of American thinking about the competition for positions from the time of the nation's creation. African Americans, maintained as a separate caste first by slavery and then by the Jim Crow system, increasingly called for an end to the caste system through equality of opportunity.

The increase in structural mobility encouraged the perception that not only did everyone have the chance to get ahead but also that everyone should be getting ahead, even though "ahead" still meant ahead of others. Government support, although still limited in the first decade and a half after the Second World War, promoted the view that government could and should help Americans move forward in the competition. While outcomes were still expected to be unequal, the logical implication of government assistance was that starting places could be politically equalized. Because winning the socioeconomic race was coming to be seen as the norm, government began to acquire the responsibility for compensating for any disadvantages that could keep people from becoming winners. The campaign for equality for African Americans picked up momentum just as Americans began to expect upward mobility as a norm and to accept government as an equalizer of competitive disadvantages. The phrase "equal opportunity" became closely associated with the African American struggle. Initially, this phrase simply referred to the breaking down of racial-caste barriers to entry into the competition.

POSTWAR ECONOMY AND STRATIFICATION

With the end of World War II, the United States had emerged as the world's greatest economic power. The major industrial nations of Europe were in ruins. The Soviet Union had suffered devastation from the German invasion, and its socialist system would have removed it as a competitor even if it had been in better condition. For the United States, though, the war had provided a tremendous fiscal stimulus. By 1950 the United States accounted for 18 percent of all the world's exports, and by 1953 the nation contributed 45 percent of all global industrial production.[1] This rapid economic growth was a consequence of structural changes in the American economy brought about by wartime production, as large corporations worked on a vast scale with the government to produce the equipment that won the war. "It was at wartime General Motors," historian Niall Ferguson has observed, "that [management expert] Peter Drucker saw the birth of the modern 'concept of the corporation.'"[2]

The extent to which we can accept this dating of the modern corporation to the postwar period is open to debate. As discussed in previous chapters, the corporatization of American society grew steadily throughout the Progressive Era and the New Deal. Nevertheless, the war did produce an unprecedented interweaving of business and government and it intensified a commitment to economic planning.

Figure 6. Gross National Product of the United States, 1940–1959, in Constant 1954 Dollars (Billions of Dollars).

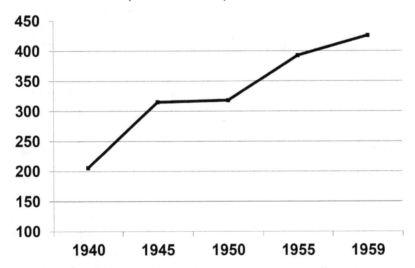

Source. US Census Bureau, *Statistical Abstract of the United States*, 1960.

As the war ended, many policymakers had feared that the United States would be plunged into recession following decreasing war spending and the return of American servicemen to an economy with insufficient employment opportunities. As figure 6 shows, the late 1940s did indeed show some stagnation in the Gross National Product (GNP) between 1945 and 1950, after a steady climb out of the nadir of 1933. Throughout the 1950s, though, the country's productivity again climbed steadily, showing steadily expanding economic activity

More production must mean benefits for someone. In theory, these benefits could go to only a few people in an economy who reap the rewards of everyone's work. This can happen, for example, when low-paid workers produce goods for a foreign market and the owners or stockholders receive most of the profits. To the extent that workers produce goods for a domestic market, though, the domestic market must have enough effective demand to support continued productivity. People must be able to buy the goods, or businesses will not keep producing more of them. In the United States of the 1950s, Americans were the greatest consumers of their own products, so that increased productivity did create steadily improving material standards of living across most of the population.

The United States also ran a trade surplus with the rest of the world until the 1970s. Not only were Americans producing for a domestic market (i.e., for themselves), they were also selling to everyone else. Recovering economies in Europe, assisted by the Marshall Plan, provided international demand for the goods produced by American companies and workers.

The postwar years were not only years of broad, growing prosperity but also of greater equality of condition, resulting from general growth in domestic consumption, made possible by more public buying power. In 1947, the US Department of the Census began measuring income inequalities among American families with the index of income inequality, also known as the Gini coefficient, which the last chapter presented as a measure of household inequality. Again, this index measures the distribution of income between 0.0, the point at which all families have equal shares of the national income, and 1.0, the point at which one family has all of the income. Looking at the Gini coefficient to determine percentage changes in income inequality each year after 1947, US Census analysts Arthur E. Jones and Daniel H. Weinberg found that income inequality among families in the United States dropped from 1947 to 1957, with brief upward spikes following the recessions of 1949 and 1953.[3] The trend toward equalization reversed with the two recessions at the end of the 1950s and beginning of the 1960s, but then family income inequality began to decrease again until the end of the 1960s. At least for the time immediately following the war, economic growth was accompanied by greater equalization of incomes, with brief downturns followed by short periods of greater inequality.

The relationship between prosperity and equality of condition is complicated, but a simplified version of it would be as follows: When production is growing, businesses have greater need of employees. When businesses had greater need of employees, they offered the latter more pay in real terms, meaning greater buying power and therefore a larger share of the nation's total income. The employees, in turn, used that buying power to purchase more goods and services, further intensifying demand for themselves. The vast foreign market for American products and relatively limited overseas competition for production meant that profits from abroad also flowed into the United States, expanding economic activity and the need for people in jobs. In the two decades following World War II, prosperity possessed a redistributive logic and only periods of faltering prosperity slowed the progressive distribution of income across a wider population.

The movement toward greater equality of incomes was not in itself what we usually think of as upward mobility. The income of janitors may increase more rapidly than that of bank presidents, but the janitors have not really moved up on the scale of desirable jobs because their comparative standards of living have improved. Indeed, part of the postwar Great Compression appears to have been a general increase in the demand for all kinds of labor, including laborers in occupations that have been the lowest paid. Economists Claudia Goldin and Robert A. Margo have argued that the rapid growth of highly educated workers, together with generally expanding production, produced a shortage of unskilled workers, driving up the real incomes of those at the bottom.[4] The prosperity of the postwar period entailed more than just a wider spread of purchasing power, though. It also involved a change in the form of the American workplace so that there were more "good" jobs available.

Figure 7. Percentages of Americans in the Labor Force in Managerial, Professional and Technical Occupations, 1930–1970.

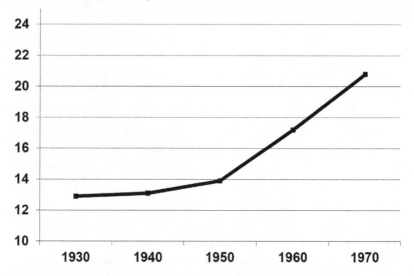

Source. Steven Ruggles, Sarah Flood, Ronald Goeken, Josiah Grover, Erin Meyer, Jose Pacas, and Matthew Sobek.2020. IPUMS USA: Version 10.0 [dataset]. Minneapolis, MN: IPUMS, 2020. https://doi.org/10.18128/D010.V10.0.

Figure 7 presents an illustration of structural upward mobility in American life in the form of proportions of the American workforce from 1930 to 1970 employed in professional, technical, and managerial occupations; in other words, the types of jobs that have the greatest prestige and the largest incomes. In the previous chapter, I argued that the 1930s were a time of general equalizing of condition. However, the Great Depression's trend of equalization of condition was not a result of widespread upward occupational mobility. The 1930s were a time of stagnating structural mobility, and professional, technical, and managerial jobs were held by only 13 percent of workers by 1940. During the 1940s, growth of the professional, technical, and managerial occupations began to recover, and then shot up dramatically from 1950 onward, growing from about 14 percent of the workforce in 1950 to over 17 percent in 1960 to 21 percent in 1970. More Americans were reaching desirable and relatively prestigious occupations, as well as obtaining greater amounts of the growing national wealth.

The sources of the simultaneous expansion of equality of condition and equality of opportunity might be debated, but the most obvious explanation is the nature of the managerial corporate economy of mass production that had reached maturity by the middle of the twentieth century. As organizational scholars Gerald F. Davis and Doug McAdam note, "In broad strokes, the post-War U.S. economy was populated by large, vertically integrated mass producers. Employment and economic power were disproportionately concentrated in a few hundred major corporations." [5]

In a review article on organizational perspectives on stratification, James N. Baron pointed out that researchers have generally found that organizational size, one of the central topics of research in this area, is related to higher wages, both in the sense that wages tend to be higher in industries made up of large companies and in the sense that the larger companies in any given industry tend to pay more. [6] The increased productivity resulting from producing large quantities of goods meant that relatively fewer people were needed on assembly lines. At the same time, the bureaucratic form of postwar corporations created greater demand for managers and analysts, while both the complexity of the organizations and the growing sophistication of technology required more workers with advanced technical skills. The work of distributing the expanding national product, or of creating demand for it, generated jobs in advertising, sales, and related fields.

In the *Los Angeles Times* in 1949, journalist Adie Suehsdorf enthused over opportunities for upward mobility that were beginning to be seen as not only equal but widely available:

> What is happening is this: a number of the nation's most progressive companies, together with the armed services, are making room at the top for promising men and women from their own ranks. Extensive new personnel plans, already in action, are offering employees wide-open opportunities for rapid advancement to all levels of management [...] Industry and the military are learning that successful people are the key to a successful enterprise. They are turning away from the old-fashioned point of view that executives grow in a special white-collar garden, unavailable to the working force. They are finding that discontent and trouble breed whenever people are not happy in their jobs, and whenever progress is not encouraged [...] In short, they are learning what Horatio Alger knew all the time. They want and need to believe in the American Dream of equal opportunity for all and a fair chance to advance on one's own merit.[7]

Greater demand for people in professional positions meant that the economy could employ a more highly educated population. The proportion of the US population completing elementary school had already reached well over 80 percent in the early twentieth century, and completion of high school had been climbing throughout the first half of the century.[8] Still, by 1940 only a minority of adult Americans (under 40 percent) had finished high school. College or university educations were even rarer. In that last census year before the war, fewer than five percent of Americans aged 25 years and older had completed four or more years of college and only 6.6 percent of those aged 20 to 24 years were enrolled in educational institutions. Although birth rates had been low during the Great Depression years, college enrollments shot up dramatically from the prewar 1939–1940 academic year to the postwar 1949–1950 academic year (figure 8), and these enrollments continued to grow as the relatively small 1930s' birth cohorts reached traditional college age throughout the 1950s. By 1960, nearly 8 percent of Americans had finished four or more years of college, and 14.6 percent of those in the 20-to-24 age group were enrolled as students.

Figure 8. College and University Enrollments, 1919–1920 through 1959–1960.

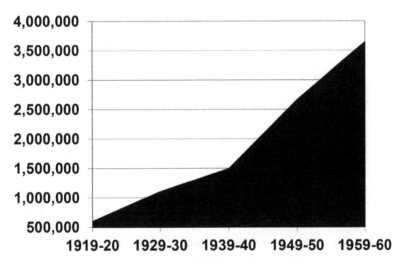

Source. National Center for Education Statistics, *Digest of Education Statistics*, Table 3. Enrollment in educational institutions, by level and control of institution: Selected years, 1869–1870 through fall 2016. Washington, D.C.: NCES, 2007.

Income, occupational prestige level, and educational attainment are the three measurements of socioeconomic status, or position in a system of stratification, used by social scientists. The three are combined into the socioeconomic index (SEI), which gives everyone a score showing where they stand in our system of structured inequality. The mean socioeconomic index score would show us roughly where the average person is located in this system. As figure 9 demonstrates, with rising incomes, better jobs, and higher levels of education, the average moved rapidly upward following the Second World War.

Figure 9. Mean Socioeconomic Index Scores of Americans in the Labor Market, 1920 to 1970.

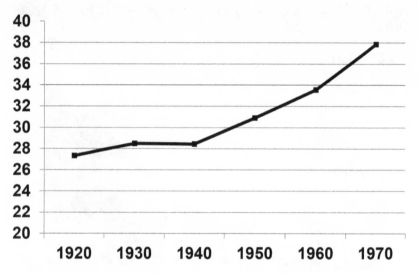

Source. Steven Ruggles, Sarah Flood, Ronald Goeken, Josiah Grover, Erin Meyer, Jose Pacas, and Matthew Sobek.2020. IPUMS USA: Version 10.0 [dataset]. Minneapolis, MN: IPUMS, 2020. https://doi.org/10.18128/D010.V10.0

Our society continued to be competitive, with individuals striving for high status, but, relative to the past, high status was more readily available even while incomes tended to be more equal. In this situation, there appeared to be no contradiction between equality of opportunity (individuals competing for more desirable positions) and equality of condition (people enjoying roughly similar rewards). American society had begun, in the eyes of many, to look like a competition with only winners.

Postwar Government Subsidies for Socioeconomic Opportunity

During the New Deal, it had become widely, although not universally, accepted that the role of government was to promote ever-improving material standards of living in every respect for everyone and by the postwar period, this high expectation for government had become standard. In the 1950 November Congressional elections, President Truman campaigned for his own party with the claim that "only the Democratic Party can make come true the American dream of better health, education, security, and recreation for all."[9]

Many Americans view homeownership as one of the marks of middle-class status. Owning a home has been indirectly subsidized by the government since the nation adopted the income tax in 1913. The home-mortgage deduction entered the tax code at the very beginning, allowing people paying mortgages to deduct their interest payments from taxes. This practice was not initially intended to encourage social ascent. Indeed, in the early years, income taxes were levied primarily on the wealthy. Only in the 1950s did the deduction become widely used in the United States, as the income tax spread to more of the population and as more people began to buy homes through more direct forms of government subsidy.

As the previous chapter discussed, the US government became a provider and guarantor of home loans at the beginning of the Great Depression. This took on larger dimensions by the late 1940s and the 1950s. New initiatives for the federal provision of readily available mortgages, placing more people into homes of their own, initially sprang from the desire to stimulate home construction. In the spring of 1946, for example, the Senate Banking Committee approved a housing program intended to build 12,500,000 units over a ten-year period. "It is tailored to the theory," observed an Associated Press article, "that private enterprise will build most of them [the units] if given easier government loans and mortgage guarantees. To that end, the Federal Housing Administration's financing would be extended in present fields and broadened to reach new ones. One provision would open the way for purchase of an FHA-financed home with a 5 percent down payment and 32 years to pay off the mortgage."[10]

The Servicemen's Readjustment Act is best known for its educational support to veterans. But another of the most important contributions of the bill to government support for upward mobility came through the Veterans Administration (VA) mortgage, which greatly extended government involvement in the housing market. The legislation provided to all veterans a federally guaranteed mortgage with no down payment.

Housing is not necessarily a positional good, even though homeownership continues to be a status marker in the United States. In theory, housing policies could make it possible for every household to own a home without promoting mobility. The main difficulty with extending homeownership through making mortgages easier to obtain is that the required capacity to repay loans drops lower as mortgages become more widely available. This problem may not become apparent if the extension of credit is matched by the movement of people into higher income levels, so that more people are actually able to afford to repay loans. However, if homeownership is subsidized by mortgage guarantees and not simply given away, loans will have to be repaid. In even the best periods of rising prosperity that we have known so far, there have always been households that cannot repay loans. Therefore, ever-widening mortgage guarantees must eventually reach a point at which defaults become a common occurrence. In addition, while the general trend of modern history has so far been toward rising prosperity, this trend has never been free of periodic reversals.

Being able to own a home, then, is closely linked to both occupational mobility and to general participation in prosperity. Being able to make mortgage payments depends on income, and income is connected to obtaining a desirable job, as well as to how well jobs in general pay in real buying power; that is, how widely national wealth is distributed by means of the demand for labor. Extending homeownership by subsidizing mortgages depends on an increasingly widespread ability to repay loans, just as extending high-prestige jobs to more people depends on the increasingly widespread availability of high-prestige opportunities. Even in a period of rapid economic growth and large-scale structural mobility, neither home loans nor occupational mobility can be universal. There are always households that cannot repay loans, and it is never possible for every worker to be at the top of the job ladder. During the postwar period, though, with incomes steadily rising and with the expectation that they would continue to do so, together with the fact that government housing subsidies were still at an early stage, the possibility of overextension seemed distant.

The clearest form of government support for occupational mobility during the two decades following the war came in the form of tuition payments for higher education. This also was initially a product of efforts to deal with the economic challenge of massive numbers of returning veterans. In addition to the mortgage guarantees, the bill provided tuition and educational expenses to veterans who had served at least 90 days. Tuition payments were sufficient to cover costs even at elite institutions, such as Harvard and Yale, making possible mobility through education to individuals who previously would have had no access to the top ranks of American educational institutions.

Economic historian Harold G. Vatter has observed that "public outlays for veterans' education were almost nonexistent before World War II; but by 1947 over $2.25 billion were already being expended for that purpose [...] The contribution of veterans' education to the training level of the U.S. labor force and to future technological development was inestimable."[11] In their study of the impact of the G.I. Bill on educational attainment, economists John Bound and Sarah Turner found that "the combined effect of military service and the G.I. Bill was to increase postsecondary educational attainment among World War II veterans above that of their non-veteran peers, with particularly large effects on college completion [...] our estimates suggest war service increased college completion rates by close to 50%."[12] Political scientist Suzanne Mettler has reported that G.I. Bill beneficiaries accounted for 49% of those enrolled in college by 1947, and that "within 10 years after World War II, 2,200,000 veterans had attended college and 5,600,000 had participated in vocational training programs or on-the-job training under the G.I. Bill."[13]

Figure 10. Receipts of Federal Funds by Institutions of Higher Education, 1939–1940, 1949–1950, and 1959–1960, in Millions of Constant 1960 Dollars.

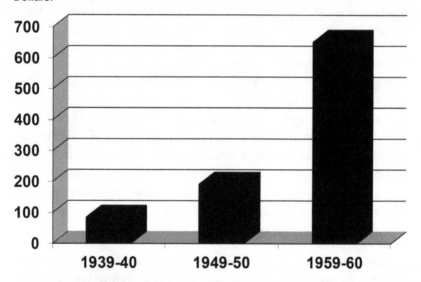

Source. US Department of Education, *Digest of Education Statistics*, 2007, Table 26.

The war in Korea helped to further extend federal support for access to higher education. On July 16, 1952, Congress passed the Veterans' Readjustment Act, which gave most of the educational benefits provided to World War II veterans to a new era of returning military service people. Veterans of the conflict in Korea who had served at least 90 days were entitled to tuition payments, as well as home loans and other benefits, for a period of one and a half times the duration of their service.

Federal outlays on higher education increased from an estimated $85 million in the 1939–1940 academic year to $192 million ten years later to $652 million by 1959–1960, in constant 1960 dollars, as shown in figure 10 (one 1960 dollar would have the estimated value of $8.80 in 2020 dollars). This sharp upward movement in federal support for higher education in particular and for all levels of education in general was driven by Cold War considerations, as well as by policies toward returned veterans from hot wars.

In October 1957, the Soviet launch of the Sputnik satellite created fear that the United States was falling behind its ideological and geopolitical rival in producing a highly trained population, especially in scientific areas. A month after the launch, President Dwight D. Eisenhower delivered a speech in Oklahoma City, in which he attributed the Soviet success to the communist power's concentration on creating an educational system that would give it an advantage in the struggle among nations. The following January, he proposed to Congress an educational program for the purpose of strengthening the nation's defense against the communist world. The president sought greater spending on the National Science Foundation, particularly for summer programs to train teachers in science and mathematics and to move more students into careers in science. He also wanted more money to be spent on the testing, guidance, and counseling of students in order to direct them into studies seen as strategically important for the United States.[14] Thus, not only would the federal government be spending money on subsidizing opportunities in higher education, it would also be greatly increasing its efforts to direct American elementary and secondary school students toward colleges and universities.

Congress adopted President Eisenhower's program in the form of the National Defense Education Act (NDEA) on August 22, 1958. Senator John J. Sparkman of Alabama referred to this new, major act of federal support for education as a historic event, saying that it was "the first time an education bill of this magnitude has cleared both houses."[15] The $900,000,000 four-year bill provided loans to college students identified as having special abilities, gave grants to the states to enhance the teaching of science, mathematics, and languages in elementary and secondary schools, funded testing and counseling for students, gave support and directed revenues to teacher-training institutes, and paid for approaches to education that used modern technologies.[16]

Credential inflation was, in theory, a possible result of government subsidies for higher education. Producing more degrees could lead to too many degrees chasing after too few jobs. As discussed earlier, though, the postwar period was a time of job growth, especially in the white-collar professions that required the credentials of higher education. General economic growth created more jobs in every sector of the economy, but both growth and the corporate structure of the American economy tended to increase demand especially for the professional, technical, and managerial occupations that were most likely to employ people with high levels of formal education. Part of the rising expectations of the postwar period, then, was that in education, as well as in the society in general, there was no contradiction between the competition to achieve and the extension of benefits to ever-increasing proportions of the population.

In addition, this rapid expansion of higher education could have lowered the quality of college education by pumping more students who were not prepared for advanced learning. This is, again, similar to the risk that overextending guaranteed mortgages can lead to a flood of bad loans. In fact, some influential commentators did fear that just such a flood of bad students would result from the government educational subsidies that began with the G.I. Bill. Robert Maynard Hutchins, president of the University of Chicago notoriously objected that the bill would turn colleges and universities "into hobo jungles." Harvard University president James Bryant Conant more diplomatically expressed his concern that the bill did not "distinguish between those who can profit most by advanced education and those who cannot."[17]

One of the reasons the fears of Hutchins and Bryant apparently went unrealized, at least in the short term, was that institutions of higher education had not really distinguished well between those who could or could not profit most by advanced education before government subsidization. While the elite institutions educated many brilliant scholars before the middle of the twentieth century, rigorous competition for entry into colleges only began with the adoption of educational tests such as the Scholastic Aptitude Test (SAT), administered by the Educational Testing Service, which began operations on January 1, 1948. Whether or not the overall level of college education was higher or lower in 1955 than it had been in 1935 is difficult to answer, but institutions such as Harvard and the University of Chicago almost certainly had better students by the middle of the 1950s than twenty years earlier. With government financial help reducing (although never eliminating) the importance of family background for enrollment, a larger pool of applicants, and a competitive means of distinguishing among those applicants, Harvard and the University of Chicago could and did select the very top students from all across the country. Subsidization had not meant they would have to accept all applicants.

This last point is important. We should note that not only was competition for entry into elite colleges by means of test scores increasing but also that government support through programs such as the National Defense Education Act was intended to identify and support students with special abilities. The goal was not to compensate for the results of historical or economic disadvantages among categories of potential students, but to promote meritocratic competition.

EDUCATION, MERITOCRACY, AND THE NEW NATURAL
ARISTOCRACY

In theory, equality of opportunity and equality of condition are generally opposite concepts. The former, understood as the chance for upward mobility, means that there are more and less prestigious positions, more and less affluent ones, and that each individual has an equal chance to occupy the better positions. To the extent that government promotes equality of opportunity, it is also promoting inequality of condition. However, this truism can be obscured by the kind of structural mobility that discussed earlier. When the proportion of desirable occupations rapidly increases, then promoting widespread meritocratic competition for them can have the effect of distributing upward mobility more widely. In an expanding economy of mass production and mass consumption with relatively high demand for many occupations considered less desirable, the competitive inequality of upward mobility tends to be offset by generally improving conditions. The situation of the postwar period made it possible for Americans to juggle these opposing ideas of equality of opportunity and equality of condition, to think of their society as a competition with only winners.

Even though the occupational system could be considered a competition, there were more ribbons available. In addition, the Great Compression meant that those who finished behind still enjoyed substantial rewards. The result was a generally positive view of meritocracy that was consistent with both equality of opportunity and equality of condition.

The British social scientist Michael Young coined the term "meritocracy" in his 1958 dystopian novel *The Rise of the Meritocracy*. In Young's imagined future, there is an elite ruling class, but it is not an aristocracy, or at least an aristocracy attained through birth. Instead, the rulers are an updated version of that old "natural aristocracy" that Jefferson and Adams had debated. Young's elite have assumed their positions in an extreme version of corporate, bureaucratic environment characteristic of the mid-twentieth century. It is a futuristic mandarinate, created by advancement in educational institutions, especially through competitive testing. Young's vision was dystopian because he foresaw a state in which —precisely because inequalities were based on intelligence and effort —the successful elite had an unlimited belief in their own virtue and therefore had little compassion or appreciation for the less successful. Although some social critics did take a similar gloomy view of American competitive equality, most people in the United States did not experience their world as one of intense struggle for scarce resources, which led to meritocracy being given a more favorable implication.

In the American context, the meritocratic competitor could be seen as an institutionalized version of the self-made man. Having achieved success through educational attainment and achievement, individuals could obtain desirable positions in business and government organizations. In their 1967 study of stratification in the United States, *The American Occupational Structure*, sociologists Peter Blau and Otis Dudley Duncan found that the educational attainment of individuals was the strongest predictor of their occupational prestige and income level. However, going back to the issue of old natural aristocracy, they found that the strongest predictor of the educational attainment of individuals was the socioeconomic status of families of origin.

As government gradually became more involved in providing access to upward mobility, squaring the circle of equal opportunity among unequal conditions would become more of a policy goal. Coming out of the mid-century experience of expanding opportunities, equalizing conditions, and more active government, this policy goal would appear realistic to many. However, as will be seen in the following chapters, mid-century economic conditions were ephemeral.

SOCIAL CRITICISM AND THE REACTION TO THE NEW STRUCTURAL MOBILITY

Despite the clear evidence of upward mobility, American civilization in the middle of the twentieth century had its share of discontents. Particularly among intellectuals, many looked around and found the land of opportunity wanting. The voices of the discontented, moreover, were influential because they spoke to shortcomings that many Americans perceived. Prosperity carried its own internal contradictions because it caused expectations to rise beyond the means of fulfilling those expectations and because it was the product of an unfamiliar, suspect social and economic system.

One should avoid romanticizing the 1950s and early 1960s as a golden age of equality and opportunity. A look back at the social criticisms of the era reminds us that it held its share of concerns, most of which became standard objections to American corporate society. In the 1950 book *The Lonely Crowd*, sociologist David Riesman and his coauthors argued that the organizational setting of the period shaped the members of America's middle class into an "other-directed" cultural type. Without tradition or strongly established personal beliefs, other-directed Americans could define themselves only by reference to other people, devoting obsessive attention to what other people wore, earned, or thought. While one might today debate the extent to which Americans really were more other-directed at the end of the 1940s and beginning of the 1950s than their predecessors had been, the popularity of Riesman's work testifies the extent to which Americans saw themselves as becoming a nation of conformists. One might also speculate that if Americans were measuring themselves against others more than in the past, this was precisely because the widespread upward mobility of the time meant that people were trying to figure where they stood in this new middle-class society.

In 1951, Riesman's fellow sociologist, C. Wright Mills, in *White Collar: The American Middle Classes*, described the white-collar workers of the time as a new class created by the rise of the corporate industrial economy.

Without denying the material benefits of the white-collar professions, he characterized them as dominated by a marketing mentality and as alienated from each other and from their work. Sloan Wilson's 1955 semi-autobiographical novel *The Man in the Gray Flannel Suit* offered a fictional portrait of the world of white-collar corporate conformity with its story of public relations executive Tom Rath.

Discomfort over public relations and advertising, activities given a new emphasis and a wider scope by the need to find markets for the abundance of mass-produced goods, appeared in Vance Packard's 1957 *The Hidden Persuaders*, a popular description and criticism of manipulative marketing techniques for promoting desire for consumer goods and managing political campaigns. Two years later, in *The Status Seekers* Packard argued that new class divisions were emerging in the economy of abundance and he expressed what had become the standard worries about alienation in the workplace, as well as criticisms of the constant striving for success and signs of success.

In 1958, economist John Kenneth Galbraith revealed worms in the apple of prosperity in *The Affluent Society*. The very productivity of the American economy, according to Galbraith, had brought an overemphasis on private consumption, largely driven by the marketing and adver-tising decried by Mills, Wilson, and Packard. While encouraging useless consumption (or, critics might say, consumption that did not accord with Galbraith's own tastes and values), the industrial system underempha-sized or ignored important public-sector spending on infrastructure, the landscape, and social benefits. Galbraith, like Packard, argued that the generally rising standard of living masked newly developing categories of the disadvantaged, who were overlooked in the obsession with mass private consumption.

In *The Other America*, published in 1962, Michael Harrington echoed the view that the massive upward mobility and social transformation of the previous seventeen years had a dark side. Harrington argued that although most Americans were better off than they had ever been before, about one in four were trapped in invisible poverty. In the society of abundance, according to Harrington, the poor were not easily identifiable by obvious markers such as dress because inexpensive goods such as clothing had become widely available. The general mobility, moreover, had left the poor in separate, isolated pockets, such as urban ghettoes or out-of-the-way rural shanties, away from the daily experience of other Americans. This isolation also kept the poor from following the mobility tracks of their fellow citizens, because they were insulated from the general culture of material self-improvement. Harrington, who apparently influenced (or at least provided justifications for) the social policies of Presidents John F. Kennedy and Lyndon B. Johnson, argued that Americans needed to turn their attention from the pursuit of private well-being and toward raising the standards of living in these pockets of poverty,

Today, we can read these influential authors as historical illustrations of the social concerns of their times, as well as commentators with whom we may agree or disagree. We should also be impressed, though, with how much their reactions to postwar American society became the standard and oft-repeated wisdom on American social problems. First, life in the new corporate culture was portrayed as materially comfortable, but as standardized, alienating, and conformist. Second, the very extent of individual opportunity tended to give Americans the illusion that no one was excluded at the same time that the pursuit of individual opportunity did exclude groups of people. Taken together, these two broad objections to American society after the mid-twentieth century might appear contradictory: life in the mainstream is purposeless and emotionally unrewarding, and not enough people can join this purposeless, unrewarding mainstream.

Rising expectations of emotional satisfaction and material prosperity for everyone, including minority groups, contributed to the undercurrent of dissatisfaction. At the same time, the ideals of universally increasing consumption and upward mobility along bureaucratic tracks conflicted with some of the older visions of American life, such as the independent individual and the self-made man. Journalist Malvina Lindsay, writing in 1949, reported that "[t]he college class of 1949 is reported in polls to want jobs working for someone else and to aspire 'only' to the achievement of a calm and ordered existence."[18] Speaking to the General Federation of Women's Clubs, the unopposed candidate for federation president Mrs. Hiram C. Houghton declared in May 1950 that "The American dream has been brought about by men and women who dared to live on the frontiers of life. Our zest for living has died down. We have gone underground in our search for security. We have become 'securocrats.'"[19]

By the middle of the twentieth century the United States had emerged from worldwide war a victor, and Americans, with substantial justification, considered themselves citizens of the world's most successful nation. At the same time, rapid suburbanization and the spread of work in big corporations created nostalgia for an older America. The Sloan Wilsons of the time tasted success and it was not enough for them; there must, they felt, be something better and more fulfilling. At the same time, the country that had overcome economic depression and war simultaneously felt both its capacities and its shortcomings. If material success was not enough for those who had achieved it, it was also not enough that only a majority of the citizenry had risen to a high standard of living.

The nostalgia for a pre-corporate America, based on the individualistic ethos of self-made and self-directed personalities, can be seen running through these criticisms. David Riesman and his coauthors contrasted the other-directed, conformist American of their own day with the inner-directed individual of earlier times, the personality type that had been identified with the image of the self-made man. C. Wright Mills, similarly, contrasted the old, self-employed middle class of previous days with the bureaucratic middle class he believed the new corporate system had brought into existence. Even in the writings of the social democrat/socialist Michael Harrington, one can see a faith in the doctrine of individual achievement. The isolation of the poor, in Harrington's view, was a consequence of the new structure of the American economy that prevented them from achieving the success of other Americans.

The popular social criticisms of postwar America, then, were reactions to the experience of widespread upward mobility in a corporate setting that drew on a legacy of ideas about individuals and the society surrounding them. While this setting enabled more people than ever before to achieve personal success, it also threatened the old "self-made man" ideal precisely because the setting was so highly organized and interdependent. The very success encouraged the belief that everyone should share in it, while at the same time Americans continued to believe that success was an individual achievement.

How would all Americans be enabled to reach the highest levels of achievement? The victories of recent historical experience had been due not only to the emergence of a large-scale corporate economy but also to the subsidization of that economy by a large-scale government. The United States defeated its enemies in World War II through close cooperation between the federal government and private business, cranking out the huge quantities of materials that enabled this country and its allies to overwhelm the Axis powers. The structural mobility resulted from the economy that was created by this cooperation.

Business-government collaboration became part of the standard criticism of postwar American bureaucratic society. C. Wright Mills' *The Power Elite*, published in 1956, provided a companion volume to *White Collar*. In the later book, Mills argued that the United States had become a controlled state, under the direction of interlocked military, corporate, and governmental elites. However, as we can see in the works of Galbraith and Harrington, other critics of the time also placed their hopes in the collaboration of government with the market economy as a means of making the widespread structural mobility universal. While Americans continued to see both big government and big business as threats to individual autonomy, they also saw these two as the means of fulfillment for all individuals. As part of its growing collaboration with the market, the federal government began its first large-scale efforts at subsidizing upward mobility in the postwar period. In doing so, it helped to prepare Americans for the view that their society could be an individualistic competition for achievement in which everyone could be a winner.

The sense of frustration with the failure of American society to rise to the expectation that each individual should be emotionally fulfilled as well as have access to all the benefits of affluence reached a particularly high pitch with writers, artists, and miscellaneous bohemians who mainly inhabited the two coastal cities of New York and San Francisco. The Beats, or "beatniks," as San Francisco columnist Herb Caen dubbed them, saw their nation as a soulless machine, or "Moloch," as poet Allen Ginsberg labeled modern America in Part II of his poem, "Howl." Influenced heavily by Walt Whitman, Ginsberg lacked the earlier poet's exuberance, and in the poem "A Supermarket in California" gave vent to his feeling that America had failed to live up to Whitman's faith in a nation of creative and self-fulfilled individuals in the turn to standardized abundance.

While the Beats rejected the society of mass consumption that surrounded them, a consumer ethic of sorts also haunted their worldviews and their work. A uniform, mass-produced suburbanizing nation had failed to provide for their spiritual and aesthetic desires. In the protest song, "Little Boxes," which Malvina Reynolds wrote for Pete Seeger in the early 1960s, Beat-affiliated protest singers decried suburban developments such as Levittown that had provided a generation of returning US servicemen and their families with their first opportunities for homeownership. The suburbs were too conformist and too standardized for the tastes of these countercultural figures. In the decades that followed the immediate postwar period, this concept of equality, in which every individual had the right to be fulfilled psychologically and spiritually, became a strong current in the national culture.

TV NATION

In the early nineteenth century, Frances Trollope had decried what she saw as the vulgarity of American culture, and she connected this in part to the influence of newspapers in the new nation. In the years following World War II, a new medium of mass communication, more homogenizing than newspapers and arguably even more influential than radios earlier in the century became deeply entrenched in the cultural life of the United States. Although the technology was first developed at the very end of the 1920s, commercial television only began to spread across the country in the late 1940s. Its diffusion was rapid. By 1955, 67 percent of US households had at least one television set. Four years later, 86 percent of US households had a TV.[20]

While television became a presence in most households during the 1950s, the programming was highly centralized and uniform, controlled by three major national broadcasting networks. As a business enterprise, television existed to sell products. The persistent and repeated commercials were, from the producers' perspective, the real point of the medium. The programs were strategies to get people to watch these commercials, and whether Americans were amused or annoyed by the constant sales pitches, seeing the USA in their Chevrolets or wearing Timex watches that took a licking and kept on ticking became part of their everyday cultural realities. Even more than during the heyday of the radio soap operas, Americans came to share in a common culture of mass consumption.

Television also contributed to further political centralization. While Washington, DC, had been a distant city in earlier decades, TV brought the federal government into homes even than Franklin Roosevelt's radio fireside chats had. Eric Burns has argued that at least part of the electoral success of President Dwight Eisenhower could be attributed to his election staff's canny use of television to sell his image.[21] The president had become a product to be sold, like cars or washing machines, and the relationship between the public and the national executive had become a relationship between consumers and a marketed image.

In a remarkably prescient observation, decades before Ronald Reagan and Donald Trump, John Crosby, a television critic for the *New York Herald Tribune*, wrote in 1951 that "[t]elevision personalities are likely to be the politicians of the future."[22] Even before TV actors became political leaders, though, political leaders were becoming political actors. A new kind of electronic populism was redefining the nature of American citizenship, blending consumerism with the direct connection of every citizen to the governmental center.

WALLS OF SEPARATION BEGIN TO CRUMBLE

The various American ideas of equality—including the equality of autonomous individuals, self-made men, equal completion in a corporate meritocracy, egalitarian participation in the state, and egalitarian treatment by the state—were all fundamentally inconsistent with the heritage of race-based slavery. From the end of the Civil War until the middle of the twentieth century, the United States had mainly dealt with this inconsistency through various versions of the separate-but-equal myth. By separating out the non-White population (which was mostly Black until the end of the twentieth century), Americans could either conceptualize their nation as equal in various ways within distinct tracks, or they could lay the problem of racial inequality aside. By the time the Second World War ended, though, this conceptual bracketing of equality across races became increasingly difficult.

In September 1940, after the military draft had been established, Walter White of the NAACP and T. Arnold Hill of the National Urban League (NUL) met President Franklin Roosevelt to discuss racial discrimination in the armed forces and in defense industries. When Roosevelt took no action, A. Philip Randolph, union leader and head of the Brotherhood of Sleeping Car Porters, began to organize a Black protest march on Washington,

DC. Under this pressure, President Roosevelt issued Executive Order 8802, creating the wartime Fair Employment Practices Committee.

Although the march was called off after Franklin Roosevelt's act, the March on Washington Movement (MOWM) remained in existence and organized small marches and nonviolent protests. After the war, Randolph, who had become America's leading civil rights activist, organized protests against segregation and discrimination in the armed services. This pushed President Harry Truman to issue Executive Order 9981, which largely desegregated the US military.

Early in 1945, Henry Lee Moon described some of the sources of the postwar movement for racial equality and expressed the initial understanding of equal opportunity as the absence of formal barriers to individual efforts. "[The] determination to achieve equality," he wrote in this last year of the war, "will certainly be re-enforced by the return of nearly a million veterans embittered by the discriminations they have encountered in the armed services."[23] Moon described the equality sought largely in terms of allowing individuals to pursue their own lives and goals unimpeded: "What do we mean when we say that we hope for equality? Simply this: that we Negroes are entitled to and must have every right, privilege, and opportunity accorded to every other citizen. We must have equal opportunity for the development of individual personality and the enjoyment of life."[24]

Assaults on the legal foundations for the separate-but-equal doctrine began in earnest in the 1950s. The war had exposed many African Americans, through the military or through jobs that became available during the war, to new experiences. The rapid spread of television brought information about the abundance of resources and opportunities into the homes of African Americans. Economic growth increased expectations.

While the African American population did enjoy some improvements in their standards of living during the expansion of the 1950s, these lagged behind the benefits accruing to other Americans. Figure 11 shows median household incomes for White and Black families in 1950, 1955, and 1960, in constant 1955 dollars. While White families added nearly $1,500 (1955 value) during the decade (an increase of close to the equivalent of $14,000 in 2019), Black families added a little under $850 (or about the equivalent of $8,000 in 2019). Absolute incomes were higher for both racial groups, but the dollar gap between them grew from $1,753 (or the equivalent of $15,000 in 2019) to $2,359 (or $22,500 in 2019 buying power). Black incomes remained relatively constant as a percentage of White incomes, from 54% in 1950 to 55% in 1960. At a time of both rising expectations and general economic equalization, Blacks were experiencing relative economic stagnation.

Figure 11. Median Black and White Family Income, 1950, 1955, 1960 (in 1955 dollars).

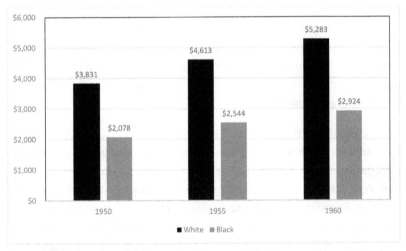

Source. US Department of Commerce, Bureau of the Census, Current Population Reports, Series P-60, Money Income of Families and Persons in the United States, nos. 105 and 157.

The war had not only exposed African Americans to new possibilities but also stimulated belief, as well as on the part of other Americans, in the capacity of government to solve social problems. Federal programs like the G.I. Bill of Rights, the Veterans Authority, and the Federal Housing Authority provided evidence of the effectiveness of government action. If the federal government could deal with all these other social issues, provide resources, and create opportunities, could it not deal with long-lasting racial inequalities?

STRIVING FOR EDUCATIONAL EQUALITY

In the early years, efforts to bring about equality of educational opportunity were aimed at treating students as individuals. School integration was less a matter of trying to create equality among categories, than it was of eliminating racial categories in education. In the historic 1954 *Brown v. Topeka Board of Education* case, the US Supreme Court declared that "[i]n the field of public education the doctrine of 'separate but equal' has no place. Separate educational facilities are inherently unequal," and that "[...] school children irrespective of race or color shall be required to attend the school in the district in which they reside and that color or race is no element of exceptional circumstances warranting a deviation of this basic principal."[25]

Commenting on the Supreme Court's decision in 1954, Justice Thurgood Marshall said that he expected it would take "up to five years" to eliminate segregation in education throughout the United States. Further, the *New York Times* reported that Marshall "predicted that, by the time the 100th anniversary of the Emancipation Proclamation was observed in 1963, segregation in all forms would have been eliminated from the nation."[26] Simply eliminating legal categories in school assignment, in this optimistic view, would place every individual student on an equal footing, without regard to race.

Faced with the resistance of many school districts to cooperate with the Court's initial *Brown v. Topeka Board of Education* decision, in 1955 the Court issued Brown II, ordering schools to move ahead with integration. Many political leaders, though, were obstinate in their rejection of the racial integration of schools. A year after Brown II, 101 southern senators signed a manifesto declaring that the Brown decisions themselves were illegal.[27] In 1957, President Dwight D. Eisenhower was forced to activate the Arkansas National Guard to escort seven Black children through an angry mob to integrate all-White Little Rock Central High School.

Beneath the conflict over the free access of individuals to educational institutions, and therefore to the upward mobility assumed to be the consequence of educational attainment, lay more profound historical contradictions. If the legal blocks to enrollment and attendance were removed, would this, in fact, eliminate racial inequalities in American society? Indeed, if all Americans could compete equally as individuals for ascension in a meritocratic educational hierarchy, would this eliminate the influence of differences in family backgrounds, neighborhood, community characteristics, and social networks?

Given that the opportunities of individuals are heavily shaped by the social structures surrounding them, a commitment to equality of opportunity could easily become a commitment to equalizing the whole of society. Since equality of opportunity produces inequality of outcomes, the effort to give all individuals the same life opportunities can lead to continuous, circular attempts to redress the consequences of individual competition for the sake of individual competition. In the following decades, as the problem of racial inequality drove egalitarianism to become the central article of American faith in education, schools would become defined as places where society is transformed into a state in which no one is ever left behind, while everyone always strives to get ahead.

Even as the country began to struggle with the categorical inequality of race, the postwar economic setting that had obscured the contradictions and complications of different ways of viewing inequality began to change. The structural mobility that had encouraged Americans to believe that everyone could compete and get ahead began to diminish. The widespread distribution of benefits that had given the impression that the competitive equality of opportunity was entirely consistent with growing equality of condition began to give way to a more polarized economy. Pursuit of categorical equality challenged whether older images of equality, independent individuals, and self-made successes had ever been realities.

NOTES

1. Frost, "Losing Economic Hegemony."
2. Ferguson, *The War of the World*, 528.
3. Jones and Weinberg, *The Changing Shape of the Nation's Income Distribution, 1947–1998*.
4. Goldin and Margo, "The Great Compression"
5. Davis and McAdam, "Corporations, Classes, and Social Movements after Managerialism," 297.
6. Baron, "Organizational Perspectives on Stratification."
7. Suehsdorf, "They're Making Room at the Top," H4.
8. Bankston and Caldas, *Public Education, America's Civil Religion*.
9. "Truman Raps Opponents," *Los Angeles Times*, May 16, 1950, 1.
10. Associated Press, "12 ½ Million Housing Bill Reported Out," *New York Times*, April 5, 1950, 1.
11. Vatter, "The Economy at Mid-Century," 4.
12. Bound and Turner, "Going to War and Going to College," 786.
13. Mettler, "Bringing the State Back in to Civic Engagement," 351.
14. Spring, *The Sorting Machine Revisited*.
15. Quoted in B. Furman, "Senate Votes Aid to Science Study," 16.
16. Ibid.
17. Hutchins and Conant, quoted in Hammond and Morrison, *The Stuff Americans are Made Of*, 290.
18. Lindsay, "Search for Safe Living," 16.
19. Quoted in "Club Leaders Want, 'Raging Epidemic of Americanism,'" *Washington Post*, May 31, 1950, B3.
20. US Census Bureau, *Statistical Abstract of the United States, 1960*, table 679.
21. Burns, *Invasion of the Mind Snatchers*.
22. Quoted in Burns, *Invasion of the Mind Snatchers*, 190.
23. Lee, "What the Negro Hopes For," 8B.
24. Ibid.
25. US Supreme Court, *Brown v. Board of Education of Topeka*, 469.
26. "N.A.A.C.P. sets advanced goals," *New York Times*, May 18, 1954, 16
27. Bergman, *The Chronological History of the Negro in America*.

CHAPTER 6

CIVIL RIGHTS AND GROUP EQUALIZATION

A NEW FOCUS ON GROUP EQUALIZATION

In the Jeffersonian vision, individuals are equal because each is indepen-dent, with no hierarchy of relations among them defining obligations among statuses and rights and privileges pertaining to statuses. This idea of equality rests on negative liberty, on each person's freedom from government interference. However, by the late twentieth century, the word "equality" had become closely associated with actions by both government and corporate organizations to advance the statuses of categories of people.

At least four major interrelated developments inspired the goal of group equalization through policy from the 1960s onward. First, the material abundance of the years following World War II encouraged many to think of the nation's primary economic challenge as one of maintaining high levels of consumption throughout the society. Second, mass communication drove high expectations for material standards of living. Third, the media of mass communication began to project thinking about social life onto a new screen of perception and understanding, giving rise to a new dominant narrative about equality as a matter of the relationships between advantaged and disadvantaged groups. Fourth, the expansion of the range of government activity tended to cast improving general living standards and equalizing conditions across groups as problems to be solved by political means.

CONSUMER EXPECTATIONS AND THE CIVIL RIGHTS ERA

As detailed in the previous chapter, the years after the Second World War saw sharply rising consumption because of a rapidly growing economy. According to US Census data, per capita disposable income in 1950 was equivalent to $12,277 in 2020, and personal income expenditures the equivalent of $11,331 in 2020. By 1960 per capita disposable income had risen to $17,434 and per capita expenditures to $16,201 (both amounts in 2020 dollars). By the end of the 1960s, per capita disposable income had shot up to a level that would equal $27,975 and expenditures to $25,581 (both amounts in 2020 dollars).[1] Although the economic growth would stagnate in the late 1970s, another decade of expansion following the immediate postwar period had conditioned Americans to think of moving upwards as the natural direction for themselves as individuals and for the nation as a whole. It also conditioned policymakers to think about economic issues in terms of how the abundance could be distributed among consumers, especially as awareness grew that some still could not reach all the expected fruits of the cornucopia.

As the previous chapter noted, by the end of the 1950s, economist John Kenneth Galbraith was characterizing the United States as an "affluent society." In this new economy, according to Galbraith, the fundamental issue was no longer how to achieve sufficient production, but how to distribute what was being produced. He argued that the nation was spending too much on private consumption, to the detriment of public goods and interests. Galbraith, later an associate and advisor of President John F. Kennedy, maintained that the production of private consumer goods without government guidance left corporations pursuing profits through advertising to increase demand for luxuries, while roads fell into disrepair and children attended badly run schools. This high private consumption also left the poor behind the rest of society. Galbraith proposed steering more investments toward public spending, especially through human investment in education.

President Kennedy identified the underprivileged segment of the country as a growing area of attention at the beginning of his own administration. When he took office, the nation was coming out of recessions in 1957 and 1960 that had slowed the remarkable rate of postwar economic growth. In his February 1961 message to Congress, President Kennedy announced an economic recovery plan that would "sustain consumer spending and increase aggregate demand now when the economy is slack."[2] Thus, in a key speech foreshadowing President Johnson's War on Poverty, Kennedy explicitly identified boosting demand through government spending, including and especially spending on the poor, as an economic strategy

The following year, in his economic message of January 21, 1962, President Kennedy announced his own expectation that policy should spread rising standards of living more widely and erase poverty. "Increasing in our lifetime," he declared, "American prosperity has been widely shared, and it must continue so. The spread of primary, secondary, and higher education, the wider availability of medical services, and the improved postwar performance of our economy have bettered the economic status of the poorest families and individuals. But prosperity has not wiped out poverty. In 1960, 7 million families and individuals had personal incomes lower than $2,000 [approximately $17,400 in 2020]. In part, our failure to overcome poverty is a consequence of our failure to operate the economy at potential."[3]

President Kennedy, then, expressed some of the basic themes that began to turn attention in an economy of high consumption toward the economically and socially marginalized. Consumer spending could resolve economic slowdowns. Since the poor had the least to spend, government could boost economic growth by improving their spending power and by targeted government investments that would ultimately bring them in from the margins and create full employment. Following Galbraith's logic, public spending would go toward benefits such as health and training so that human resources could be developed with full efficiency. When all were employed and enjoying salaries, demand would push the country's productive capacities to their maximum. Kennedy's attention to the poor reflected distributional expectations, as well as ideas about the relationship between demand and production. In the land of plenty, there should be no shortages for anyone. Prosperity must not only be widely shared, but it must also wipe out poverty completely.

TELEVISION AND NATIONAL NARRATIVES

Television had penetrated deeply into American culture during the 1950s, and by the 1960s and 1970s it had become a dominant cultural force. Since the time that the Nielson Corporation began tracking the number of hours Americans spent watching television, time in front of the small screen increased steadily well into the twenty-first century. By 1960, American households were viewing over five hours a day, on average. By the beginning of the 1970s, this reached over 6 hours per day, increasing to over 7 hours each day by the early 1980s.[4] From 1960 to 1987, according to an annual lifestyle poll conducted by the Gallup Organization, more Americans had cited watching television as their favorite way to spend their evenings than any other activity. This preference reached its peak in 1966, when almost half (48 percent) of Americans said that watching television was their favorite evening pastime.[5]

One consequence of the cultural influence of television was to feed the trend of rising consumer expectations. As pointed out earlier, taking the perspective of TV as a business enterprise, advertising was the source of profit for broadcast organizations and the economic reason for the medium's existence. Beyond advertising, simply seeing idealized versions of other people and households in the programming encouraged Americans to see their society as one of abundant consumption. Television also offered a means of dramatizing social events.

Over the course of the twentieth century, electronic media had given rise to new ways of shaping and perceiving reality. Human beings never see their world as a collection of raw facts. They make sense of their surroundings by shaping these into meaningful stories. This does not mean that all social narratives are equally fictitious: political propaganda, the self-justifying myths nations and societies tell themselves about history, and efforts to understand the world through historical research or careful reporting approximate reality to vastly differing degrees. Of necessity, though, interpretation involves a selection of facts. People evaluate their facts, and social facts motivate people by taking dramatic form. The means of communication are fundamental to shaping and emphasizing social dramas.

One of the commonplace observations about the 1960 US presidential election is that television boosted the campaign of the telegenic John F. Kennedy, perhaps even enabling him to defeat Richard M. Nixon, who cast a less charismatic persona over the airwaves. It is difficult to measure the extent to which this observation may have been true. Nevertheless, the importance of television in making a shared drama of national life became a topic of commentary by the early 1960s.

Daniel Boorstin, in the 1962 book *The Image: A Guide to Pseudo-Events in America*, argued that the mass media, especially television, had replaced real events with mass-communicated "pseudo-events," in which broadcasters created a world of illusions through the need to fill the airwaves with constant programming. Among other observations, Boorstin coined the insightful definition of a celebrity as someone who is well-known for being well-known.

Boorstin probably went too far in seeing the mass media of his day as weavers of illusions. Television news reporters usually did attempt to provide information on actual occurrences. Print media had also never been an unfiltered, unbiased window on objective reality. But television's combination of sight and sound, its potential presence throughout the waking hours, and its geographic ubiquity gave it a special power for presenting its own realm of flickering images.

Television drew on and revised an inherited stock of ideas. Davy Crockett, for example, the frontiersman and self-made man mentioned in chapter 2, became the inspiration for a popular craze of coonskin hats in the early years of the medium and later the protagonist of a fictional series. But television also introduced new protagonists and dramatic narratives, in its reporting of current events, as well as in its fictions. Most notably, through television, the civil rights drama became a dominant narrative about the nature of equality and inequality.

THE CIVIL RIGHTS DRAMA

At the factual level, television presented Americans with visual evidence of the inconsistencies in national ideals and the contradictions between many of those ideals and national realities. At the level of shaping facts into meaningful stories, television helped to recast thinking about equality as a historical morality play about the liberation of victimized categories of people. In the nineteenth century, the expansion of popular media, especially newspapers, had spread the idea of equality of individuals as self-made men. In the mid-twentieth century, mass media brought racial inequality to the center of national attention Newspapers intensified their coverage of events in locations around the country but, even more importantly, television brought the entire nation into homes. The civil rights movement of the late 1950s and 1960s was, above all else, a televised drama. The same economy of mass consumption that had emphasized the distribution of goods and services as the fundamental characteristic of economic life also distributed one particularly critical good, the television, in almost every home. Television supported itself as a means of advertising, but it had a cultural force beyond stimulating desires for products. It became a medium for presenting local civil rights struggles to the nation as a whole.

In 1960, protestors, primarily students, participated in widespread sit-in demonstrations against segregated lunch counters and other segregated public facilities. This began on February 1, when students from the North Carolina Agricultural and Technical College took seats at a lunch counter in the Woolworth variety store in Greensboro and refused to leave until served. The sit-in movement was quickly taken up in other cities. Events in one location became nationwide through the new medium of televised broadcast.

The Freedom Rides grew out of the sit-in movement and had the same goal of desegregating facilities. These began in 1961 when the Congress of Racial Equality (CORE) sponsored a bus tour to desegregate terminals. Others began freedom rides on the railways. These activities pushed the Interstate Commerce Commission to prohibit discrimination in interstate buses and bus facilities in September 1961.

In 1963, protests against racial segregation in Birmingham, Alabama, appeared on television screens in homes around the country. The Birmingham police responded to the peaceful protests by turning fire hoses on them and attacking them with police dogs. Here was an episode displayed with powerful televised images that readily lent themselves to a narrative of heroes and villains, of oppressed and oppressors.

The televised and heavily reported events of the March on Washington in August 1963 brought attention and moral authority to the cause for Black advancement. At the Lincoln Memorial, the Reverend Dr. Martin Luther King, Jr. gave his most influential and memorable speech, one that came to rival and perhaps even surpass other statements of national ideals. In his "I Have a Dream" speech, Dr. King evoked the memory of President Lincoln and the Emancipation Proclamation. He described the Declaration of Independence and the Constitution as "a promissory note" of unalienable rights and declared that by denying these rights to its Black citizens, the United States had defaulted on its moral debt. Dr.

King's oratory placed the group advancement pursued by organizations such as the NAACP at the center of American goals.

Dr. King's assassination in April 1968 added martyrdom to the televised drama of the civil rights struggle. Following this murder, riots broke out in more than 100 Black communities around the United States, all captured on the small screen. If historically entrenched racial inequality could be pushed into the corners of the national consciousness in earlier decades, by the end of the 1960s it had become central to many Americans' framing of their shared past.

The power of the civil rights movement as a moral narrative in the mass media made it a model for thinking about social relations in general, moving it beyond the quest for equality for African Americans. By the late twentieth century, the retelling of the story of the struggle against the Jim Crow system and segregation had become a standard theme on small and large screens, presented as the modern morality play, with the lines between the virtues of the oppressed and the wrongs of the oppressors always clearly drawn. Statistical inequalities between races still existed, although substantial upward mobility by minority group members had occurred. But the image of oppressed categories of people had emerged as one of the shaping concepts of the national consciousness. Providing full access to the society of abundance for historically disadvantaged groups became part of the views on how to achieve equality of distribution, even though it was often unclear whether the goal was to redistribute competitive opportunities or actual conditions of life.

LEGISLATING GROUP EQUALITY

In June 1963, responding to the growing influence of the civil rights movement, President John F. Kennedy sent a civil rights bill to Congress. Pressure from civil rights groups and the leadership of President Lyndon B. Johnson helped move the Civil Rights Act of 1964 forward. Title VI of the new legislation carried forward the intentions of Kennedy's

Executive Order. It prohibited discrimination on the basis of race, color, and national origin for all programs receiving federal funding. It provided for the termination of federal assistance or the initiation of legal action by the Department of Justice in cases of discrimination and it enabled those who believed themselves victims of discrimination to complain to the funding agency or to file suit in Federal court.

Title VII of the act made it unlawful for any employer with fifteen or more employees to discriminate against any individual on the basis of race, color, national origin, religion, or sex. Title VII contained a section prescribing remedies for cases of discrimination, in which judges were given authority to order "such affirmative action as may be appropriate," such as punitive damages or reinstatement of employment for discrimination victims. Further, Title VII defined the mandate of the Equal Employment Opportunity Commission (EEOC), which had been initiated by President Kennedy's Executive Order 10925, as suing on behalf of those believed to have suffered discrimination.

Title VII stirred debate in Congress. To some, the provisions of this part of the act infringed on the rights of employers and businesses to hire and serve those they deemed appropriate. Republican Senator Everett Dirksen asked whether the legendary Harlem Globetrotters could legally maintain a racial identity under Title VII. Democratic Senator Sam Ervin wanted to drop Title VII because it would "make members of a particular race special favorites of the laws."[6] Others, such as Republican Senator Norris Cotton and Republican Senator Carl Curtis, opposed Title VII because they believed its antidiscrimination language would prohibit the preferential hiring of members of minority group, which they believed would be necessary to compensate for historically created racial inequality.

The Civil Rights Act appeared to equivocate between dedication to nondiscrimination and intervention to raise disadvantaged categories of people, President Johnson clearly took the side of egalitarian social reformation. In a now famous speech at Howard University in 1965, President Johnson proclaimed, "you do not take a person who for years has been hobbled by chains and liberate him, bring him up to a starting line of a race and then say, 'you are free to compete with all the others,' and still justly believe that you have been completely fair." This frequently quoted remark contained the implication that government should not simply eliminate discrimination against individuals based on race, national origin, gender, or religion, but should intervene in society to eliminate the consequences of past discrimination.

President Johnson's Howard University speech involved a new turn in older ideas about self-made individuals and competitive equality. People were to continue to find their own places in the American society and economy through competition, as if they were runners in a race. But this competitive equality could only be established if historical disadvantages could somehow be eliminated or if the race could be rigged so that those presumed to be handicapped by those disadvantages could somehow receive compensatory advantages.

President Johnson contributed to the extension of categorical equalization of opportunity beyond Black Americans. His Executive Order 11246, issued in the same year as his Howard University speech, required that organizations with more than fifty employees with over $50,000 in federal revenue come up with yearly affirmative action plans to increase the hiring of underrepresented minorities and women. Taken with the Howard University speech, these targets reflect a major shift in governmental civil rights policies beginning in the mid-1960s. Although still expressed in the language of anti-discrimination, emerging efforts at addressing racial inequalities were moving toward social reconstruction, toward governmental action to eradicate categorical disadvantages in society. Once the society had been reshaped to eliminate the disadvantages created by centuries of exclusion and discrimination, then individuals would presumably be free to compete in a setting of equal opportunities.

These efforts to use policy to eliminate categorical disadvantages, initially concerned chiefly with African Americans became known as "affirmative action." This term became part of the vocabulary of governmental responses to racial inequality in March of 1961, when President John F. Kennedy used the term "affirmative action" in his Executive Order 10925, creating the Committee on Equal Employment Opportunity. The order required federally funded projects "take affirmative action" to avoid racial bias in hiring and employment.

Although the early civil rights movement was mainly aimed at ending racial discrimination, the idea expressed by President Johnson's Howard University speech was already current among civil rights activists, who began to push for racial preferences in hiring to compensate African Americans for past discrimination. As early as 1962, the Congress for Racial Equality (CORE) issued demands that employers begin to hire Blacks in specified percentages, and it organized boycotts of businesses to push the hiring of Blacks. When James Farmer, a CORE leader, appeared before Congress in the summer of 1962, Farmer testified that although CORE did not believe in racial quotas, "we do believe, however, in aggressive action to secure the employment of minorities."[7] Asked by Democrat Peter Rodino if he thought qualifications and education should be the basis of hiring, Farmer elaborated:

> [...] if two people apply for a job and are equally qualified and generally or roughly have the same qualifications, one is Negro and one is white, and this is a company which historically has not employed Negroes, I think then that company should give the nod to a Negro to overcome the disadvantages of the past [...] Negroes have received special treatment all of their lives. They have received special treatment for 350 years. All we are asking for [...] is some special treatment now to overcome the effects of [...] the past.[8]

Farmer's words reveal that already, in the early 1960s, the anti-discrimination goals of civil rights activists were beginning to shade into goals for compensation to move toward equalization of condition across racial categories. Simply achieving the right to vote, or having schools and universities open their doors without regard to race, or getting employers to hire in a nondiscriminatory manner would not bring about actual equality. The more that activists struggled to be free of the bonds of discrimination, the more true equality became their goal.

Although advocates of individual-level nondiscrimination views of equality would later cite Martin Luther King's famous call to judge individuals based on their character rather than the color of their skin, Dr. King supported economic redistribution as a way to achieve greater racial equality. In this respect, he had more in common with Malcolm X, an exponent of Black Nationalist identity politics than many of those citing him recognize.[9]

The calls of activists evoked some governmental responses. The Civil Rights Act of 1964 became the basis of a widening pattern of governmental interventions for the sake of categorical equality. For example, the Equal Employment Opportunities Commission (EEOC), created by the Civil Rights Act of 1964, became a major means of attacking inequality based on group membership in employment. The organization initially had little power beyond investigating cases of discrimination. In 1972, however, Congress amended the Civil Rights Act to give the EEOC power to sue in court. The EEOC received even greater power in 1976 when Congress gave it responsibility to protect pregnant women from job discrimination and in 1978 when Congress gave it responsibility over cases of age discrimination.

THE POLITICAL QUANDARY OF SEEKING CATEGORICAL EQUALITY

The shift in American racial policy from eliminating discriminatory laws to governmental intervention to establish racial equality was a new movement from the idea that equality simply means the official treatment of every individual in the same manner to the idea that equality means doing things to put those individuals on the same social and economic level. The civil rights movement created a demand for governmental action to equalize racial groups by raising expectations of actual equality, and not simply formalizing equality of treatment. But what did actual equality mean in a nation with such a long-standing reality of racial castes? And how could it be achieved?

From the inception of the modern civil rights movement, the pursuit of equality across racial categories became a central problem in American political life. In a frequently quoted lament, after signing the Civil Rights Bill of 1964, President Johnson remarked to his press secretary, Bill Moyers, that the Democrats had lost the South to the Republicans for a generation. Although President Johnson's exact words are uncertain, Moyers affirmed in a November 2008 interview with radio host Terry Gross that the president did say something along these lines.[10] The civil rights era did, in fact, mark a particularly important episode in the realignment of American national politics, but it went deeper than the North-South division and it involved the intertwining of the shift in federal support for categorical equality from occupational and class groups to racial groups with racial attitudes and with differing philosophical views on the nature of political and legal equality.

In 1948, Strom Thurmond, of the breakaway States Rights Democratic Party, which blended state control with an explicitly segregationist stance, won Louisiana, Mississippi, Alabama, and Thurmond's own state of South Carolina. Republican Barry Goldwater's 1964 electoral college victories were an expanded version of Thurmond's, taking the states of Louisiana, Mississippi, Alabama, Georgia, South Carolina, and Goldwater's home state of Arizona. Similarly, in 1968 George Wallace's American Independent Party took Louisiana, Mississippi, Alabama, South Carolina, Georgia, and Arkansas.

Richard Nixon's campaigns during the 1968 and 1972 elections sought to draw Southern voters to the Republican Party with the "Southern strategy," a term often credited to Republican strategist Kevin Phillips. Although the Republicans did succeed in turning the formerly Democratic South into a Republican stronghold following the late 1960s, identifying the party's approach as specifically Southern may be a mislabeling because it also helped in making advances among White voters outside the South. Moreover, although White racial anxiety was part of the political realignment, reducing this realignment to racial prejudice or resentment would be as simplistic as claiming that race played no part at all in American politics after the 1960s.

Pinning down voter motivation is always difficult, especially because individuals may have multiple motivations and theoretically distinct views are often associated in actuality. But the election results of Thurmond, Goldwater, and Wallace did show some commonalities. All had their victories concentrated in the Deep South, where hostility toward federal efforts at achieving racial equality were greatest. However, in contrast with Thurmond and Wallace, there is no reason to suspect Senator Goldwater of consciously exploiting any racial animus or of having any sympathy for racial discrimination. In opposing the Civil Rights Act of 1964, Goldwater apparently acted on the basis of his disagreement with the practice of using government intervention in pursuit of categorical equality.

Responding to a Black college student in February 1964, presidential candidate Goldwater said that he supported the section of the legislation that would grant more power to the attorney general to enforce school-integration orders. These orders were still at that time largely understood as requiring public schools to accept and treat students without regard to race. However, Goldwater opposed the section that would bar discrimination in public accommodations[11]. Goldwater further explained his views in June of that year when he declared to the Senate that he saw its public accommodations and equal employment opportunity provisions as unconstitutional because these "[...] will require for the effective execution the creation of a police state. And so, because I am unalterably opposed to any threats to our system of government and the loss of our God-given liberties, I shall vote 'No' on this bill."[12]

There is no good reason to refuse to take Goldwater's statement of principles as a subterfuge for White racial politics. He was dedicated to the concept of equality as independence, as the freedom of each individual to live without the imposition of hierarchical authority. Still, even at the time many would have argued that there was a real-world contradiction in this concept of equality. How could a large set of citizens enjoy an equality of independence among other citizens while being kept in a state of inequality of condition by both a heritage of discrimination and by continuing discrimination by nongovernmental actors in private and public life?

Although Goldwater's political philosophy was arguably not at all racist, it could serve the interests of those who wanted to maintain a system of racial inequality. After Goldwater's speech, Southern Democratic senators Strom Thurmond and John L. McClellan, both staunch segregationists, walked over to shake Goldwater's hand. [13] Leading up to the 1964 election, worries about increasing the intrusive power of the federal government to promote greater racial equality were mixed with both irrational racial anxiety and rational self-interest on the part of Whites. The concerns that Goldwater would voice about the increasing power of government combined with matters such as White homeowners' angst over what antidiscrimination enforcement in housing would mean for home values and with suspicion or outright hostility toward Blacks and other minorities.

In October 1963, when President Kennedy was still the presumptive 1964 Democratic candidate, *The Washington Post* reported that politicians in both parties saw a growing "white backlash" to the then-incipient civil rights measures of the Administration. The newspaper quoted a Northern Democratic senator as saying "For the first time, I'm getting mail from white people saying, 'wait a minute. We've got some rights too.' The cloakroom talk in the Senate is that this is true in every Northern state. The southerners are chuckling at us."[14]

That racial attitudes among Whites did contribute to the Republican vote in 1964 is borne out by more than just state voting patterns. According to the Harris Poll taken at the time of the campaign, Goldwater supporters were much more likely than Americans in general to hold negative views of race relations in the United States, to oppose the right to demonstrate by civil rights activists, and to see the civil rights movement in general as an attempt by Blacks to use political power to obtain preferential treatment.[15]

Racial hostility toward the civil rights movement was even clearer four years later in the third-party campaign of Alabama's George Wallace. Wallace had risen to national prominence precisely because of his opposition to racial integration at a time when his state was a national focal point of racial tension and anti-Black violence. Gary Orfield, who would later become one of the foremost academic advocates of racial equality and was then an assistant professor at the University of Virginia, opined in July 1968 that Wallace had "found a way to translate the raw racism of Alabama politics into a potent expression of the uncertainties, discontents, and hates of millions of Americans." Orfield observed that Wallace was presenting his opposition to the equalization of Blacks as resistance to "social engineering" by federal bureaucrats and he wrote that "[b]ehind the platitudes about local sovereignty is a clear determination to let local Whites put the Blacks back in their place again."[16] Orfield warned that through his influence on Electoral College votes, Wallace could inject his racial politics into the national political future, a warning that in hindsight appears as prophetic as President Johnson's reported lament.

It is clear that racism had moved to the forefront with the Wallace campaign. However, this very clarity can lend itself to the reductionism of arguing that all localism equals racism or that every reservation about the pursuit of categorical equality through policy is simply racial animosity in disguise. Certainly, everyone opposed to racial equality would also oppose laws against housing discrimination, efforts at school desegregation, and affirmative action policies. But it does not follow that everyone who believes in local control is motivated by the goal of keeping Blacks down or that critics of affirmative action are always seeking to maintain an existing racial hierarchy.

The political debate over civil rights and the political realignment that followed it illustrated the complexity of racial inequality in the United States, and it presaged how future political divisions would grow out of ideas about the nature of equality and racial identity politics. The debate also encapsulated a quandary created by the nation's historical ideals and realities. If the federal government did not intervene to mandate categorical equality, then it would be at the very least compliant in maintaining a state of inequality for many of its citizens. If it did intervene, then it would be violating the foundational principle of individual independence from hierarchical authority.

CATEGORICAL EQUALITY IN LAW

The conflict between trying to eliminate the categorical disadvantages created by past discrimination and treating all individuals as equals in the same manner became a thorny legal issue as well as a political issue. American law has consistently recognized that making distinctions based on race does indeed constitute discrimination and that Whites as well as Blacks are constitutionally protected from discrimination. The Supreme Court has made it clear that neither the Fourteenth Amendment nor the Civil Rights Act of 1964 could be seen as aimed exclusively at improving the conditions or opportunities of disadvantaged groups but provided guarantees of procedural uniformity in the treatment of all individuals. Efforts at categorical equalization were increasingly coming into conflict with the idea of the equal treatment of all individuals.

In *McDonald v. Santa Fe Trail Transportation Co.* (1976), the court faced the issue of whether attempts at categorical equalization entailed discrimination against Whites. The Santa Fe Trail Transportation Company had discharged two White employees who had misappropriated cargo. However, a Black employee who had been charged with the same offense was not discharged. The two discharged employees attempted to address the perceived discrimination through their union and filed complaints with the EEOC. They sued based on Title VII and of section 1981 of Title

42 of the US Code, which guarantees all persons equal rights. A district court had dismissed the suit, on grounds of categorical equalization, concluding that section 1981 was intended specifically for Black workers and did not cover discrimination against Whites. Therefore, the facts stated by the petitioners did not constitute a claim under Title VII. Justice Thurgood Marshall wrote the decision for the Court, holding that Title VII did indeed prohibit discrimination against Whites as well as nonwhites.

The idea that equal protection of the law should apply to all individuals, regardless of the racial, ethnic, or gender categories of those individuals, posed a problem for using preferences in employment or education to improve the situations of individuals in disadvantaged categories. Treating every individual in the exact same manner, though, may overlook the built-in advantages of those who have wealth, personal connections, or who may simply fit in to opportunities in jobs or schooling better than other people because they are like those who already make up the majority of those in occupations or institutions.

Legal debates over race-conscious governmental policies increasingly concerned this question of the nature of equal protection and discrimination, as defined by the Fourteenth Amendment and the Civil Rights Act of 1964. A report of the US Commission on Civil Rights, published in 1981, observed that the movement toward affirmative action by the federal government had been a movement away from simple nondiscrimination, noting that "among the most significant changes [in the enforcement of civil rights] is a shift of primary attention from individual to institutional discrimination and from the test of intent to that of results."[17]

The idea of using law to promote equality of results for categories was far from a matter of universal agreement. This legal question became a fundamental dividing line that could be clearly seen on the Supreme Court, the nation's ultimate arbiter. On affirmative action cases, the Supreme Court was nearly always narrowly divided between those dedicated to nondiscrimination and those dedicated to equalization. In coming years, this would make appointments to the Supreme Court an intensely divisive partisan matter, closely related to identity politics.

EDUCATION, THE PURSUIT OF CATEGORICAL EQUALITY, AND THE PROBLEM OF INDIVIDUAL EQUALITY

During the years following World War II, the term "equality of opportunity" had become ever more closely linked to chances for advancement through education. Again, the term "meritocracy," coined in the 1950s, referred specifically to those who achieved upward mobility and entered elite status through success in schooling. If education was the main track on which individuals were competing, then equal opportunity meant equality of educational opportunity. But how could the latter be achieved, especially with regard to Black Americans, who had long been denied access to educations equal to those of Whites?

The earliest efforts to establish equality of educational opportunity, during the 1950s, had involved simply eliminating the legal enforcement of separate schools for Blacks and Whites. A year after the 100th anniversary of the Emancipation Proclamation, the Civil Rights Act of 1964, along with the equal protection clause of the Fourteenth Amendment, became a mainstay of efforts to achieve equality in schools and other American institutions. Title VII of the legislation contained language that appeared to show a procedural commitment to individual equality under the law: "No person in the United States shall, on the ground of race, color, or national origin, be excluded from participation in, be denied the benefits of, or be subjected to discrimination under any program or activity receiving Federal financial assistance." The threat of withholding funds from institutions that engaged in discrimination intensified the following year when the Elementary and Secondary Education Act (ESEA) of 1965 offered billions of dollars to school districts through new initiatives such as Head Start, the free and reduced-price meal program, and other Title I programs for disadvantaged schools. The financial push, together with the judicial prohibition of racial discrimination in schooling, largely ended de jure segregation in most parts of the country.

As explicit discrimination against minority individuals decreased, it became more evident that this decrease did not establish the desired state of equality of educational opportunity. In 1966, sociologist James Coleman and his associates published a study of influences on educational outcomes, known as *Equality of Educational Opportunity*. The report indicated that if the law were interested in promoting the opportunities of minority children, and not simply their rights to attend schools without regard to race, it would need to concern itself with the racial composition of schools. The report found that family socioeconomic status was the most important influence on school achievement and that socioeconomic status was highly correlated with race. Moreover, Coleman and his collaborators found that the socioeconomic levels of schoolmates, not just the backgrounds of the students themselves, affected school achievement. The report indicated that students brought social resources from homes to schools, where those resources were pooled and magnified. These social resources included such intangibles as familiarity with middle-class norms, reading habits, and high educational expectations.[18]

By the late 1960s, it had become evident that bringing together students of different racial backgrounds would not be achieved by a laissez-faire approach. School districts would need to engage in active redistribution of students. However, when, if ever, this redistribution should cease became increasingly problematic. In *Green v. County School Board* in 1968, the Supreme Court both struck down the practice of simply opening admissions to all students equally and established a theoretical end point of mandated redistribution. The Supreme Court ruled that a freedom-of-choice plan in New Kent County, Virginia, was unconstitutional because it had not resulted in Whites volunteering to attend the all-Black school in the county or in Blacks volunteering to attend the all-White school. The Supreme Court ordered the school board to devise a plan that would lead to schools being integrated realistically. Following *Green v. County*

School Board, federal courts began to pursue aggressively the societal goal of creating truly integrated educational institutions.

While educational desegregation advocates still used the language of individual-level anti-discrimination from the late 1960s onward, decisions about race in schools increasingly involved efforts to create schools that would ultimately remove race as a basis for the inequalities created by past discrimination. Along these lines, *Green v. County School Board* introduced the concept of unitary status to determine when school districts had reached the state of true racial desegregation. The Supreme Court ruled that school boards "were clearly charged with the affirmative duty to take whatever steps might be necessary to convert to a unitary system in which racial discrimination would be eliminated root and branch [...]"

The *Green v. County School Board* decision introduced a paradox into the question of race in school assignment. If taking race into consideration in school assignment was a way to reach a state in which the effects of previous intentional discrimination had been eradicated, and if the declaration of unitary status amounted to recognition that these effects had been eliminated, then it would be difficult to justify the use of race-conscious decisions after unitary status was attained. One could argue that after a school achieved this status, it had satisfied its social ends and should therefore concentrate on the question of whether or not individuals were treated according to the same processes. However, from the time of *Brown v. Topeka Board of Education* onward, the use of social scientific research had supported thinking about the racial composition of schools in terms of achieving social goals beyond simply overcoming the structural effects of past discrimination. If the goal was to promote interracial interaction or to equalize academic achievement believed to be related to racial composition, then societal goals would require racial redistribution, regardless of whether de facto racial concentrations could be attributed to past discrimination or not. Redistributing students according to race, though, meant assigning students to schools according to racial categories.

By the 1970s, debates over race-based assignments of students increasingly concerned the nature of equal protection and discrimination, as defined by the Fourteenth Amendment and the Civil Rights Act of 1964. If differential treatment according to race constituted racial discrimination, then presumably providing or denying seats in an educational institution on the basis of race would be legally prohibited.

With the concept of unitary status, the potential for conflict between the individual discrimination rationale and the goal of categorical equalization became greater. Categorizing students according to race and placing them in schools had generally been justified from the late 1960s through the 1970s on the grounds that this was undoing past, intentional discrimination. If a district had not been found guilty of past discrimination or if the effects had been eradicated in the eyes of the law, then the justification would not be valid. One answer to this would be to turn solely to the principle of equal official treatment of individuals and declare that treatment on the basis of racial classifications not only could not be mandated following unitary status, but it could also not even be permitted. However, in many cases this would have meant giving up on ambitious social goals and accepting any de facto segregation or racial inequality that could not be clearly attributed to specific discriminatory public policies.

HIGHER EDUCATION AND THE DIVERSITY COMPROMISE

By the late 1960s, education, especially higher education, had become the accepted route to upward mobility. The ideal of equality of opportunity meant that access to higher education should be available to all. The postwar experience of structural mobility had conditioned Americans to believe that ever-increasing numbers of people should be able to win the socioeconomic race, if only their competitive positions could be equalized. The years of the civil rights movement had drawn attention to the fact that the competitive positions of different categories of Americans, especially Blacks and Whites, were not equal. So how should the nation's institutions respond to categorical inequality? If they simply left the race to individuals, then the institutions would be ignoring the disadvantages created by a long history of oppression and discrimination. If they allowed compensatory advantages to members of disadvantaged categories, then they would not be treating all individuals in the same way.

The answer to this conundrum was a new approach to balancing race-based policies in higher education, aimed at creating a society of more equal opportunities, with the uniform and equal treatment of individuals. This approach came from developments in higher education. The formula that would become the most influential attempt to balance the two goals appeared in the critical case *Regents of University of California v. Bakke*. The case originated in 1973 when Allen Bakke, a White man, applied for admission to the medical school at the University of California, Davis.

Under its affirmative action program, UC Davis had reserved sixteen of one hundred seats for minority or socioeconomically disadvantaged applicants, who were judged by a committee separate from the one that judged regular applicants and who could be admitted with lower grade point average (GPA) and Medical College Admissions Test (MCAT) scores than regular applicants. After Bakke was denied admission, he wrote to the chairman of the admissions committee complaining because he had not been considered for a reserved seat for the disadvantaged and because no Whites received these reserved seats. Bakke applied again in 1974, this time with a substantially higher MCAT score and was again denied admission, although minority applicants with lower scores and GPAs were admitted through the separate special admissions process. Bakke sued in the California Superior Court, maintaining that he had experienced discrimination, in violation of the equal protection clause and Title VI of the Civil Rights Act of 1964, as well as the California constitution. The case went before the California Supreme Court, which decided in Bakke's favor by eight to one.

UC Davis then appealed to the Supreme Court, maintaining that it was justified in using race as a factor in admissions and that its separate admissions program was a legitimate way of doing so. Bakke maintained, again, that reserving places violated his right to equal treatment and subjected him to discrimination. Justices William Brennan, Byron White, Thurgood Marshall, and Harry Blackmun supported the use of race in admissions to educational programs for explicit categorical equalization, in order to provide a remedy to minorities for the present-day consequences of past discrimination and racial prejudice. Chief Justice Warren Burger and Justices Potter Stewart, John Paul Stevens, and William Rehnquist maintained an individual-level view of legal equality and opined that the admissions policy at UC Davis violated Bakke's rights under the equal protection clause and the Civil Rights Act. Justice Lewis Powell provided the pivot that moved the case toward admitting the use of race when argued that treating individuals differently on the basis of race requires a compelling state interest.

Justice Powell wrote the opinion of the Supreme Court, in which the four justices who favored race-conscious admissions joined in part (i.e., accepted partially and with reservations). A special admissions quota, such as the one employed by UC Davis, could not be used because it constituted discrimination. Race could be treated as a factor but was subject to strict scrutiny. The *Regents of University of California v. Bakke* decision therefore meant that educational institutions could continue to seek to increase their admissions of members of racial minorities or other underrepresented groups, but only to increase diversity and not to compensate for past discrimination. Moreover, membership in an underrepresented group could be only one of many factors in an admissions decision. The Supreme Court had recognized the individual-level right to equal and identical procedural treatment but asserted that this right could be trumped by the societal-level rationale of compelling state interest.

On its surface, the compelling state-interest justification seemed to move away from efforts to seek categorical equality because compensation, or trying to place all individuals at the same starting point, could no longer be used as a justification for differential treatment of people in different categories. Ostensibly, institutions could give preferential admissions in order to improve the educational environment for all students. However, it is difficult to take this at face value as the main reason for differential admissions policies. First, advocates of affirmative action in higher education consistently opposed efforts to scale it back precisely because this would lessen the opportunities of Black and later Hispanic students. Second, diversity was almost always defined in terms of increasing the representation of specific protected categories, not as increasing overall demographic variety. When Justice Sandra Day O'Connor reaffirmed the *Regents of University of California v. Bakke* decision in writing the opinion on a key case in 2003, she justified the continued use of racial preferences by claiming that these had to continue until underrepresented groups would become fully represented, presumably twenty-five years later.[19]

THE EXPANSION OF CATEGORICAL EQUALITY

During the 1950s and 1960s, the term "civil rights" referred mainly to efforts to achieve equality for Black Americans. The idea of establishing social as well as political equality rapidly came to include other categories as well. As historian Anthony J. Badger has noted," the rights African Americans achieved became the basis for a rights revolution which extended rights to other disadvantaged groups: women, gays, lesbians, the disabled and immigrants."[20] The National Indian Youth Council (NIYC) and the American Indian Movement (AIM) began to stage protests against discrimination and White domination in the late 1960s and early 1970s. Among Hispanics and Latinos, organizations such as the United Farm Workers, the Raza Unida Party, the Alianza Hispano-Americana, and the Brown Berets began to assert economic and social rights at the same time. The Mexican-American Legal Defense and Education Fund emerged to become the chief mainstream Hispanic civil rights organizations. As the concept of achieving civil rights expanded to include these other groups, Latinos and Hispanics moved from the margins of civil rights efforts to the center. As a consequence of the huge growth in the Latino population in the years following the civil rights movement, which will be examined more closely in the next chapter, affirmative action, as an outgrowth of the movement, came to include Latinos along with African Americans as the largest group of affirmative action's beneficiaries.

The women's movement had a long history in the United States. As early as the nineteenth century the women's movement had connections to struggles against slavery and racial oppression. However, the women's movement also began to take on new energy after the civil rights movement, and many began to draw parallels between the social and economic situations of women and those of ethnic and racial minorities. The massive entry of women into all areas of the American labor force, beginning at the same time as the civil rights movement, encouraged the inclusion of women in programs aimed at eliminating categorical inequalities.

Many gays and lesbians began to see their sexuality as a civil rights issue in the years following the civil rights movement. The rise of the gay liberation movement saw outspoken challenges both to prevailing popular attitudes toward same-sex behavior and to medical definitions. In 1973, the American Psychiatric Association (APA) dropped its official position that homosexuality was a psychiatric disorder.[21]

The precise meaning and motivation of the change is open to question, and there were many mental health professionals who continued to see homosexuality as a manifestation of a psychological problem. Nevertheless, taken together with the evidence on public opinion, it does seem that the APA decision was part of a major shift in social norms and in the codification of social norms through law and through medical definitions of acceptable behavior. Following this trend in social norms, in 1979 the Surgeon General of the United States stated that the United States Public Health Service (USPHS) would no longer regard homosexuality as an illness or psychiatric defect.[22]

Gay activists sought antidiscrimination legislation and other forms of civil rights protection. A 1993 march on Washington for gay and lesbian rights was attended by an estimated 300,000 people. By the early twenty-first century, sexual minorities, frequently known by the acronym LGBT (lesbian, gay, bisexual, transgender), were often accorded the civil rights protections of many local, state, and federal laws. Affirmative action policies in employment and education generally did not include the representation of sexual minorities, although the goal of seeking greater categorical diversity implied that affirmative action could be extended to sexuality by some organizations.

Disability also became a civil rights matter. The Rehabilitation Act of 1973 and the Education for All Handicapped Children Act of 1975 required businesses and school receiving government funds to follow government guidelines, including affirmative action guidelines, in hiring or admitting disabled workers or students. Under pressure from activists, Congress passed the Americans with Disabilities Act of 1990, which required businesses and public spaces to change or remove features of architecture or transportation that presented barriers to the disabled.

By the 1970s, the widening scope of civil rights activities and organizing based on categorical identities led to the rise of ethnic consciousness and multicultural movements. Not only African Americans, but also women, ethnic and national-origin minorities, LGBT-identified people, and others became interest groups that saw themselves and were seen by many others as having a moral right to entry into full equality in all areas of American society.

GENDER AND CATEGORICAL EQUALITY

The ever-widening civil rights model provided a pattern for thinking about categorical inequality in the late twentieth century. This model did not dispense with older ideas of equality as a matter of individual rights and opportunities. But it portrayed those rights and opportunities as threatened because of categorical identities. People who understood themselves to be members of relatively disadvantaged categories asserted shared interests and sought protection and advancement of these interests by political means, giving rise to the concept of protected categories of citizens.

Women came under the legal definition of a protected category with Title VII of the Civil Rights Act of 1964, which made it unlawful for any employer with fifteen or more employees to discriminate against any individual based on race, color, national origin, religion, or sex. According to some accounts, Democratic senator Howard Smith added the clause prohibiting discrimination based on gender to alienate those opposed to governmental involvement in gender relations and thereby torpedo the entire act. Others have argued, though, that Senator Smith may have been opposed to racial equality, but that he was a supporter of gender equality and that he introduced the clause on the urgings of the National Women's Party.[23] Whatever its origins, the inclusion of women within the Civil Rights Act would work together with the rising women's movement during the late 1960s and 1970s and the simultaneous large-scale entry of women into the labor force to define women in terms of the civil rights model.

I have argued that the question of gender equality became relevant to the extent that men and women were considered comparable. As long as people accepted the view that men and women occupied separate spheres; delving and spinning, public action and private, the household and the field; they were not widely understood to be comparable. Movements for women's political rights in the early twentieth century had accompanied the decline of family farms, urbanization, the rise of public schooling, public schooling as part of child rearing, and an increase in women's employment. The employment of women did not begin, of course, in the late twentieth century. However, this was the time when, along with an expanding concept of equality as a categorical issue, women moved into the same sphere of activity as men in ever larger numbers.

Figure 12 shows the trend of women's entry into the labor force from 1960 to 1990. At the beginning of this period, a large proportion of traditionally working-age women (25 to 64) were labor force participants, but working women still constituted a minority at 40%. A decade later, this had risen to nearly half. By 1980, a substantial majority of working-age women were labor force participants, and this reached about 70% by 1990. Although many of these women were in "pink collar" or gender-identified jobs, it was no longer plausible to think about men and women as modern-day versions of hunters and gatherers,

Figure 12. Percentage of Women Aged 25–64 Participating in the US Labor Force, 1960–1990.

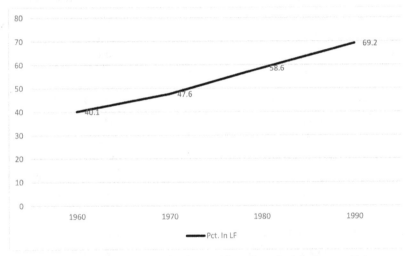

Source. Steven Ruggles, Sarah Flood, Ronald Goeken, Josiah Grover, Erin Meyer, Jose Pacas and Matthew Sobek.2020. IPUMS USA: Version 10.0 [dataset]. Minneapolis, MN: IPUMS, 2020. https://doi.org/10.18128/D010.V10.0

The entry of most women into work outside the household was not accompanied by an equalization of pay. In fact, during the 1960s, the median income of employed women shrank from 63 cents on the dollar earned by men to just over 50 cents. Much of this shrinking, of course, was probably due to the very fact that more women were working; many were entering the labor force at lower levels or were taking part-time work. The gap decreased only slightly by 1980, mostly because the median income of women had not stagnated as much as that of men during the economic slowdown of the late 1970s. By 1990, although most adult women were part of the workforce, they still had a median income of about 60 cents to the dollar earned by men.

If the massive influx of women into the labor force increasingly put women into the same sphere of activity as men, heightening the problem of gender inequality, it did not put an end to the heritage of separate spheres. One complication, that would receive greater attention in later decades, was that many people, especially men, tended to view their coworkers as members of the opposite sex, rather than as fellow employees. Although sexual harassment by individuals of the same sex has always occurred, the most common type has been the harassment of women by men.

In addition, while the view that "women's place is in the home" became much less common in American society in the second half of the twentieth century, an underlying association of women with domesticity continued. In the 1989 sociological study, *The Second Shift: Working Families and the Revolution at Home*, Arlie Hochschild documented the contradictions that had been introduced by the mainstreaming of women's employment outside the home. Hochschild argued that the growth in the non-domestic employment of women had been something of a social revolution. But older patterns of family life continued. Women who were employed full-time were also burdened with a greatly disproportionate share of housework and childcare.

The intimate interpersonal nature of family relations entailed difficult complications for efforts to achieve categorical equality between men and women. If women suffered disadvantages due to perspectives on gender relations, both conscious and unconscious, and due to family roles, then policies intended to eliminate those disadvantages would logically involve redesigning interpersonal and family relationships. But that would involve policymakers or activists deciding how people should live their private lives, which could fundamentally contradict American traditions of independence from bureaucratic intervention.

CIVIL RIGHTS, DEMOGRAPHIC CHANGE, AND CATEGORICAL EQUALITY

The concern with categorical inequality inspired by the events of the civil rights era helped in bringing about policy changes that transformed American society from the mid-1960s onward. In 1965, encouraged by President Lyndon Johnson, Congress amended its immigration policy, dropping national-origins quotas of immigrants that had been in place since the 1920s. Democrat Philip Hart, one of the sponsors of the 1965 Hart-Cellar immigration reform, declared that the effort to maintain American norms of the equality of individuals and to protect the American political heritage "require that our immigration policy be brought in line with the moral and ethical principles upon which our democracy is based."[24] When he signed Hart-Cellar Act of 1965, President Lyndon Johnson explicitly cited the nondiscrimination principles of civil rights. In the years that followed, the act opened the way for the massive wave of Latin American and Asian immigration of the late twentieth and early twenty first centuries, so that late twentieth and early twenty-first century immigrants are generally known among immigration scholars as the post-1965 wave.

The post-1965 immigration wave began to bring large numbers of people into the United States during the 1970s, setting a trend for the following decades. From 1971 to 1980, 4,493,000 immigrants were admitted into the country, an increase of 1,171,000 people from the decade 1961 to 1970. Admissions increased to 7,338,000 during the 1980s and 9,095,500 in the 1990s. In addition, those who arrived as legal permanent residents were only part of the demographic change due to migration. Numbers of unauthorized immigrants, especially from Mexico and Central America, began to grow quickly from the 1970s onward.

Before the 1965 wave, most immigrants had come to the United States from Europe. However, the demographic composition of immigrants changed following the 1960s. About half of post-1965 immigrants came from Latin America and about one quarter from Asia. This added a new dimension to categorical inequality. Latin America's geographic position bordering the United States, along with its economic difficulties, made it a source of low-wage labor for the United States. While immigrants from Asia were diverse in background, they were generally more highly educated, higher-paid workers.[25]

In the two decades following the civil rights movement, shifts in the American economy led to the establishment of a large Spanish-speaking working class, especially in the lower levels of the working class. Seasonal agricultural labor had long been associated with immigrants from Latin America, as well as with African Americans. With increasing numbers of relatively disadvantaged people of Latin American background, the civil rights–oriented emphasis on Latin Americans as a category would increase. Along with African Americans, Latinos and Hispanics would become a focus of policies aimed at group equalization, even as the number of immigrants of Latin American heritage grew ever more rapidly in number, creating expanding challenges for these policies.

The quest for categorical equality meant that members of protected group should not be concentrated at a comparatively low socioeconomic level, and that social policy should promote upward mobility for groups that were underrepresented in more remunerative and prestigious occupations. At the same time, though, economic demand drew immigrants from different regions into different social classes. As I noted in *Immigrant Networks and Social Capital*, social networks tend to reproduce classes within families and communities. Attempts to achieve equality across categories became part of a continuing struggle in the face of economic and social trends, which will be examined in the next chapter.

POLICY VERSUS SOCIETY

In several books on school desegregation, Stephen J. Caldas and I have argued that attempts at desegregating schools have generally had very limited success because schools exist in the larger society and as long as the larger society remains segregated, the schools tend to remain segregated.[26] Black, White, and Hispanic Americans often live in different places. These different places vary in their access to jobs and family resources, as well as in the kinds of information that flow along network lines. The efforts to achieve categorical equality through policy that grew out of the civil rights era ran up against the problem that the society itself was categorically unequal precisely because people in different groups lived in different places, had different social connections, and often moved along different life tracks.

One of the best studies of residential segregation in the United States is *American Apartheid* by Douglas S. Massey and Nancy A. Denton. As they convincingly demonstrate, racially segregated neighborhoods in the United States were not simply the consequence of preferences of individuals, but resulted from a long history of housing discrimination, including discriminatory government policies. As noted in chapter 4, the New Deal—in many ways the beginning of governmental social activism in the twentieth century—not only permitted but even encouraged racial discrimination and separation, including and most notably in housing.

The federal government began attempting to undo this heritage of discrimination and separation during the 1960s, first by mandating the end of discrimination in federal housing and later by officially prohibiting it in housing and in general. Massey and Denton note:

> The 1968 Fair Housing Act committed the federal government to the goals of open housing. Within private housing markets, it expressly prohibited the kinds of discrimination that had evolved over the years to deny blacks equal access to housing: it made it unlawful to refuse to rent or sell a home to any person because of race; it prohibited racial discrimination in the terms or conditions

of any rental or sale; it barred any and all discrimination in real estate advertising; it banned agents from making untrue statements about a dwelling's availability in order to deny a sale or rental to blacks; and it contained specific injunctions about blockbusting, prohibiting agents from making comments about the race of neighbors or those moving in in order to promote panic selling.[27]

On paper, this was a radical turnaround from the earlier years of government support for racial discrimination in housing. The problem, Massey and Denton argue, was that the act lacked adequate enforcement. They make this case well, and I believe they are right. However, to maintain that residential segregation in the United States would have been eliminated if only the federal government had engaged in more intensive and extensive intervention to reshape the society it had helped to create over a long stretch of time is to make a counterfactual argument, however morally justifiable that argument may be. We cannot know how things would have been different if efforts to enforce the FHA policies had been more aggressive. If resistance to the active desegregation of housing led to undermining the legislative mandate, what type or degree of coercion would have been required to overcome that resistance? And who among the agency officials or elected representatives could have been empowered to exercise that coercion?

Historical analysis can provide reasonable explanations of trends and occurrences and help us understand our present. That our present would have been preferable in some way if only individuals and institutions had acted differently is untestable speculation. While the period succeeding the civil rights era did see the rise of a Black middle class and greater residential mobility for Black middle-class families, many neighborhoods, especially in central urban areas, remained intensely segregated after the 1960s.

Within those racially segregated neighborhoods, different community structures tended to predominate. In 1965, as questions of categorical inequality were moving to the center of national attention, Daniel Patrick

Moynihan touched off a storm of controversy when he pointed out that Black Americans had much higher rates of single-parent, female-headed families than other Americans (at the time a little over a quarter of Black children lived in single-parent families) and argued, in an ill-chosen phrase, that this high proportions threatened Black children with a "tangle of pathologies."[28] Some of his critics denounced his views as racist; others claimed that his concerns embodied patriarchal and anti-feminist assumptions about the superiority of male-headed households. In the ensuing years, the conventional wisdom purveyed by sociology textbooks has consistently held up *The Moynihan Report* as an example of the "culture of poverty theory," which is identified as a reactionary line of thought that "blames the victim" of social injustice by claiming that socially disadvantaged statuses are products of inferior cultures.[29]

However, the eminent sociologist William Julius Wilson acknowledged in the insightful 1996 volume *When Work Disappears* that Moynihan did recognize that the unstable Black family was the consequence of the American socioeconomic structure.[30] In a history of *The Moynihan Report*, the controversy over it and its influence, from its early days to the Obama era, James T. Patterson argued in 2010 that politicians, academics, and activists lifted quotes out of context to make accusations against Moynihan. Far from "blaming the victim," from this perspective, Moynihan simply maintained that, having been produced by an unequal and discriminatory economy, one-parent families yielded unfortunate results of their own.[31]

Within the social isolation of segregated inner-city neighborhoods, a new kind of poverty emerged, one characterized by single-parent families, high crime rates, and extremely high unemployment, especially male unemployment. William Julius Wilson argued that this last characteristic, the absence of jobs, was the structural factor at the root of the new poverty. According to Wilson, the post-industrial disappearance of urban jobs left members of minority groups concentrated in neighborhoods where work had largely disappeared. This tended to undermine marriage, and it led to a wide range of "ghetto-related behaviors."[32] Without working and without employed role models, minority young people were growing up deprived of opportunities, experiences, and expectations that might lead to upward mobility.

The relationship between minority isolation and the failure of policy efforts to desegregate American society was circular. The more minority group members were concentrated in locations with little access to larger opportunities and social networks, the more their family and community structures were shaped by limited expectations and frustrations, giving rise to a multitude of social problems. The more minority neighborhoods were associated with social problems, the greater the resistance to breaking down racial segregation in the society at large.

The late twentieth-century recognition of categorical inequality existed uneasily with the nation's heritage of equality as a matter of independent individuals, with the idea that all could make their own destinies, with expectations for widespread upward mobility. But the stubborn persistence of categorical inequality also raised questions about to what extent it was really within the power of policy to restructure society and when the use of policy would entail and justify discarding fundamental American political values. In the years that followed the era of civil rights, the "return-of-the-repressed" categorical inequalities would complicate ever more the nation's ideas about the meaning of equality. These categorical inequalities would not only entail contradictions for inherited views of just what equality entailed, they would also prove stubbornly resistant to change and continue to be focal points of dispute in a nation that was becoming more diverse and polarized, socially, politically, and economically.

Notes

1. US Census Bureau, *Census of Population and Housing, 1970.*
2. Quoted in "Text of the President's Message on Economic Recovery and Growth," *New York Times,* February 3, 1961, 10
3. Quoted in "Goal of growth: Assets Must Be Shared More Widely," *New York Times,* January 22, 1962, C6.
4. Madrigal, "When Did TV Watching Peak?."
5. Carroll, "Family Time Eclipses TV as Favorite Way to Spend an Evening."
6. Quoted in Rubio, *A History of Affirmative Action, 1619–2000,* 145.
7. Farmer, quoted in Anderson, *The Pursuit of Fairness,* 77.
8. Ibid., 77–78
9. Peniel, *The Sword and the Shield.*
10. National Public Radio, "Bill Moyers' View of Contemporary America."
11. "Goldwater Sees Harm in Civil Rights Measure," *Los Angeles Times,* June 23, 1964, 3.
12. Quoted in Albright, "Sen. Goldwater to Vote Against Civil Rights Bill," A1.
13. Ibid.
14. Roberts, "Politicians Taking a Wary Attitude Toward the Civil Rights Question," A1.
15. Harris, "Goldwater Rights Views Given Minority Rating."
16. Orfield, "A Proposal for Outfoxing Wallace," B2
17. U.S. Commission on Civil Rights, *Promises and Perceptions,* 1
18. Coleman, Campbell, Hobson, et al., *Equality of Educational Opportunity.*
19. Bankston, "Grutter v. Bollinger: Weak Foundations."
20. Badger, "How Did the Civil Rights Act Change America? 2007, 13.
21. Conrad and Schneider, "Homosexuality: From Sin to Sickness to Lifestyle," 208.
22. Ibid., 209–210.
23. See, for example, Osterman "Origins of a Myth" on the question of Smith's motivations.
24. Quoted in Shanks, *Immigration and the Politics of American Sovereignty, 1880–1990,* 170.
25. Bankston, *Immigrant Networks and Social Capital.*

26. See, for example, Bankston and Caldas, *Controls and Choices: The Educational Marketplace and the Failure of School Desegregation*; and Caldas and Bankston, *Still Failing.*
27. Massey and Denton, *American Apartheid*, 195.
28. Moynihan, The Moynihan Report, 1965, 29.
29. See, for example, Greenbaum, *Blaming the Poor*; and Ryan, *Blaming the Victim.*
30. Wilson, *When Work Disappears*1996.
31. Patterson. *Freedom is Not Enough.*
32. Wilson, *When Work Disappears*, 51–86.

CHAPTER 7

CATEGORICAL INEQUALITY IN AN ERA OF POLARIZATION AND CONTRADICTION

THE ECONOMIC SETTING

By the end of the 1970s, the Great Compression was clearly over. Figure 13 uses a common measure of income inequality, the Gini coefficient, to show family income inequality in the United States from 1947 to 2018. By this measure, inequality in incomes among families reached its lowest point during the 1960s and began a steady rise thereafter. This increase in inequality of incomes stretched across the Republican and Democratic administrations of Richard Nixon, Gerald Ford, Jimmy Carter, Ronald Reagan, George H.W. Bush, Bill Clinton, George W. Bush, and Barack Obama.

Figure 13. Measures of Family Income Inequality (Gini Coefficients), 1947–2017.

Source. US Census, Current Population Reports, Historical Income Tables: Income Inequality: Households. Table F4. https://www.census.gov/data/tables/time-series/demo/income-poverty/historical-income-families.html#

The long-term bipartisan trend should make us cautious about attributing it entirely to any particular set of economic policies. Although it is possible that policies such as tax cuts on higher incomes during the Republican administrations of the 1980s may have contributed to this trend and exacerbated it, the extended nature of the trend should lead to look for its root cause in deeper structural changes in the American economy. Policies were less fundamental causes of growing income inequality than they were responses to those deeper structural changes and interactions with them.

Two bursts of speculative investment during the 1990s illustrated the developing nature of the American economic structure in the late twentieth and early twenty-first centuries. First, the dot-com bubble took off as the United States became a center of new communication technology and investors rushed to put their money into this new industry, inflating stock values. This bubble did not really burst because investment in communication technology did not disappear, although it did contract suddenly. Another bubble in the housing market was expanding at that same time. Housing prices jumped in the early 2000s, but the rapid growth in the price of houses began in the middle of the 1990s.

The Clinton administration took aggressive steps to end real and perceived discrimination in housing, making lenders more reluctant to refuse to make loans. More importantly, the administration encouraged mortgage lending to lower-income borrowers to promote more widespread homeownership. In 1995, the Department of Housing and Urban Development (HUD) enabled Fannie Mae and Freddie Mac to obtain affordable housing credit for buying subprime loans to low-income and risky borrowers. The idea was that homeownership was one of the keys to membership in the middle class and that making homeownership easier would broaden the middle class. Mortgage policy, among other things, was an updated version of President Johnson's War on Poverty.

This policy approach encouraged the mortgage industry to extend loans to even those most likely to default. The growing industry absorbed investments from all over the world, and the values of homes and the increasingly sophisticated financial instruments that carried debt shot up. Investors believed that spreading out reliable and risky loans across complicated bundles would protect against a crash due to a wave of defaults and ensure continuing growth in value. The debt bundles themselves became items of speculative investment, with market values driven by the expectation of future profits by investors, rather than by the underlying worth of products and services.

The ideological appeal of subsidizing widespread entry into the middle class through lenient mortgage lending along with the demand of capital for new sources of investment drove speculation in the housing market. The expansion of economies in other countries, most notably in the rapidly accelerating Chinese economy, resulted in surpluses of capital seeking new sources of investment. Since the United States continued to be the largest consumer economy, with imports exceeding exports from the 1980s onward, these surpluses were generally in the form of dollars. Foreign and domestic capital pushed the opening of new investments, so that financial interests in expanding access to housing and related loans were, at least on the surface, consistent with the ideological goal of moving more people and new categories of people into the American middle class.

THE TECHNOLOGY-FINANCE ECONOMY AND INEQUALITY OF OPPORTUNITIES

It would be an exaggeration to suggest that production in the United States was completely hollowed out by the end of the twentieth century and that all factory goods were either purchased from foreign companies or produced overseas by companies headquartered in the United States. Nevertheless, the comparative advantage of the United States in many areas of production did decrease. However, the United States continued to have a strong comparative advantage in two sectors: technology and finance.

If the availability of land was the driving force of the early American economy, by the early twenty-first-century technological innovation and finance had become the nation's new economic frontier. As Özgür Orhangazi notes in *The Financialization of the American Economy*, "total income acquired by the finance, insurance, and real estate (FIRE) sector has been increasing since the early 1980s. While in the 1952–1980 period the share of national income that went to the FIRE sector hovered between 12 and 14 percent, by the 2000s it had approached 20 percent."[1] Orhangazi observes that total employment in the financial sector expanded from 3 percent in 1952 to about 5 percent in 1980, then leveling off to about 4 to 5 percent thereafter. However, the compensation of those in the financial sector continued to increase sharply from 1980 on. As more of the nation's resources and activities became concentrated in finance, so too did wealth and income become concentrated in the hands of those in the financial sector, leaving smaller shares to those outside it.

While finance and technological innovation occupied a larger part of the GNP, there was also growth in other industries, such as more labor-intensive ones, although these offered fewer rewards than the factory jobs of the past. Technological change in construction diminished the need for highly skilled workers and increased demand for the semi-skilled.[2] Other new industries that required relatively low-skilled labor also emerged. During the 1970s and 1980s, for example, the American meat-processing industry became more consolidated, controlled by fewer and larger firms at just the time when skill requirements were falling in highly mechanized, large-scale meat-processing plants. The plants moved out of their old urban locations and began to look for cheaper labor. At the same time, what remained of the American textile and carpet industries moved out of the urban centers to Southern rural areas and sought cheap labor as well as technological efficiency to remain competitive in a global market.

The structural mobility that had created opportunities for individual upward mobility in the postwar era was no longer evident in the increasingly bifurcated economy of the late twentieth and early twenty-first centuries, with relatively small but highly remunerative positions in areas such as technology and finance and many more positions in service and low-paid labor. In May 2018, according to the Bureau of Labor Statistics, the ten largest occupations in the United States, in descending order of number of workers were retail salespersons; food preparation and service workers, including fast food workers; cashiers; general office clerks, registered nurses; laborers and freight, stock, and material workers; customer service representatives; waiters and waitresses, general and operations managers, and personal care aides. With more of nation's resources in finance and technology, it was top-heavy in assets and remuneration but bottom-heavy in occupational opportunities. The situation was unlikely to change. The Bureau of Labor Statistics projection of jobs to see the greatest growth in the 2018–2028 period looked very much like the list of the largest occupations, consisting mainly of jobs in service and low-wage labor.

Workers in low-wage labor and service jobs were especially vulnerable to economic downturns. When the coronavirus pandemic spread throughout much of the world in the spring of 2020, many investors in the stock market were adversely affected, tut the greatest negative impact was on low-income earners because they were subject to the massive layoffs and wage freezes. The ideal of universal upward mobility, subsidized by government policy, had come into conflict with the realities of opportunity.

FROM MASS MEDIA TO SOCIAL NETWORKS

In the nineteenth century, newspapers had played a large part in shaping American ideas of citizenship and of the self-made man. In the twentieth century, first radio and then television had promoted the understanding of the nation as massive community of citizen-consumers, enjoying opportunities for material abundance, and connected by uniform, centralized media of communication. At the very end of the twentieth century, though, new means of communication spurred the growth of the technology-finance economy and produced a new environment of information distribution.

Once again, a large and active government sector played a key role. The internet grew out of work at the federal Defense Advanced Research Projects Agency (DARPA) during the 1960s. By the late 1980s, the Federal Networking Council had been established to coordinate the efforts of federal agencies in building the infrastructure of the internet. As the internet became a widespread and popular means of communicating during the 1990s, many internet enthusiasts proclaimed individualist, libertarian ideals, believing that this would free information from bureaucratic control, but at virtually every step the internet was fostered and subsidized by agencies of the federal government.

While the development of the internet was federally subsidized, its takeoff in the mid-1990s was closely linked to profit-seeking capital investment. In an expedited version of the evolution of the market economy a century earlier, individual entrepreneurship led to the emergence of huge corporations. During the 2000s, the technology began to connect individual users, first with sites such as MySpace and Linkedin, and by 2006 with Facebook and Twitter. The introduction of the iPhone in 2007 by Apple, an entrepreneurial endeavor that had become a massive corporation in the twenty-first century, freed users from larger devices and made communication possible at all times and virtually everywhere.

Social network and related internet media were at once centralizing and decentralizing. In terms of market control, Facebook, Google, Twitter, and similar companies were oligopolistic. They concentrated ownership and profits, benefitting their highly skilled knowledge workers and directing enormous wealth to top management and investors. The 2020 coronavirus pandemic that had hit lower earners hardest also reinforced the highly concentrated, oligopolistic character of social media and related technology-based companies. Stay-at-home orders meant that consumers were much less likely to spend time and money outside of their homes, relying on the big internet companies even more for social lives. Instead of shopping at brick-and-mortar businesses, consumers turned to ordering online, most notably from the internet retail giant Amazon.

At the same time that it concentrated business control, the online world produced a boutique marketplace of communication in which users could exchange thoughts and perceptions instead of receiving information from a limited number of television or radio broadcasters. The decentralizing aspect might be expected to lend itself to an updated type of individual equality of independence, given the freedom from hierarchical control. In effect, though, the boutique marketplace of communication encouraged users to sort themselves out by interests, opinions, and social identities, feeding the growing identity politics of the time. In addition, the very decentralization, the breakdown of the old communication hierarchies, paradoxically lent themselves to the variety of centralization known as "populism."

Populism, in the sense the word was usually used by the second decade of the twenty-first century meant an appeal by leaders to masses of followers, bypassing organizational structures. The eclipse of the broadcasting hierarchy meant that movements or political leaders could address themselves directly to atomized individuals and to the self-created interest groups of these individuals, with limited organizational mediation. Social media gave an added impetus to a tendency noted during the television era, the ability of celebrities to turn themselves into political figures. The social media–driven populism of the era drew heavily on a disenchantment with established government produced by the perception of many Americans that government was a vast, intrusive entity that did not serve their own interests. It also entailed a particular kind of identity politics, an ethno-nationalism connected to this disenchantment with government, based on the perception that the pursuit of categorical equality was an alliance between bureaucratic elite patrons and minority group clients.

The disenchantment with established bureaucracies extended beyond government to the more traditional media of newspapers and television. Newspapers became more concentrated in the hands of a small number of corporate owners, wiping out many of the local news sources, closely connected to communities, which generally held the trust of citizens. A populist leader, appealing to those atomized and alienated from established nationwide institutions, could, when shown in an unfavorable light by the so-called mainstream media, portray these as elite-dominated conspiracies, working together with anti-democratic government bureaucrats.

STRUCTURAL MOBILITY AND SUBSIDIZED MOBILITY

By the second half of the twentieth century, Americans had largely come to see equality as equality of opportunity, with the understanding that this specifically meant universal chances for upward mobility. The focus on historically disadvantaged or oppressed categories of people placed attention on the representation of those categories in desirable occupational positions. Equality of opportunity was still an idea rooted in competition among individuals, but it was a competition that required policy manipulation in order to boost the representation of the underrepresented at the higher socioeconomic levels. Encouraging the expansion of mortgage lending through policy in the mid-1990s was one of the ways in which the United States attempted to subsidize upward mobility, especially for historically disadvantaged categories of people. Policymakers also attempted to broaden the middle class by subsidizing mobility through employment and education.

The legal history of affirmative action in the twenty-first century illustrates the problems and contractions of subsidized upward mobility. In the 2003 affirmative action case *Grutter v. Bollinger*, Justice Sandra Day O'Connor, speaking for the court, explained that part of the reason the University of Michigan law schools' minority admissions policy met the criterion of a compelling national interest was that "universities, and in particular, law schools, represent the training ground for a large number of our Nation's leaders." The case was not about trying to change the racial or ethnic composition of all levels of American society, but specifically about trying to increase the number of minority group members in a high-prestige, generally high-income profession among the nation's natural aristocrats.

Of course, the main reason that White Michigan resident Barbara Grutter brought her lawsuit after being rejected by the University of Michigan was that she too wanted to enter a desirable occupation and a training ground for leadership. This is a desire shared by many, including those who have been traditionally underrepresented in fields such as law.

During the nearly four decades from 1970 to 2007 census data show that attorneys grew from about a quarter of a million to well over one million individuals, an increase from 3 out of every 100 people in the labor force to 7 out of every 100. Minority ("nonwhite") attorneys made up only 2 percent of the American legal profession in 1970, but 10 percent in 2007. Only one out of every twenty attorneys was a woman at the beginning of this period, but over one-third were women by the end. White men went from 93 percent of lawyers to 62 percent, with slow rates of growth in absolute numbers from 1990 onward.[3]

Judged from the perspective of inclusion, the composition of the legal profession made great advances over those four decades. Minority members and women were much better represented in the 2000s than in the 1970s. This undoubtedly represented an extension of the opportunity to serve in the legal profession. It is also clear that the entry of new groups of people into this profession was a large source of its overall growth. Apart from the question of opportunity, one might have asked: how many lawyers did the United States really need? For that matter, how many leaders did the nation need?

If there was any limit to the number of lawyers (or leaders) the country needed, that might imply that creating greater diversity means that policymakers would have to somehow discourage people from the profession's traditional demographic pools as well as encourage people from traditionally underrepresented groups. Otherwise, policymakers would continually pump up the competition for hotly desired positions by subsidizing those at a competitive disadvantage, producing oversupplies of attorneys or leaders in various fields.

Efforts at categorical equalization through affirmation action in the United States began with the idea that the impediment of discrimination should be removed to enable African Americans to compete as individuals in the national labor market. As President Johnson observed in his Howard University speech, genuinely competitive equality across categories, judged by outcomes, could not be achieved simply by eliminating discriminatory laws because categorical inequality was not just maintained by law but ingrained in the structure of the society.

Following the 1960s, programs aimed at giving compensatory advantages to those judged to have been historically disadvantaged in getting ahead in American life generally came in two areas. One of these was employment. Encouraged by the federal government, businesses tried to find ways to place minority members in desired jobs or make more promotions available to them. The other area was education. Since education was critical to getting ahead in the race, getting more African Americans and members of other groups deemed to have been historically disadvantaged became a primary strategy for increasing minority upward mobility.

The United States had moved away from allowing the competition for upward mobility and toward finding ways to subsidize mobility. Although the competition and the subsidization took place at the level of the individual, there was a societal-level logic to the process. When enough minority-group members had moved into widely desired, high-status jobs, the historical disadvantage would presumably have been removed from American society, and then socioeconomic race could proceed without handicapping.

The desire to enable the disadvantaged to move ahead often had echoes of the self-made man ideology because those who had come from disadvantaged backgrounds, like Booker T. Washington, could be seen as having overcome greater obstacles than those who had enjoyed the benefits of abundant family resources. Subsidizing categorical mobility, then, may be presented as cancelling out social disadvantages to enable individual effort.

The rise of affirmative action–type policies as strategies for squaring the circle of competitive equality in an unequal society involved a number of problems and contradictions. Americans in general did not believe that everyone should be equal, just that everyone should have equal chances to become unequal. But even in a race, a runner's chances in placing depend on quality of training, coaching, and time free from other pursuits, as well as on the placement of carefully staggered starting points on a circular track. Life is much more complicated than a footrace. In life, placing in the race of mobility takes place across generations, so that parents often run their own races hard to give children better starting points. To equalize the game for every generation, a society would have to intervene constantly and eternally to redistribute any gains made by all previous generations.

Subsidizing upward mobility also tends to overvalue the positions at the top of the prestige scale. Policies that try to enable more people to move into preferred positions consequently move them away from the growing number of jobs with less prestige. In a footrace, one may be able to encourage everyone to place first. An irony of attempting to subsidize mobility is that it can ultimately increase inequality in the name of equality through intensifying competition for scarce opportunities.

Middle-class parents generally use all the resources at their disposal to try to place their own children in middle-class jobs. Affirmative action–type policies tried to place government or institutions in the role of substitute families by giving students or job applicants from poor and working-class families the resources their own families did not have. By spreading the opportunity to be in middle-class jobs more widely, both families and policymakers increased the demand for those jobs, ratcheting up the competition in an increasingly polarized economy.

Perhaps one of the most evident problems with political attempts to adjust the competition was that other competitors could see it as rigging the race against them. As early as the 1970s, some Whites began to object that although they had been winners, the prizes had been taken from them and given to others. That those making these objections generally had their own unearned advantages was a perfectly legitimate response, and one that proponents of categorical equalization often made. However, that response did not erase the perception or the resentment that accompanied it. Despite the desire to readjust the competition, the

United States had not abandoned the idea that it should be a competition among individuals. In a society of narrowing opportunities, intensified competition along categorical lines helped to spur political polarization along those lines.

CATEGORICAL EQUALIZATION AND POLITICAL ALIGNMENT

During the New Deal, the government, in particular the federal government, had begun to take an active role in providing economic benefits to citizens. This development had come primarily from the Democratic Party, which drew much of its strength from the urban working class in the North and from the nearly monolithically Democratic White segregationist South. Democratic support for the civil rights movement during the Kennedy and Johnson administrations, however tardy and temperate this support may have been, broke apart this morally dubious but pragmatic alliance. In public perception and to some extent in reality, the pursuit of categorical equality through government policy became a matter of race, rather than class.

As figure 14 illustrates, in the years following the civil rights era, partisan voting behavior was clearly closely associated with race. From 1972 through 2016, more than eight out ten Black men and women voted Democrat in presidential elections, except in 1988, when electorally weak candidate Michael Dukakis still held on to well over three-quarters of Black votes, according to self-reports in the General Social Survey. While scant majorities of White women voted Democrat in 1976 (Jimmy Carter vs. Gerald Ford), 1996 (Bill Clinton vs. Bob Dole), and 2008 (Barack Obama vs. John McCain), the Democrats took slight majorities of White men only in 1976 and 1996.

Figure 14. Percentages Voting Democrat, by Race and Gender, 1972–2016.

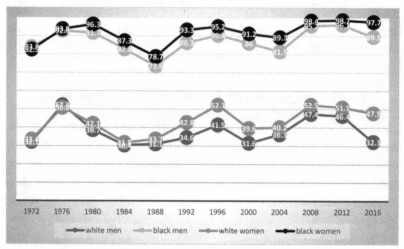

Source. Tom W. Smith, Michael Davern, Jeremy Freese, and Steven Morgan, General Social Surveys, 1972–2018 [Machine-readable Data File]. https://gss.norc.org/.

The elections showed a gender divide as well as a racial divide, but the racial gap in party politics was much greater over all these years. Third-party votes in some years suggest that low White support for Democrats was at least partly more disenchantment with that party than it was pro-Republican. In 1980, John Anderson took 5.3 percent of the White male and 6.8 percent of the White female vote, probably drawing most votes away from the Republicans. In 1992, the White vote was split between George H.W. Bush and H. Ross Perot. Among White men 43.1 percent voted for Bush and 21. 3 percent voted for Perot, and among White women 42.6 percent voted for Bush and 15.0 percent voted for Perot. Perot split the White vote again in 1996, taking 15 percent of White men and 13.6 percent of White women. Ralph Nader may have affected the Electoral College outcome in 2000 because of the narrowness of that election, but he received only small percentages of the national vote in any demographic category (third-party votes not shown in this figure).

The racial element of support for the major American political parties had implications for the goals and policies of those parties. It would be an overstatement to say that the Democrats became the party of minority voters, while Republicans became the party of Whites, especially White men. Still, minority voters, especially Black voters provided a critical base for the Democrats, while White voters provided a similar base for the Republicans. Partisan politics were heavily shaped by racial politics.

Figure 15. Beliefs on the Responsibility of Government, by Race, General Social Survey 1984*.

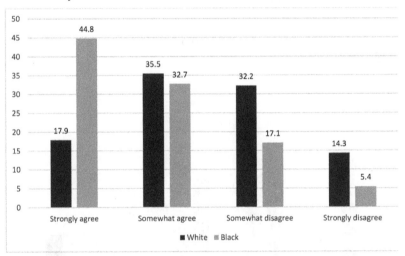

Source. Tom W. Smith, Michael Davern, Jeremy Freese, and Steven Morgan, General Social Surveys, 1972–2018 [Machine-readable Data File]. https://gss.norc.org/.
*Respondents were asked to what degree they agreed with the statement that "It is the responsibility of government to meet everyone's needs, even in the case of sickness, poverty, unemployment, and old age."

Because of their differing historical experiences, Whites and Blacks tended to see the role of government in addressing social and economic inequalities differently. In 1984, the General Social Survey asked its respondents about the responsibility of government for meeting economic needs. While majorities in both races at least somewhat agreed that government was responsible for meeting a wide range of needs among citizens, Blacks were much more likely to agree, especially strongly agree (figure 15).

Over thirty years later, the two races still tended to hold differing views on government benefits. In the years 2016–2018, White respondents to the General Social Survey were significantly more likely than Black respondents to agree that social benefits from government make people lazy (figure 16). Over 53 percent of Whites agreed with this statement, compared to 38 percent of Blacks.

Figure 16. Social Benefits from Government Make People Lazy, by Race, 2016–2018.

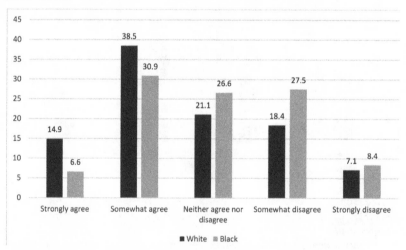

Source: Tom W. Smith, Michael Davern, Jeremy Freese, and Steven Morgan, General Social Surveys, 1972–2018 [Machine-readable Data File]. https:// gss.norc.org/.

As stark as the partisan statistical divides were, statistics understated the intensity of political polarization during the 2016 election. On November 6, 2016, the *New York Times* described the campaign as a clash of two different realities, observing that "the two parties did not just disagree on how to solve the country's problems; they also had radically different ideas about what those problems even were."[4] Candidate and later President Donald Trump's main support rested on a deeply committed, almost entirely White base, facing another deeply committed opposition, with a relatively limited number of swing voters between the two unswayable parties.

The ideological divide associated with questions of racial equalization were an evident part of partisan politics of 2016 and beyond. It would be simplistic to reduce the Clinton-Trump competition to matters of race. Those who supported each candidate did so for many reasons. Hillary Clinton supporters linked her to the relative economic prosperity of her husband's years in office, had favorable views of her years of governmental experience, supported having a woman as president, or simply had strongly negative views of her opponent's character and background. Trump supporters thought that he would promote economic growth by pursuing pro-business policies, believed in his television celebrity image as an extraordinarily successful entrepreneur, cast votes for him out of anger and alienation in the globalizing economy of the twenty-first century, saw him as an anti-politician opposed to the political establishment, or just disliked him less than they disliked Clinton.

While avoiding reductionism or ad hominem claims about individual voters, though, it is clear that ideological views connected to race and policies of racial equalization did mark partisan outcomes. Nearly two-thirds of those who voted for Democrat candidate Hillary Clinton said that they believed racial differences were due to discrimination. By contrast, eight out of ten Trump voters said that racial differences did not result from discrimination (figure 17).

The 2016 election marked a clear split on policies related to sources of racial inequalities and policy responses to these. This was part of a more general polarization in American society related to the identity politics that had arisen around questions of categorical inequality.

Figure 17. "Racial Differences are Due to Discrimination" by Vote in 2016 Presidential Election.

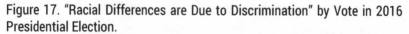

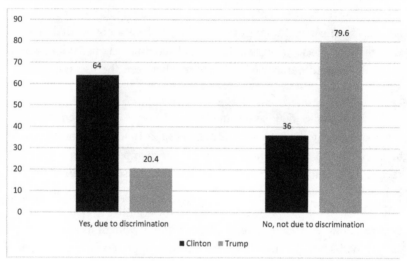

Source. Tom W. Smith, Michael Davern, Jeremy Freese, and Steven Morgan, General Social Surveys, 1972–2018 [Machine-readable Data File]. https://gss.norc.org/.

These views on the sources of categorical inequality were naturally reflected in differing views on governmental responses. While most voters on both sides were against racial preferences in hiring for jobs (figure 18), over two-thirds of Trump voters strongly opposed preferences, compared to one-third of Clinton voters. Nearly a quarter of those in the Clinton camp strongly favored such preferences, compared to a tiny percentage of Trump voters.

Figure 18. Support for Racial Preferences in Hiring by Vote in 2016 Presidential Election.

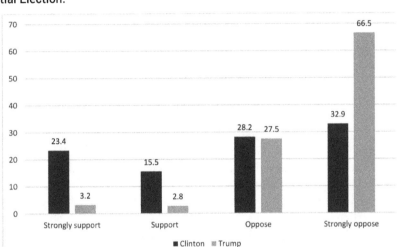

Source. Tom W. Smith, Michael Davern, Jeremy Freese, and Steven Morgan, General Social Surveys, 1972–2018 [Machine-readable Data File]. https://gss.norc.org/.

IDENTITY POLITICS AND POLARIZATION

As categorical inequality moved from the margins of public consideration to the center, some Americans came to the conclusion that achieving true equality would mean more than simply trying to adjust equality of opportunity by subsidizing the upward mobility of historically disadvantaged groups. It would mean completely unravelling and reweaving the fabric of American society. Joe Feagin, a former president of the American Sociological Association, described the country as fundamentally racist in all its institutions, primarily against Black Americans but also against all who could be classified as people of color. To begin the work of redesigning the nation, Feagin called for rejecting the existing constitutional order and establishing a new constitutional convention that would represent the group interests and rights of all nonwhites, and for individual and group reparations.[5]

For the most ambitious advocates of categorical equality mandated by law, the goal of civil rights legislation became the complete restructuring of American society by political means. At the 2002 annual symposium of the Albany Law Review, Miranda K.S. Massie, an attorney associated with the group By Any Means Necessary (BAMN), argued:

> The only way we have moved forward in this nation—which is defined by the maintenance of a caste system in which White people get preferences and privileges every day based only on the fact they are White—is because of the progress of the Civil Rights Movement. We have democratic aspirations to be a nation in which there is true equality and in which we have real democracy—not just formal democracy. That is our foundational tension. It has been built into the Constitution, and it has been built into our moments of historical progress and regress.[6]

Massie went on to characterize racism as fundamental to the character of American democracy, and she described the civil rights program of affirmative action as far more than just an attempt to eliminate discrimination against individuals or provide opportunities to members of minority groups. Instead, she maintained that affirmative action is part of a continuing movement aimed at fundamentally restructuring the whole of American society.

The uncompromising nature of these demands for a basic reorganization of American society lent itself to an intransigent identity politics. In 1995, Constance Horner, a member of the US Commission on Civil Rights, remarked on the cultural climate that had come to surround discussions of debates about affirmative action policies:

> One of the dilemmas confronting people in public life critical of affirmative action has been the concern that calling it into question would be viewed by black Americans as, at best, indifference to their historic plight or, at worst, a contributor to resurgent

racism. Some proponents of affirmative action have, over several decades, taken advantage of this concern to enforce a politically correct silence that has precluded the incremental correction of a public policy gone awry that is preservative of peaceful democratic change. Indeed, some of the explosive force of the current critique results from the unleashed resentment over this intimidation.[7]

During the second decade of the twenty-first century, a series of well-publicized events encouraged a view of the world as a matter of support for the marginalized versus bigotry. Police shootings of Black men, a number of which appeared to be unjustifiable, called public attention to continuing racial inequality and resulted in protests and riots across the country. The racially motivated murder of Black churchgoers in Charleston, South Carolina, by a young White man sparked renewed questioning of the nation's racial history. Two years after the Charleston murders, a demonstration staged by White supremacists that resulted in violent clashes with anti-racist counterdemonstrators and the death of a young woman among the counterdemonstrators intensified feelings about race, group justice, and bigotry in the country.

At universities, student activists who had grown up with recorded images from the civil rights movement, staged demonstrations and presented their institutions with lists of demands. Prominent among these demands were the insistence that the universities immediately increase their hiring of faculty and their recruitment of students from all marginalized groups. The anti-racist and anti-sexist official climate that followed the civil rights era tended to portray the advancement of all formerly excluded or underrepresented groups as a critical institutional imperative. Because this advancement could be hampered by employees, faculty members, or fellow students who had biases or were even insufficiently supportive of the institutional goal, organizations often tended to try to get all their members to hold and express opinions consistent with the institutional imperative. Within the universities, this led to claims that the institutions were intolerant of intellectual diversity.

Outside the universities, this led to perceptions that higher education itself was a bastion of uniform identity politics.

Even as racism, ethnocentricity, and sexism became recognized in many sectors as the fundamental flaws in American society requiring aggressive tactics of categorical equalization, resentment toward "political correctness" combined with reactions against rapid cultural change in other sectors to create a generalized sense of opposition and alienation. As Stephen J. Caldas and I have observed in *Public Education, America's Civil Religion*, for many Americans the US Constitution was not just a framework for laws but a sacred text that symbolized national existence.[8] For these citizens, calls for a new ethnically based constitutional convention were more than arguments for legal reform; they were denials of national identity.

Public-opinion issues related to categorical equalization became more polarized, as reflected in the 2016 election. On the one hand, policies to advance equalization based on race, ethnicity, and gender became deeply institutionalized in many corporations and universities. On the far side of support for race-based policies, activists and organizations such as BAMN advocated racial, ethnic, and gender preferences intended to completely restructure the society. On the other side, the pervasive, subtle institutional demands for ideological conformity, along with the more radical activist claims alienated many Whites and other non-beneficiaries of preferences, feeding a reactionary White identity politics.

The pursuit of categorical equality appeared to some White Americans as systematically preferring categories other than their own, as well as a turning away from individualistic ideas of equality. In an article on White evangelical support for Trump, a journalist said of one of her interviewees: "the years of the Obama presidency were confusing to her. She said she heard talk of giving freedoms to gay people and members of minority groups. But to her it felt like her freedoms were being taken away. And that she was turning into the minority [...] we spent eight years, if not more [she said] with our freedoms taken away under the guise of giving freedoms to all.'"⁹

IMMIGRATION, DEMOGRAPHIC DIVERSITY, AND ETHNIC STRATIFICATION

The United States has always had racial and ethnic inequality. The most obvious form, of course, is the Black-White caste system, first in the overt form of slavery and later in massive segregation and discrimination. Native Americans or Amerindians have been placed outside of the American polity for most of the nation's history. Ideas about equality have been maintained by excluding these groups from the consciousness of the dominant majority.

As discussed in chapter 3, large-scale immigration at the end of the nineteenth and beginning of the twentieth centuries, responding to the demands of an emerging corporate economy, brought a new dimension of ethnic stratification: the working classes became identified with the new immigrant groups from eastern and southern Europe. The great wave of immigration to the United States beginning in the late twentieth century combined with the technology-finance heavy economy of the era to give rise to yet another form of ethnic inequality.

The demand for semi-skilled workers in construction and in new industries such as meat packing and carpet making created an informal, flexible sector at the bottom of the economy. At the same time, growing technological sophistication together with the expansion and centralization of financial activities opened up positions for the highly skilled. Sociologist Ivan Light has described how this shapes ethnic inequality:

> [...] globalization attracts two types of migrants to the developed core countries. A minority are skilled professionals, who earn high incomes. The Asian Indian migrants [...] belong to this class, as do the Korean and Chinese immigrants [...] The majority, however, are poor people from the developing world, who flood into big

cities in response to demand for informal sector jobs (such as nannies, gardeners, roofers, construction workers) on the part of newly wealthy households. The Mexican and Central American immigrants belong to this category.[10]

The only modifications I would make to Light's observation are that it overemphasizes the big cities at a time when immigrants were spreading out to new suburban and rural destinations and that the new immigrant working class did not work only as employees of wealthy individuals.

Within the new global economic arrangement, it had become easier than ever to import and export people, as well as capital and goods. Reed Ueda has observed that the new processes of the world economy have reconfigured immigration, noting that "American immigration has occurred in a worldwide environment of rapid resource and asset flow that involves international capital, transcultural images and ideas, and technology and human capital flows. Advanced transportation and communication systems, transnational social networks, and migrant facilitators and traffickers have multiplied the possible pathways for the movement of populations into and out of the country." [11]

Whether large-scale immigration was a cause or consequence of increasing inequality in general and across ethnic and racial groups remains a legitimate topic for debate. My own view is that immigrant labor responded to a workplace that was becoming more stratified. Others, most notably economist George J. Borjas, have maintained that the intensified competition produced by immigrants reduces the wages of native-born workers. Since the largest number of immigrants were in working-class sectors, this mainly lowered the wages of the native-born working class, while benefits flowed primarily to those in higher-income sectors who were employing cheaper labor or enjoying cheaper services. Borjas has also produced some evidence that highly skilled immigrants, specifically those earning doctorates in the United States, lowered opportunities and outcomes for natives in specific knowledge-intensive areas.[12]

Regardless of how we answer the cause-and-effect question, it is evident that immigration was part of the trend of expanding inequality. It was also part of a trend of a new form of categorical inequality. People from just south of the US border were geographically situated to meet the new North American demand for low-wage labor in the rapidly growing construction industry, in the new industries, and in personal services. The housing boom, stimulated by the nation's role as an international financial center, created an intense demand for construction laborers who could provide a largely seasonal and flexible labor force. By 2004, foreign-born Hispanics comprised 7 percent of the total US labor force, but over 15 percent of the construction labor force. Just three years later, foreign-born Hispanics had increased to 19 percent of all workers in the American construction industry.[13]

A large part of the Spanish-speaking working class in the United States occupied a distinct position because of legal status as well as occupational specialization. As the US economy became more tightly integrated with other nations, control over the movement of labor loosened. In particular, unofficial flows of immigration from Mexico, which shares a long land border with the United States, became highly sensitive to economic trends in both countries. Over 70% of Mexico's export revenues came from oil at the beginning of the 1980s. As the price of oil declined beginning about 1982, Mexico had less revenue coming in, provoking a debt crisis, and the country's already existing problems of poverty became worse. Undocumented immigration from Mexico began to move upward rapidly, from a little over 621,000 in the decade 1970–1979 to over one million in the 1980s.

The Immigration Reform and Control Act (IRCA) in 1986 encouraged some Mexicans in the United States without authorization to remain by offering amnesty, and it encouraged others to move into the United States on a long-term basis by intensifying control of the border, making it more difficult to move back and forth. The longer-term orientation led many workers to move further north, away from the border. In 1994, a second economic shock hit Mexico, with the devaluation of the peso, which caused dramatic inflation and a decline in living standards. Both Mexico's economic problems and US demands for casual labor continued into the new century, and undocumented immigration skyrocketed.

Political disorder in Central America tended to shift undocumented immigration from workers to refugees after 2015. This was partly due to earlier migration because the violence apparently began with members of ethnic gangs formed in the United States deported to their countries of origin. Still, a strong association between Mexican and Central American national origin and relatively disadvantaged status continued to exist, and the undocumented were a significant percentage of people of such national origins.

At the other end of the American economy, non-refugee Asian groups tended to be heavily overrepresented in the highly skilled, knowledge-intensive jobs created by the technology-finance environment. In income, educational attainment, and occupational prestige (the three measures of occupational attainment), Asian groups on average showed not only more advantageous situations than other nonwhite groups but also more advantageous situations than White non-Hispanics. According to the 2013–2017 American Community Survey, Asian Indians had the highest socioeconomic index scores in the United States (59.37). People classified as Chinese in what the census calls detailed race categories scored 52.66 and those classified as Pakistani averaged 52.10. Non-Hispanic Whites showed an average of 46.59. Black non-Hispanics came in at 37.92, lower than non-Hispanic Whites, but substantially higher than Mexicans, Hondurans, and Guatemalans (32.50, 26.52, and 26.00, respectively).

Intergenerational transmission made this pattern of racial and ethnic inequality likely to persist into the future. As Stephen J. Caldas and I have documented, the socioeconomic inequalities associated with adult socioeconomic positions in different categories are also associated with educational outcomes in younger generations.[14] In grades and standardized tests throughout the schooling years, Asians tend to show better outcomes than non-Hispanic Whites. Moreover, as the populations of Asian and Latin American background have grown in the United States, achievement gaps between students of Asian and Latin American origins, the two fastest-growing segments of the population, have widened.

The concept of categorical inequality, along with policies aimed at achieving greater categorical equality, had developed in response to recognition of the historic oppression of African Americans. The demographic change that resulted from immigration, though, along with the expansion of the civil rights model to include categories of people other than African Americans, both responded to the economic structure that was creating greater inequality and intensified the inequality across categories. In addition, the perception that the benefits of large, centralized government went chiefly to people in nonwhite or Latin American–origin groups created resentment among many non-Hispanic Whites, who saw themselves as being excluded. This perception was especially strong among those most affected by the economic changes of the time, notably those in blue-collar occupations that did not require higher-education credentials. The additional perception that non-Hispanic Whites were overwhelmingly native-born and that the numbers of the Latin Americans and Asians had grown as a result of immigration intensified the impression among some of the White working class that their own identity group was being left behind in the political distribution of opportunities and resources.

Unease with cultural change associated with high levels of immigration compounded economic anxieties. The "new destinations" trend in immigration to the United States meant that locations that had previously had little experience of ethnic or linguistic diversity became home to large immigrant settlements. The September 11, 2001, terrorist attacks and the events that followed these exacerbated the cultural unease. Some Americans reacted with hostile stereotypes of Muslims, and more worried that migrants from Muslim dominant countries could include terrorists.

While the US population of people from North Africa and the Middle East had been very small before the twenty-first century, the American military invasions following the September 11 attacks made the region a major source of national-origin diversification for the United States. To give examples from three of the most notable sending countries, according to the 2017 US *Yearbook of Immigration Statistics*, between 2015 and 2017, the number of people from Afghanistan admitted into the United States annually as permanent residents grew from 8,328 to 19,538, eclipsing South Korean immigrants by the latter year. Iraqis admitted as US permanent residents numbered 21,107 in 2015, 18,904 in 2016, and 14,203 in 2017. Somali immigrants were about 7,000 each year. Others from the region were also admitted as refugees: 5,000 from Afghanistan during these three years, nearly 30,000 from Iraq, and more than 15,000 from Somalia. The United States was becoming much more ethnically diverse at the same time that ethnic stratification was growing along with worries about how immigration might be changing American life.

In her 2016 book, *Strangers in their Own Land: Anger and Mourning on the American Right*, perhaps the best effort by a scholar to examine the Tea Party and Trump supporters sympathetically, sociologist Arlie Hochschild found that the feeling of exclusion from the benefits of big government was a driving force of political attitudes among those in her study. Immigrants and members of racial and ethnic minorities were not foremost in their denunciations, but they did see minorities as among those whom government support enabled to jump the line ahead of deserving, hardworking Americans. We should remember that the Louisiana region where Hochschild did her investigation had a long history of racial discrimination and had supported George Wallace in 1968. It is entirely possible, then, that norms of social acceptability in the twenty-first century led Hochschild's respondents to downplay, even in their own minds, the influence of race and ethnicity on their political views.

It is clear, though, that by the 2016 election, the perception that federal bureaucracy had become too large, intrusive, and inconsistent with the interests of average Americans that existed alongside a growing undercurrent of anti-immigrant emotions, consisting of cultural concerns that the United States was becoming an alien land for native-born, English-speaking citizens and economic concerns that members of the native-born working class were being displaced by the arrival of foreign workers and the export of jobs to foreign workplaces. Outsider firebrand Donald Trump explicitly based his seemingly implausible candidacy for president on denunciations of the federal bureaucracy, calls for extreme measures to halt undocumented immigration, along with extremely negative characterizations of Muslims and people from Latin America, and protectionist economic measures.

Candidate and later President Trump's promise to take dramatic action to reinforce the US-Mexico border with a massive wall appealed to those who felt left out in America's changing population, who believed that the federal government favored minority ethnic groups at the expense of the majority, and who worried about immigrants as competitors for jobs. Trump's slogan, Make America Great Again, was, like any effective slogan, vague enough to be interpreted differently by different people. However, given the emphases of his campaign and his policies, much of what it meant was a promise to return the nation to an idealized past before the increase in ethnic diversity through immigration, when the majority population enjoyed the equality of opportunity available in the postwar Great Compression and when government bureaucracies were less focused on categorical equalization.

Immigration, then, tended to undermine goals of categorical equalization in at least two ways. First, immigrants from different regions tended to reflect bifurcating demand in the workforce, creating greater ethnic stratification. Second, it contributed to a growing perception by a substantial segment of the White population that they were becoming strangers in their own country and that their federal government did not serve their interests. This reinforced the discomfort of many Whites with minority identity politics. These two ways were connected because the feeling of alienation was often strongest among those working-class Whites who were most affected by the emergence of the finance-technology dominant economy.

CATEGORIES AS NETWORKS AND INTEREST GROUPS

Efforts at categorical equalization were also undermined by members of categories themselves, including not only the broad categories of race, class, and gender but also families, religious affiliations, and friendship groups. Neither equality of opportunity nor equality of condition can be established by proclamation. Nor do opportunities and conditions result from the heroic efforts of individuals, although individual ability and effort are certainly relevant to each person's life outcome.

The structure of opportunities establishes what positions may be available at a given point in time. I have argued that the settlement of land, the rise of a market economy, the growth of bureaucracies, the economy of mass production and consumption, and the dominance of finance and technology produced different kinds and numbers of positions, forming and reshaping a legacy of ideas about equality. However, access to those positions depends to a large extent on each individual's social connections.

Social networks serve to maintain what Douglas S. Massey has called "opportunity hoarding," a practice clearly beneficial to insiders and harmful to outsiders. Massey identifies opportunity hoarding as one of the main mechanisms for perpetuating inequality among categories and groups of people, noting that "*opportunity hoarding* occurs when one social group restricts access to a scarce resource, wither through outright denial or by exercising monopoly control that requires out-group members to pay rent in return for access. Either way, opportunity hoarding is enabled through a *socially defined process of exclusion*."[15] Members of every group, not just native-born Whites, concentrate resources and advantages among group members and thereby diminish the relative access of outsiders, undermining efforts to establish categorical equality by policy.

Informal interpersonal networks channel people in ethnic groups into occupational niches. Roger Waldinger, studying immigrants in professional occupations in New York City, argued that professional niche concentrations of people from India grew through informal network mechanisms as well as formal recruiting of professionals into places unfilled by natives. After jobs in the city bureaucracy opened to immigrants and some found positions, network recruiting of kin, friends, and other coethnics brought immigrants into professional jobs, operating transnationally as well as locally. Waldinger quotes an executive in an engineering agency:

> There seems to be a tremendous network of friends and family; real contacts socially. Even in the past when we were first conducting our own provisional hiring pools, with no lists, we would post or gather resumes, send out call letters, and have them come to hiring pools. We would invite 50 people and 80 would show up, "Oh, my brothers' friends' cousin called and said there would be a position." Once we had a recruitment for managers and engineers by invitation only. And there was somebody who flew in from India that day."[16]

Waldinger found that as immigrants became insiders, they became privy to vacancies and passed on news about these vacancies to their family and community members. Individual ability and preparation did come into play. Waldinger noted that immigrants who concentrated in the bureaucracy were good test-takers and therefore able to do well on civil service tests, but selective information channels brought them to the tests.

Information channels pose a basic problem for categorical equalization. If individuals' chances at placement in occupational positions depend at least in part on information and if information flows along lines of social connection frequently defined by group membership, then giving everyone a truly equal opportunity would mean having to somehow redistribute these family and friendship networks or eliminating those altogether.

The ideal of categorical equalization, then, not only challenged many of the nation's inherited ideals of equality but also had its own built-in contradictions. How could group equalization be reconciled with the competitive nature of mobility, especially when desirable opportunities were narrowing? How could those opportunities be made equally available to members of all social categories when life opportunities were heavily influenced by interpersonal relationships?

The fact that inequalities were embedded in interpersonal relationships went beyond race and ethnicity, and even beyond socioeconomic status measures. The deepest and in some ways the most intransigent inequality, perpetuated through interpersonal relationships, may have been the oldest and the most intimate. This was the inequality of gender.

THE POLITICS OF ME TOO

When Thomas Jefferson proclaimed the innate equality of men, or the equal right of every individual to live a life free of hierarchical domination by others, he conveniently put the category of men that he dominated (slaves) outside of consideration. Jefferson also avoided the ambiguity of the word "men," which has historically been used to refer both to human beings in general and to male human beings. Women, like Blacks, were consigned to a place outside of his attention. This was possible because of a mental distinction between the public sphere, where male humans acted and where questions of power relations were relevant, and the domestic sphere, where in the worldview of the time distinct roles defined the statuses and activities of men and women.

When later generations began to see equality as a matter of equality of opportunity among self-made men and of equality of participation in a bureaucratizing, rationalizing society, women were still frequently defined in ways that implicitly excluded them. Commitment to domesticity generally motivated resistance to pressures to extend concepts of equality to include women even to matters of basic political participation, such as voting. The feminine domestic role and the masculine public role constituted the foundation of society.

This view of separate spheres for women and men diminished over time but persisted. During the 1970s, in the struggle over the Equal Rights Amendment, a proposed constitutional amendment that would seek to establish gender equality as fundamental in American law, opponents, many of whom were women, argued that the amendment was anti-family because it would dissolve the gender roles that they saw as essential to maintaining family as the basis of society. They extended this argument to broader categories of sexuality, arguing that the dissolution of gender roles would enable same-sex couples to marry and raise children, unraveling the social fabric.

Even as the defense of domesticity remained the rationale for separate gender roles, women were becoming increasingly active outside the domestic realm. As discussed in the previous chapter, the late twentieth century saw the massive entry of women into the labor force. Among the dilemmas this presented were the continuing inequality of women in wages and occupational mobility as well as the challenge of "the second shift." In the workplace, though, the idea that all people should have the same opportunities and experiences came into conflict with complications of interpersonal relations.

Sociolinguist Deborah Tannen argued in a series of influential books published from the 1980s onward that the influences of gender and social class on the workplace went beyond the allocation of opportunities and even beyond access through networks. People from different backgrounds, she maintained, had different styles of communication, and these created complications and misunderstandings in the workplace. In particular, according to her analysis, men and women tended to communicate in different ways, posing particular challenges for women in male-dominated work environments.

However, the greatest difficulties posed by gender-based interpersonal relations in the workplace came from the volatile combination of organizational power and sexuality. Employers, managers, and employees interact in ways outside of their official job descriptions. In addition to treating one another with differing degrees of friendship and rivalry, they also frequently exhibit desire and domination. The presence of men and women together in most workplaces, along with twenty-first century media of communication, brought this aspect of categorical inequality to the forefront of public attention.

THE MEDIA AND THE ME TOO MOVEMENT

Sexual harassment and exploitation did not begin with the spread of women through the workplace, nor have these ever been exclusive to male-female relationships. Public attention to these problems, though, has accompanied the increase in men and women operating together in the same environments. Although both men and women have appeared as harassers and harassed, and sexual exploitation has occurred between people of the same sex as well of different sexes, most cases have involved men as perpetrators and women as targets.

Sexual harassment became an issue that attracted widespread public attention in higher education primarily during the second decade of the twenty-first century. The legal foundations of responses to this issue, though, derived from governmental efforts at categorical equalization coming out of the civil rights era. Title IX of the Education Amendments of 1972 forbade discrimination based on sex to any educational program or activity receiving federal assistance. In the late 1970s, students at Yale University filed a lawsuit, alleging that they had been pressured for sexual favors by faculty and athletic staff, arguing that this constituted discrimination under Title IX. In the 1980 *Alexander v. Yale* case, a federal appeals court ruled that sexual harassment was indeed a violation of the law covered by Title IX, extending the scope of the legislation and making institutions responsible for maintaining harassment-free environments.[17]

Sexual harassment as a Title IX violation on campuses became a common issue after the beginning of the twenty-first century. My search of the term "Title IX" with "sexual assault" or "sexual harassment" in the online *Newspaper Source Plus* database shows that newspaper articles with these terms began to appear after the year 2000. By 2009, Title IX complaints based on sexual harassment or sexual violence were almost equal to complaints about unequal access to athletic participation, a primary focus at the time the 1972 amendments were adopted. During the 2000s, allegations of sexual assault and demonstrations against sexual harassment became commonplace on college campuses.[18]

In April 2011, the US Department of Education's Office for Civil Rights released its "Dear Colleague" letter. Describing education as "the great equalizer in America," the letter attempted to define sexual discrimination, harassment, and violence, and it outlined the responsibilities of colleges and universities to provide institutional remedies to create environments free of these gender-based interpersonal inequalities.[19] Although this letter was withdrawn by the Department of Education of the Trump Administration, offices created by colleges to address gender-based harassment and violence as well as other initiatives concerned with discrimination by gender categories continued.

Critics of the efforts to remedy sexual harassment argued that these often equated accusation with guilt and denied the rights of the accused. The critics maintained that "no tolerance" approaches aimed at eradicating sexual harassment systematically denied the rights of accused to face their accusers and lowered standards of proof. Responding to the critics, defenders of these approaches argued that traditional, individual-rights based treatment of gender-harassment cases could not respond to deeply entrenched gender-based inequalities and left the burden of proof on victims, generally members of protected gender categories, creating a double victimization.

The obligation of employers to maintain environments free of sexual harassment also grew out of principles of categorical equality established in the wake of the civil rights era. In the 1986 *Meritor Savings Bank v. Vinson* case, the Supreme Court ruled that workplace sexual environment constituted a violation of Title VII of the Civil Rights Act of 1964. The Supreme Court ruled that permitting the sexual harassment of employees created a hostile work environment based on sex was a form of discrimination. This made employers, and not simply individual coworkers, legally responsible for the interpersonal behavior of employees.

Many of the nation's largest employers accepted the idea, at least officially, that they were responsible for regulating interpersonal relations to eliminate hostile work environments. When an engineer at the tech company Google wrote a notorious memo in 2017, in which he argued that the company's efforts to increase female participation were misdirected because male predominance of the field was the consequence of biological predispositions, he was widely condemned and promptly fired. Ironically, part of his argument was that Google had become an "ideological echo chamber," with no tolerance for non-conforming opinions. Although there were no allegations that the engineer had sought sexual favors from anyone or denied anyone a promotion or raise because of gender, defenders of Google's action argued that the company had acted correctly because the expression of opinion had contributed to a hostile work environment for women.

The issue of sexual harassment, including sexual violence, reached into all parts of American society as well as in other countries with the rise of the "Me Too" movement, mainly in the second decade of the twenty-first century. Sexual harassment and violence on campus and in the workplace had become increasingly common public issues of categorical inequality. The phrase "Me Too" is generally traced to the social media protests of activist Tarana Burke in 2006.[20] This is an important point because it makes clear the central role of new media of communication in shifting how Americans thought about inequality, placing a heightened emphasis on interpersonal relations as a source of opportunities and experiences.

The "Me Too" slogan acquired a much broader use in 2017, when actresses and others in the film industry accused producer Harvey Weinstein of numerous acts of sexual abuse. The phrase became a hashtag of responses from women who identified with the experiences of the Weinstein accusers. A movement that had begun on social media then spread when it became associated with the entertainment industry and with celebrities who embodied and expressed social ideas and tensions.

BLACK LIVES MATTER AND THE ANTI-RACISM MOVEMENT

Philosophy professor Christopher J. Lebron, in the 2017 book *The Making of Black Lives Matter: A Brief History of an Idea* has pointed out that the Black Lives Matter movement dates from 2013, when it arose as a response to the not-guilty verdict in the case of George Zimmerman, who had shot and killed Black teenager Trayvon Martin. Although the movement bearing that name was new, Lebron observed, the motivations and emotions behind it had a long history. Black Lives Matter, in his account, was the latest expression of a desire by Black citizens for a complete equality that would go beyond mere equality of individual rights to encompass complete equality of dignity and respect in American institutions and in the minds of other Americans.

The movement grew in the years following the Zimmerman-Martin case in the wake of a series of highly publicized deaths of Black men at the hands of police. In August 2014, a police officer in Ferguson, Missouri, shot and killed another young man, Michael Brown. Despite claims that the officer had murdered Brown while the latter held up his hands in surrender, a grand jury ruled that evidence did not warrant bringing criminal charges. Ferguson broke out in protests that turned into violent riots.

Those protesting the Brown shooting had two interconnected levels of outrage. One level concerned the perception that in this particular case a police official had gunned down a young man without cause, or without sufficient cause. The second concerned the sense that this specific incident was part of a broader pattern of racial profiling and discriminatory violence by law enforcement.

The evidence turned out not to support claims of an unjustifiable killing. A detailed Department of Justice investigation found that Michael Brown did not have his hands up at the time of the shooting. An autopsy supported the officer's assertions that Brown was, in fact, charging at him at the time of the incident. The investigation discredited the testimonies of the supposed eyewitnesses who claimed to have seen cold-blooded murder.

The Department of Justice investigation did find a substantial basis for the second level of popular anger, though. It found that law enforcement in Ferguson was more likely to stop and question or search Black residents and that officers often maintained an adversarial relationship with local Black citizens. This may have distorted national perceptions of the specific incident because Michael Brown quickly became, in the lore of the Black Lives Matter movement, one more martyr to systemic racism. Another way of looking at this development, though, is that in the increasingly polarized setting of thinking purely in terms of categorical inequality, there could be no shades of gray, but only heroes and villains, victims and victimizers. These roles were inflexibly fitted to group identities.

The Martin, Brown, and other incidents reached widespread public attention through social media. Jonathan M. Cox, using interviews with college-age individuals, found that most of his respondents had received their information about Black Lives Matter from social media.[21] Social media were also essential to bringing protestors out into the streets in Ferguson and other locations. Social media, along with universally available video recordings of controversial police actions, also made it possible to give stirring visual evidence of real or apparent police violence against Black men and to publish this evidence in ways that would have been inconceivable with earlier forms of media.

The greatest intensification of the Black Lives Matter demand for categorical equality followed the recording of the death of George Floyd in Minneapolis in May 2020. Responding to a report that Floyd had used a counterfeit bill to pay for cigarettes at an urban corner grocery store, police confronted him. According to the officers, Floyd appeared to be highly intoxicated and was resisting arrest, but these claims have been questioned. When ordered to get in the police car, Floyd refused, reportedly saying that he was claustrophobic. Officers forced Floyd to the ground and Officer Derek Chauvin proceeded to subdue him by kneeling on his neck. Despite Floyd's pleas and cries that he could not breathe, Chauvin kept his knee on the neck until the man went limp and died.

Again, social media were the key to what became a nationwide response. The sight of the policeman with his knee on a helpless and dying man's neck was captured by an onlooker's video and almost immediately promulgated around the country. For many, this was a shocking illustration of the historic and ongoing oppression of African Americans, part of a continuous heritage of racial brutality from the beginning of American history.

Protests erupted in cities not only in the United States but also around the world. While most of these protests remained entirely peaceful, in some locations within the United States they turned into ferocious anti-police rioting, accompanied by extensive destruction. The police responded with truncheons, tear gas, and military assault tactics. Black Lives Matter had previously aimed at police reforms, but in an environment of growing radicalization, more activists began to call for defunding or abolishing police departments altogether.

On the other side of the divide in worldviews, pro-police demonstrators faced off against Black Lives Matter demonstrators, frequently waving American flags and paraphernalia showing support for the reelection of

Donald Trump. The religious and rural-urban splits already characterizing positions on identity politics became wider and more clearly defined.

The Black Lives Matter movement, concentrated on questions of law enforcement but grounded in a wider goal of achieving complete categorical equality, became closely linked to a development known as anti-racism. The latter aimed at a complete reorganization of American society to achieve equality across racial and ethnic categories. Ibram X. Kendi's 2019 book *How to be an Antiracist* was a foundational text of the new anti-racism. Kendi's worldview was almost Manichean in its stark division of society into two polarities. Kendi argued that all people, organizations, and social institutions that were not actively anti-racist were racist. There could be no middle ground. To be anti-racist, moreover, did not mean advocating the legal equality of individuals or nondiscrimination. Instead, it meant aggressive compensatory discrimination in every area of American society. A long and continuing history of anti-Black discrimination, in this line of reasoning, required conscious actions and policies of extensive pro-Black discrimination.

The anti-racist position was morally compelling for many people, especially following the Floyd video and other social media shocks. It also raised problems. One was that the practice of compensatory discrimination as a universal tactic for social change, rather than as a limited and selective program of affirmative action, did not extend historical concepts of equality to previously excluded groups so much as it repudiated those historical concepts. Americans who still held the older views of equality were now, by definition, "racists" in the with-us-or-against-us worldview of anti-racism. In addition, political societies are expressions of interests as well as of moral arguments. It is difficult to see how a thoroughgoing compensatory discrimination in favor of nonwhites would be in the interest of Whites.

The latest developments in the pursuit of categorical equality encouraged stark divisions in American society created an environment for political opportunism that would exploit and intensify those divisions.

As the 2020 election approached, soon-to-be ex-President Donald Trump faced a difficult reelection because of the tandem health and economic crises created by the coronavirus pandemic. Using language seen by many as racially coded, President Trump accused Democrats, who governed many of the urban areas where protests and riots had taken place, of permitting or even fomenting destructive mobs.

An Era of Polarization and Fragmentation

No idea was as fundamental to the American political project as that of "equality," a word employed at the beginning of the American Declaration of Independence to justify the very existence of the nation. But from the beginning, equality was a troublesome concept. If it meant that each individual was equally free from inherited hierarchy, then how could this be reconciled with the competition unleashed by that freedom? More importantly, how could a society with the subordination of entire categories of people maintain a commitment to some kind of equality?

Over the course of American history, the answers to these questions entailed adapting ways of thinking about human equality to changing circumstances, on the one hand, and bracketing off consideration of the subordinated groups, on the other. But the adaptations involved their own versions of old contradictions. These contradictions were often obscured by abundance. Equality of opportunity might logically be the opposite of equality of condition, but people could maintain faith in both if the opportunities were expanding while conditions improved. The self-made man might differ from a participant in a bureaucratic organization, but office holders could still see themselves as self-made if they could be portrayed as rising through the ranks by their own efforts and abilities. Self-sufficient meritocracy might clash with government subsidies, but the subsidies could be understood as equalizing competitive opportunities.

By the early twenty-first century, shared views of America as an egalitarian nation gave way to a period of polarization and fragmentation.

The structural mobility that had persuaded Americans their society could be one in which everyone could and would get ahead had given way to a setting of greater concentration of resources and contracting life chances. A belated recognition of categorical inequality had brought the greatest challenge to national ideals from the margins to the center of awareness, even as the benefits to be distributed in order to address the disadvantages of the repressed categories shrank. Competition for those benefits combined with a proliferation of identity groups, with claims and resentments both reasonable and unreasonable fostered by the decentralizing cultural effects of economically centralizing communication technologies, splintered the population. Some called for a return to a nostalgic past, including the denial of categorical inequality in addition to a re-creation of postwar abundance, while others demanded a complete rewriting of the social contract.

Predictions are likely to be proven wrong. It may be that the country will find a new way of juggling its contradictory ideals of equality. But it seems more likely that the ideological fragmentation of the country will continue and that we will have to live without common agreement on the most basic of American values.

As mentioned in the introduction, the goal of this book has not been to prescribe solutions, but rather to try to understand, interpret, and describe how American concepts of equality have evolved, often in contradictory directions. I want to conclude, though, by suggesting that precisely because we have varying ways of saying what "equality" means, there is no such thing as an ideal egalitarian society on which we can all agree and that should be the goal of public policy. Rather, in a representative political system, the aim, which itself can be only imperfectly achieved, should be to represent the views and interests of all parties and interests and to try reach livable compromises when those are in conflict.

Notes

1. Orhangazi, *Financialization and the US Economy*, 11.
2. Thieblot, "Technology and Labor Relations in the Construction Industry."
3. Bankston, "Engineering the Competition: Affirmative Action as Subsidized Mobility."
4. "The Biggest Turning Points in a Polarizing Campaign," *New York Times,* November 6, 2016, 1.
5. Feagin, *Racist America.*
6. Massie, "Standing on the Promise of Brown and Building a New Civil Rights Movement," 507.
7. Horner, "Reclaiming the Vision: What Should We Do After Affirmative Action?," 8.
8. Bankston and Caldas, *Public Education, America's Civil Religion.*
9. Dias, "Christianity Will Have Power," 21.
10. Light, *Deflecting Immigration*, 46.
11. Ueda, "Immigration in Global Historical Perspective," 25–26.
12. Borjas, "Labor Market Impact of High Skill Immigration."
13. Pew Research Center, *Construction Jobs Expand for Latinos Despite Slump in Housing Market.*
14. Caldas and Bankston, *Still Failing.*
15. Massey, *Categorically Unequal*, 6 (italics in the original).
16. Waldinger, "The Making of an Immigrant Niche," 22.
17. Juliano, "Forty Years of Title IX."
18. Ibid.
19. United States Department of Education, "Dear Colleague" (2011). https://www2.ed.gov/about/offices/list/ocr/letters/colleague-201104.pdf.
20. Me Too Movement website, https://metoomvmt.org/.
21. Cox, "The Source of a Movement."

BIBLIOGRAPHY

Adams, John. "Letter XXXII", *Massachusetts Gazette,* September 4, 1787.

Age, The. "Democratic Candidates for President, Martin Van Buren, the Self-Made Man." November 2, 1836.

Albright, Robert C. "Sen. Goldwater to Vote Against Civil Rights Bill." *The Washington Post,* June 19, 1964.

Anderson, James D. *The Education of Blacks in the South, 1860–1935.* Chapel Hill: University of North Carolina Press, 1988.

Anderson, Terry H. *The Pursuit of Fairness: A History of Affirmative Action.* New York: Oxford University Press, 2004.

Antin, Mary. *The Promised Land.* New York: Houghton Mifflin, 1912.

Associated Press. "12 ½ Million Housing Bill Reported Out. *New York Times,* April 5, 1946.

Atlanta Constitution. "WPA Makes Beggars, Bilbo Asserts." February 21, 1937.

Badger, Anthony J. *The New Deal: The Depression Years, 1933–1940.* New York: MacMillan, 1989.

_____. "How Did the Civil Rights Movement Change America?" *Historian* 94, Summer (2007): 6–13.

Bailyn, Bernard, ed. *The Debate on the Constitution: Federalist and Antifederalist Speeches, Articles, and Letters During the Struggle over Ratification.* Part 2. New York: Literary Classics of the United States, 1993.

Baltimore Sun. "The Gates of Opportunity in America Open to Immigrants." July 14, 1918.

Bankston, Carl L. "Engineering the Competition: Affirmative Action as Subsidized Mobility." *Society* 47, no.4 (2010): 312–321.

Bankston, Carl L, III. "Grutter v. Bollinger: Weak Foundations?" *Ohio State Law Journal* 67, no, 1 (2006): 1–13.

_____. *Immigrant Networks and Social Capital.* London: Polity, 2014.

_____, and Stephen J. Caldas. *Public Education, America's Civil Religion: A Social History.* New York: Teachers College Press, 2009.

_____, and Stephen J. Caldas, *Controls and Choices: The Educational Marketplace and the Failure of School Desegregation.* New York: Rowman and Littlefield, 2015.

Baron, James N. "Organizational Perspectives on Stratification." *Annual review of Sociology* 10 (1984): 37–69.

Beecher, Catherine E. "An Essay on Slavery and Abolition Addressed to Miss A.E. Grimke." In *Against Slavery: An Abolitionist Reader,* edited by Mason Lowance, 207–220. New York: Penguin Books, 2000 [1837].

Bellamy, Edward. *Looking Backward.* New York: Ticknor & Co., 1888.

Bergman, P. M. *The Chronological History of the Negro in America.* New York: Harper Collins, 1969.

Berle, Adolf A., and Gardiner C. Means. *The Modern Corporation and Private Property.* New York: MacMillan, 1944 [1932].

Berlin, Ira. *Generations of Captivity: A History of African American Slaves.* Cambridge, MA: Belknap Press of Harvard University Press, 2003.

Blau, Peter, and Otis Dudley Duncan. *The American Occupational Structure.* New York: John Wiley & Sons, 1967.

Blumin, Stuart. "The Historical Study of Vertical Mobility." *Conference Proceedings, International Social Science Council* 8, no.1 (1969): 43–57.

Boorstin, Daniel. *The Image: A Guide to Pseudo-Events in America.* New York: Random House, 1962.

Borjas, George J. "Labor Market Impact of High Skill Immigration." *The American Economic Review* 95 (2005): 55–60.

_____. "The Long-run Convergence of Ethnic Skill Differentials: The Children and Grandchildren of the Great Migration." *Industrial and Labor Relations Review* 47, no. 4 (1994): 553–573.

Bound, John, and Sarah Turner. "Going to War and Going to College: Did World War II and the GI Bill Increase Educational Attainment for Returning Veterans?" *Journal of Labor Economics* 20 (2002): 784–815.

Bourne, Randolph S. *The Gary Schools.* Boston: Houghton Mifflin, 1916.

Brinkley, Alan. "The New Deal and the Idea of the State." In *The Rise and Fall of the New Deal Order, 1930–1980,* edited by Steve Fraser and Gary Gerstle, 85–121. Princeton: Princeton University Press, 1989.

Bronstein, Jamie L. *Two Nations, Indivisible: A History of Inequality in America.* Santa Barbara, CA: Praeger, 2016.

Burke, Edmund. *Speech on Conciliation with America.* New York: Hammond Lamont, 1897 [1795].

Burns, Eric. *Invasion of the Mind Snatchers: Television's Conquest of America in the Fifties.* Philadelphia: Temple University Press, 2010.

Caldas, Stephen J., and Carl L. Bankston. *Still Failing: The Continuing Paradox of School Segregation.* New York: Rowman & Littlefield, 2015.

Carroll, Joseph. "Family Time Eclipses TV as Favorite Way to Spend an Evening." *Gallup News Service,* March 10, 2006. https://news.gallup. com/poll/21856/Family-Time-Eclipses-Favorite-Way-Spend-Evening. aspx?g_source=position3&g_medium=related&g_campaign=tiles.

Carson, John. *The Measure of Merit: Talents, Intelligence, and Inequality in the French and American Republics, 1750-1940.* Princeton: Princeton University Press, 2007.

Cappon, Lester J., ed. *The Adams-Jefferson Letters: The Complete Correspondence Between Thomas Jefferson and Abigail and John Adams.* Chapel Hill: University of North Carolina Press, 2012.

Cawelti, John G. *Apostles of the Self-Made Man.* Chicago: University of Chicago Press, 1965.

Chapman, John Jay. "Emerson." In *The Shock of Recognition: The Development of Literature in the United States Recorded by the Men Who Made It,* edited by Edmund Wilson, 600–658. New York: The Modern Library, 1955 [1897].

Chase, Stuart. *A New Deal.* New York: The MacMillan Co., 1932.

City Gazette & Commercial Daily. "Mr. Van Buren." March 12, 1830.

Cohen, Sol. *Education in the United States: A documentary history.* Volume IV. New York, Random House, 1974.

Coleman, James S., Ernest Q. Campbell, Carol J. Hobson, James McPart-land, Alexander M. Mood, Frederic D. Weinfeld, and Robert L York. *Equality of Educational Opportunity*. Washington, DC: U.S. Government Printing Office, 1966

Conrad, Peter, and Joseph W. Schneider. "Homosexuality: From Sin to Sickness to Lifestyle." In *Deviance and Medicalization: From Badness to Sickness* by Peter Conrad, 172–214. Expanded edition. Philadelphia: Temple University Press, 1992.

Cooper, John Milton, Jr. *Woodrow Wilson: A Biography*. New York: Alfred A. Knopf, 2009.

Cornell, Saul. *The Other Founders: Ant-Federalism and the Dissenting Tradition in America, 1788–1828*. Chapel Hill: University of North Carolina Press, 1999.

Counts, George S. *The Schools Can Teach Democracy*. New York: John Day, 1939.

Cox, Jonathan M. "The Source of a Movement: Making the Case for Social Media as an Informational Source Using Black Lives Matter." *Ethnic and Racial Studies* 40 (2017): 1814–1830.

Crawford, James. *Hold Your Tongue: Bilingualism and the Politics of "English Only."* Reading, MA: Addison-Wesley, 1992.

Cremin, Lawrence A. *The Transformation of the School: Progressivism in American Education, 1876–1957*. New York: Alfred A. Knopf, 1961.

Crockett, Davy. *An Account of Col. Crockett's Tour to the North and Down East, In the year of Our Lord One Thousand Eight Hundred and Thirty-Four*. Philadelphia: E.L. Carey and A. Hart, 1835.

_____ [or Augustin S. Clayton, ghostwriter]. *The Life of Martin Van Buren*. Philadelphia: R. Wright, 1836.

_____. *A Narrative of the Life of David Crockett ... Written by Himself*. Philadelphia: E.L. Carey and A. Hart, 1834.

Croly, Herbert. *The Promise of American Life*. New York: MacMillan, 1909.

Damrosch, Leo. *Tocqueville's Discovery of America*. New York: Farrar, Strauss and Giroux, 2010.

Davis, Benjamin Jefferson. "New Deal Viewed as a Dirty Deal," *The New York Amsterdam News*, June 12, 1935.

Davis, Gerald F., and Doug McAdam. "Corporations, Classes, and Social Movements after Managerialism." *Research in Organizational Behavior* 22 (2000): 195–238.

Davis, John P. *Corporations: A Study of the Origin and Development of Great Business Combinations and of their Relation to the Authority of the State.* New York and London: G.P. Putnam's Sons, 1905.

Dewey, John, and Evelyn Dewey. *The Schools of Tomorrow.* New York: Dutton, 1962 [1916].

Dias, Elizabeth. "Christianity Will Have Power: How a Promise by Trump Bonded Him to White Evangelicals." *The New York Times.* August 9, 2020.

Edsforth, Ronald. *The New Deal: America's Response to the Great Depression.* Maldan, MA: Blackwell, 2000.

Ellis, Joseph J. 1 *American Sphynx: The Character of Thomas Jefferson.* New York: Alfred A. Knopf, 1996.

Feagin, Joe. *Racist America: Roots, Current Realities, and Future Reparations.* New York: Routledge, 2000.

Ferguson, Niall. *The War of the World: Twentieth Century Conflict and the Descent of the West.* New York: Penguin Press, 2006.

Fischer, David Hackett. *Albion's Seed: Four British Folkways in America.* New York: Oxford University Press, 1989.

Foner, Eric. *Reconstruction: America's Unfinished Revolution, 1863–1877.* New York: Harper & Row, 1989.

France, Anatole. *Le Lys rouge.* Paris: Caimann-Lévy, 1894.

Douglass, Frederick. *Frederick Douglass' Paper.* Rochester, NY: Frederick Douglass, 1851.

Frost, Raymond M. "Losing Economic Hegemony: U.K. 1850–1891 and U.S. 1950–1991." *Challenge* (July/August 1992): 30–34.

Furman, B. "Senate Votes Aid to Science Study." *New York Times,* August 23, 1958.

Galbraith, John Kenneth. *The Affluent Society.* New York: New American Library, 1958.

Gibson, Campbell, and Kay Jung. *Historical Census Statistics on Population Totals by Race, 1790 to 1990, and Hispanic Origin, 1970 to 1990, for Large Cities and Other Urban Places in the United States.* Washington, DC: U.S. Census Bureau, 2005.

Goldfield, David. *America Aflame: How the Civil War Created a Nation.* Bloomsbury, 2013.

Goldin, Claudia, and Robert A. Margo."The Great Compression: The Wage Structure in the United States at Mid-Century." *Quarterly Journal of Economics* 107 (1992): 1–34.

Gullett, Gayle, "Women Progressives and the Politics of Americanization in California, 1915–1920. *Pacific Historical Review* 64 (1995): 71–94.

Greenbaum, Susan D. *Blaming the Poor: The Long Shadow of the Moynihan Report on Cruel Images about Poverty.* New Brunswick, NJ: Rutgers University Press, 2015.

Hammond, Josh, and James Morrison. *The Stuff Americans are Made Of.* New York: MacMillan, 1996.

Hampshire Gazette. "A Self Made Man." February 22, 1837.

Harper's Weekly. "The College Commencement Season." June 27, 1885.

————. "A Distinguished Young Colored Man." August 30, 1902.

————. "Harvard's Two-Hundred and Fiftieth Birthday." August 21, 1886.

————. "Samuel D. Warren." May 26, 1888.

Harrington, Michael. *The Other America: Poverty in the United States.* New York: Macmillan, 1964.

Harris, Louis, "Goldwater Rights Views Given Minority Rating." *The Washington Post.* July 20, 1964.

Hercovici, Steven. "Migration and Mobility: Wealth Accumulation and Occupational Change among Antebellum Migrants and Persisters." *Journal of Economic History* 58, no. 4 (1998): 927–956.

Hilkey, Judy. *Character Is Capital: Success Manuals and Manhood in Gilded Age America*. Chapel Hill: University of North Carolina Press, 1997.

Hill, Joseph A. *Women in Gainful Occupations 1870–1920, Census Monography 9*. Washington, DC: U.S. Government Printing Office, 1929.

Hiltzik, Michael. *The New Deal: A Modern History*. New York: Free Press, 2011.

Hirschman, Charles, and Elizabeth Mogford, "Immigration and the American industrial revolution from 1880 to 1920". *Social Science Research* 38 (2009): 897–920.

Hochschild, Arlie. *The Second Shift: Working Families and the Revolution at Home*. New York: Viking. 1989.

_____. *Strangers in their Own Land: Anger and Mourning on the American Right*. New York: The New Press, 2016.

Hofstadter, Richard. "Abraham Lincoln and the Self-Made Myth," In *The American Political Tradition and the Men Who Made It* by Richard Hofstadter, 93–136. New York: Vintage, 1948.

_____. *The Age of Reform: From Bryan to FDR*. New York: Alfred A. Knopf, 1955.

Holton, Woody. *Unruly Americans and the Origins of the Constitution*. New York: Hill & Wang, 2007.

Horner, Constance. "Reclaiming the Vision: What Should We Do After Affirmative Action?" *The Brookings Review* 13, no, 3 (1995): 6–11.

Hughes, Rupert. "The Vice of Generalizing." *Harper's Weekly*. August 18, 1906.

Ickes, Harold L. *Back to Work: The Story of the PWA*. New York: MacMillan, 1935.

Jaycox, Faith. *The Progressive Era*. New York: Facts on File, Inc., 2005.

Jefferson, Thomas. "Letter to John Holmes" (April 22). In *The Works of Thomas Jefferson*, edited by Paul L. Ford. New York: G.P. Putnam's Sons, 1905 [1820].

_____. "A Summary View of the Rights of British America." In *The Papers of Thomas Jefferson*, vol. 1, edited by Julian P. Boyd, 121–137. Princeton: Princeton University Press, 1950 [1774].

Jenks, Jeremiah W., and W. Jett Lauck. *The Immigration Problem: A Study of American Immigration Conditions and Needs*. New York and London: Funk and Wagnall, 1913.

Johnson, Samuel. *Taxation No Tyranny: An Answer to the Resolutions of the American Congress*. London: T. Cadell, 1775.

Jones, Arthur F., Jr., and Daniel H. Weinberg. *The Changing Shape of the Nation's Income Distribution, 1947–1998*. Washington, D.C.: U.S. Census Bureau (Current Population Reports, P60-204), 2000.

Jones, Maldwyn A. *American Immigration*. 2nd edition. Chicago: University of Chicago Press, 1992.

Joseph, Peniel E. *The Sword and the Shield: The Revolutionary Lives of Malcolm X and Martin Luther King, Jr.* New York: Basic Books, 2020.

Juliano, Margaret E. "Forty Years of Title IX: History and New Applications." *Delaware Law Review* 14, no. 1 (2013): 83–90.

Kagan, Robert. *Dangerous Nation: America's Place in the World from the Earliest Days to the Dawn of the Twentieth Century*. New York: Penguin Random House, 2006.

Katznelson, Ira. *Fear Itself: The New Deal and the Origins of Our Time*. New York: W.W. Norton, 2013.

Kendi, Ibram X. *How to Be an Antiracist*. New York: One World, 2019.

Kolko, Gabriel. *Main Currents in American History*. New York: Harper & Row, 1976.

Kaufman, Bruce. "Wage Theory, New Deal Labor Policy, and the Great Depression: Were Government and Unions to Blame?" *Industrial and Labor Relations Review* 65, no. 3 (2012): 501–532.

Klemesrud, Judy. "Women's Movement at Age 11: Larger, More Diffuse, Still Battling." *New York Times*, November 15, 1977.

Kornbluth: Gary J., and Murrin, John M. "The Making and Unmaking of an American Ruling Class." In *Beyond the American Revolution:*

Explorations in the History of American Radicalism, edited by Alfred F. Young, 27–79. DeKalb, IL: Northern Illinois University Press, 1993.

Landale, Nancy, and Avery Guest, "Generation, Ethnicity, and Occupational Mobility in Late 19th Century America." *American Sociological Review* 55, no. 2 (1990): 280–296.

LeBron, Christopher J. *The Making of Black Lives Matter: A Brief History of an Idea.* New York: Oxford University Press, 2017.

Lee, Henry Moon. "What the Negro Hopes For." *Cleveland Call and Post,* January 13, 1945.

Lenthall, Bruce. *Radio's America: The Great Depression and the Rise of Modern Mass Culture.* Chicago: University of Chicago Press, 2007.

Light, Ivan. *Deflecting Immigration: Networks, Markets, and Regulation in Los Angeles.* New York: Russell Sage Foundation, 2006.

Lindsay, Malvina "Search for Safe Living," *The Washington Post,* June 16, 1949.

Linklater, Andro. *The Fabric of America: How Our Borders and Boundaries Shaped the Country and Forged Our National Identity.* New York: Walker & Company, 2007.

Los Angeles Times. "Goldwater Sees Harm in Civil Rights Measure." June 23, 1964.

————. "Truman Raps Opponents of Party 'Dream.'" May 16, 1950.

Loviglio, Jason. *Radio's Intimate Public: Network Broadcasting and Mass-Mediated Democracy.* Minneapolis: University of Minnesota Press, 2005.

Madrigal, Alexis. "When Did TV Watching Peak?" *The Atlantic.* May 30, 2018. https://www.theatlantic.com/technology/archive/2018/05/when-did-tv-watching-peak/561464/.

Main, Jackson T. "Social Mobility in Revolutionary America." In *Three Centuries of Social Mobility in America*, edited by Edward Pessen, 12–33. Lexington, MA: D.C. Heath & Co. 1974.

Majewski, John. *Modernizing a Slave Economy: The Economic Vision of the Confederate Nation.* Chapel Hill: University of North Carolina Press, 2009.

Massie, Miranda K.S. "Standing on the Promise of Brown and Building a New Civil Rights Movement: The Student Intervention in Grutter v Bollinger." *Albany Law Review* 66 (2003): 505–518.

Massey, Douglas S. *Categorically Unequal: The American Stratification System.* New York: Russell Sage Foundation, 2007.

_____., and Nancy A, Denton. *American Apartheid: Segregation and the Making of the Underclass.* Cambridge: Harvard University Press, 1998.

Me Too Movement website. https://metoomvmt.org/.

Mettler, Suzanne. "Bringing the State Back in to Civic Engagement: Policy Feedback Effects of the G.I. Bill for World War II Veterans. *American Political Science Review* 96 (2002): 351–365.

Michel, Virgil. "Defining Social Justice." *Commonweal.* February 14, 1936. https://www.commonwealmagazine.org/defining-social-justice.

Mills, C. Wright. *The Power Elite.* New York: Oxford University Press, 1956.

_____. *White Collar: The American Middle Classes.* New York: Oxford University Press, 1951.

Minns, Chris. "Income, Cohort Effects, and Occupational Mobility: A New Look at Immigration to the United States at the Turn of the Twentieth Century." *Explorations in Economic History* 37 (2000): 326–350.

Moynihan, Daniel P. *The Moynihan Report: The Negro Family—The Case for National Action.* New York: Cosimo Reports, 1965.

Morgan, Edward S. *The Genuine Article: A Historian Looks at Early America.* New York: W.W. Norton, 2004.

Nackenoff, Carol. *The Fictional Republic: Horatio Alger and American Political Discourse.* New York: Oxford University Press, 1994.

National Center for Education Statistics. *Digest of Education Statistics, 2018*. https://nces.ed.gov/programs/digest/d18/tables/dt18_104.10.asp.

National Public Radio. "Bill Moyers' View of Contemporary America." November 2008. https://www.npr.org/templates/story/story.php?storyId=96648963.

Nevins, Allan. *Study in Power: John D. Rockefeller*. New York: Charles Scribner's Sons. 1953.

New York Herald Tribune. "The Agricultural College Act." June 21, 1862.

————. "Jersey City German Republicans." September 9, 1856.

New York Times. "The Biggest Turning Points in a Polarizing Campaign." November 6, 2016.

————. "Editorial Views: Welfare Limitations." January 27, 1935.

————. "The Freemen's Great Want." April 1, 1870.

————. "Goal of Growth: Assets Must Be Shared More Widely." January 22, 1962.

————. "Ickes Portrays New Social Order." June 4, 1933.

————. "Miss Perkins Urges Job Security Plans." January 1, 1937.

————. "N.A.A.C.P. sets advanced goals" May 18, 1954.

————. "Stuart Chase, 97." November 7, 1985.

————. "Text of the President's Message on Economic Recovery and Growth." February 3, 1961.

Ohio Daily Statesman. "Amos Kendall." November 6, 1837.

Oregon State Journal. "A Self-Made Man." July 3, 1880.

Orfield, Gary, "A Proposal for Outfoxing Wallace." *The Washington Post*. July 7, 1968.

Orhangazi, Ozgür. *Financialization and the US Economy*. Northampton, MA: Edward Elgar, 2008.

Osterman, Rachel. "Origins of a Myth: Why Courts, Scholars, and the Public Think Title VII's Ban on Sex Discrimination was an Accident." *Yale Journal of Law and Feminism* 20 (2009): 409–505.

Packard, Vance. *The Hidden Persuaders*. New York: David McKay, 1957.

_____. *The Status Seekers*. New York: David McKay. 1959.

Parkman, Francis. *Some of the Reasons Against Woman Suffrage*. Reprinted by Northridge Facsimile Series VIII. Northridge, CA: Santa Susana Press, California State University, Northridge, 1977 [1901].

Patterson. James T. *Freedom is Not Enough: The Moynihan Report and America's Struggle Over Black Family Life – From LBJ to Obama*. New York: Basic Books, 2010.

Perkins, Frances. "Social Security: The Foundation." *The New York Times*, October 18, 1935.

Pessen, Edward. *Three Centuries of Social Mobility in America*. Lexington, MA: D.C. Heath & Co., 1974.

Pew Research Center. *Construction Jobs Expand for Latinos Despite Slump in Housing Market*. March 7, 2007. https://www.pewresearch.org/hispanic/2007/03/07/construction-jobs-expand-for-latinos-despite-slump-in-housing-market/.

Powers, Jane Bernard. *The "Girl Question" in Education: Vocational Education for Young Women in the Progressive Era*. London & Washington, DC: Falmer Press, 1992.

Riesman, David. *The Lonely Crowd*. New Haven: Yale University Press, 1950.

Roberts, Chalmers M. "Politicians Taking a Wary Attitude Toward the Civil Rights Question." *The Washington Post*. October 20, 1963.

Rubio, Philip F. *A History of Affirmative Action: 1619–2000*. Jackson: University Press of Mississippi, 2001.

Rugg, Harold. *Democracy and the Curriculum: The Life and Program of the American School*. New York: D. Appleton Century, 1939.

_____. *Foundations for American Education*. New York: World Book Co., 1947.

Ruggles, Steven, Sarah Flood, Ronald Goeken, Joshua Grover, Erin Meyer, Jose Pacas, and Matthew Sokek. IPUMS USA: Version 10.0 [dataset]. Minneapolis, MN, 2020.

Ryan, William. *Blaming the Victim*, New York: Vintage Books, 1976.

Salem Gazette. "Mr. Davis." October 2, 1833.

Selden, Dudley. "Who are the Aristocrats?" *New York Commercial Advertiser*, July 27, 1836.

Shanks, Cheryl. *Immigration and the Politics of American Sovereignty, 1880–1990.* Ann Arbor: University of Michigan Press, 2001.

Skarloff, Lauren Rebecca. *Black Culture and the New Deal: The Quest for Civil Rights in the Roosevelt Era.* Chapel Hill: The University of North Carolina Press, 2009.

Smiley, Gene. *Rethinking the Great Depression: A New View of Its Causes and Consequences.* Chicago: Ivan R. Dee, 2002.

Smith, Adam. *The Wealth of Nations, Vol. II.* London: Everyman's Library, 1954 [1776].

Smith, Tom W. Michael Davern, Jeremy Freese, and Steven Morgan, General Social Surveys, 1972–2018 [Machine-readable Data File]. https://gss.norc.org/.

Smith, Jason Scott. *A Concise History of the New Deal.* New York: Cambridge University Press, 2014.

Snyder, Thomas D. *120 Years of American Education: A Statistical Portrait.* Washington, DC: National Center for Education Statistics, 1993.

Spring, Joel. *The Sorting Machine Revisited.* White Plains, NY: Longman, 1989.

Stansell, Christine. *The Feminist Promise: 1792 to the Present.* New York: The Modern Library, 2010.

Storing, Herbert J., ed., *The Complete Anti-Federalist.* Chicago: University of Chicago Press, 1981.

Strayer, George D., and Frank P. Bachman. *The Gary Public Schools: Organization and Administration.* New York: General Education Board, 1918.

Suehsdorf, Adie. "They're Making Room at the Top." *Los Angeles Times*, October 16, 1949.

Taylor, Frederick Winslow. *The Principles of Scientific Management.* New York: Harper & Brothers, 1911.

Taylor, John. *Inquiry into the Principles and Policy of the Government of the United States.* Fredericksburg, VA: Green and Cady, 1814.

Thernstrom, Stephan. *Poverty and Progress: Social Mobility in a Nineteenth Century City.* Cambridge, MA: Harvard University Press, 1964.

Thieblot, A. J. "Technology and Labor Relations in the Construction Industry." *Journal of Labor Research* 23, no. 4 (2002): 559–573.

Thomas, Norman. "Is the New Deal Socialism? A Socialist Leader Answers." *The New York Times,* June 18, 1933.

Thoreau, Henry David. "Civil Disobedience." Boston: D.R. Godine, 1969 [1849].

————. *A Week on the Concord and Merrimack Rivers.* New York: Quality Paperback Book Club. 1997 [1849].

Tocqueville, Alexis de. *Democracy in America.* Translated by Arthur Goldhammer. New York: Library of America 2004 [1835].

Trollope, Frances. *Domestic Manners of the Americans.* Vols. 1 & 2. London: Whittaker, Teacher & Co, 1832.

Tull, Charles J. *Father Coughlin & the New Deal.* Syracuse, NY: Syracuse University Press, 1965.

Tunnell, Ted. *Crucible of Reconstruction: War, Radicalism, and Race in Louisiana, 1862–1877.* Baton Rouge: Louisiana State University Press, 1984.

Ueda, Reed. "Immigration in Global Historical Perspective." In *The New Americans: A Guide to Immigration since 1965,* edited by Mary C. Waters and Reed Ueda with Helen B Marrow, 14–18. Cambridge, MA: Harvard University Press, 2007.

U.S. Census Bureau. *Census of Population and Housing, 1930.* Washington, DC: U.S. Census Bureau, 1931.

U.S. Census Bureau. *Census of Population and Housing, 1940.* Washington, DC: U.S. Census Bureau, 1941.

U.S. Census Bureau. *Census of Population and Housing, 1970.* Washington, DC: U.S. Census Bureau, 1971.

U.S. Census Bureau. *Census of Population and Housing, 1990.* Washington, DC: U.S. Census Bureau, 1991.

U.S. Commission on Civil Rights. *Promises and Perceptions: Federal Efforts to Eliminate Employment Discrimination through Affirmative Action.* Washington, DC: U.S. Commission on Civil Rights, 1981.

United States Department of Education. Rescinded letter dated April 4, 2011, from Russlynn Ali, Assistant Secretary for Civil Rights. https://www2.ed.gov/about/offices/list/ocr/letters/colleague-201104.pdf.

U.S. Department of Homeland Security, *Yearbook of Immigration Statistics: 2017.* https://www.dhs.gov/immigration-statistics/yearbook/2017.

U.S. Supreme Court. *Brown v. Board of Education of Topeka* 347 U.S. 483, 1954.

U.S. Supreme Court. *Green v. County Sch. Bd.,* 391 U.S. 430, 442, 1968.

U.S. Supreme Court. *McDonald v. Santa Fe Trail Transportation Co., 427 U.S. 273,* 1976.

U.S. Supreme Court, *Regents of University of California v. Bakke,* 438 U.S. 265, 1978.

U.S. Supreme Court. "Elementary and Secondary Education Act (ESEA) of 1965", *Pub. L.* No. 89-10, 79 *Stat.* 77 (codified at 20 U.S.C. 240), 2000.

Vatter, Harold G. "The Economy at Mid-Century." In *History of the American Economy Since World War II,* edited by Harold G. Vatter and John F. Walker, 3–23. Armonk, NY: M.E. Sharpe, 1996.

Vermont Phoenix. "See How the People's Money Goes. the Gold Spoon Story." August 7, 1840.

Waldinger, Roger. The Making of an Immigrant Niche." *International Migration Review* 28 (1994): 3–30.

Washington, Booker T. *Up from Slavery.* New York: Doubleday, 1901.

Washington Post. "Club Leaders Want 'Raging Epidemic of Americanism.'" May 31, 1950.

Weed, Thurlow. *Autobiography of Thurlow Weed.* New York: Houghton Mifflin & Co, 1883.

Weiss, Richard. *The American Myth of Success: From Horatio Alger to Norman Vincent Peale.* Chicago: University of Illinois Press, 1969.

Wilson, Sloan. *The Man in the Gray Flannel Suit.* New York: Simon & Schuster, 1955.

Wilson, William Julius. *When Work Disappears: The World of the New Urban Poor.* New York: Knopf, 1996.

Wilson, Woodrow. "The Study of Administration." *Political Science Quarterly* 2 (1887): 197–222.

Wood, Gordon S. *The Creation of the American Republic, 1776–1787.* Chapel Hill: University of North Carolina Press, 1969.

Wood, Gordon S. *The Radicalism of the American Revolution.* New York: Vintage Books, 1992.

Wylie, Irvin G. *The Self-Made Man in America: The Myth of Rags to Riches.* New Brunswick: Rutgers University Press, 1954.

Young, Michael. *The Rise of the Meritocracy.* London: Thames and Hudson, 1958.

Zietlow, Rebecca E. *Enforcing Equality: Congress, the Constitution, and the Protection of Individual Rights.* New York: New York University Press, 2006.

INDEX

CPSIA information can be obtained
at www.ICGtesting.com
Printed in the USA
LVHW010057050521
686548LV00006B/376